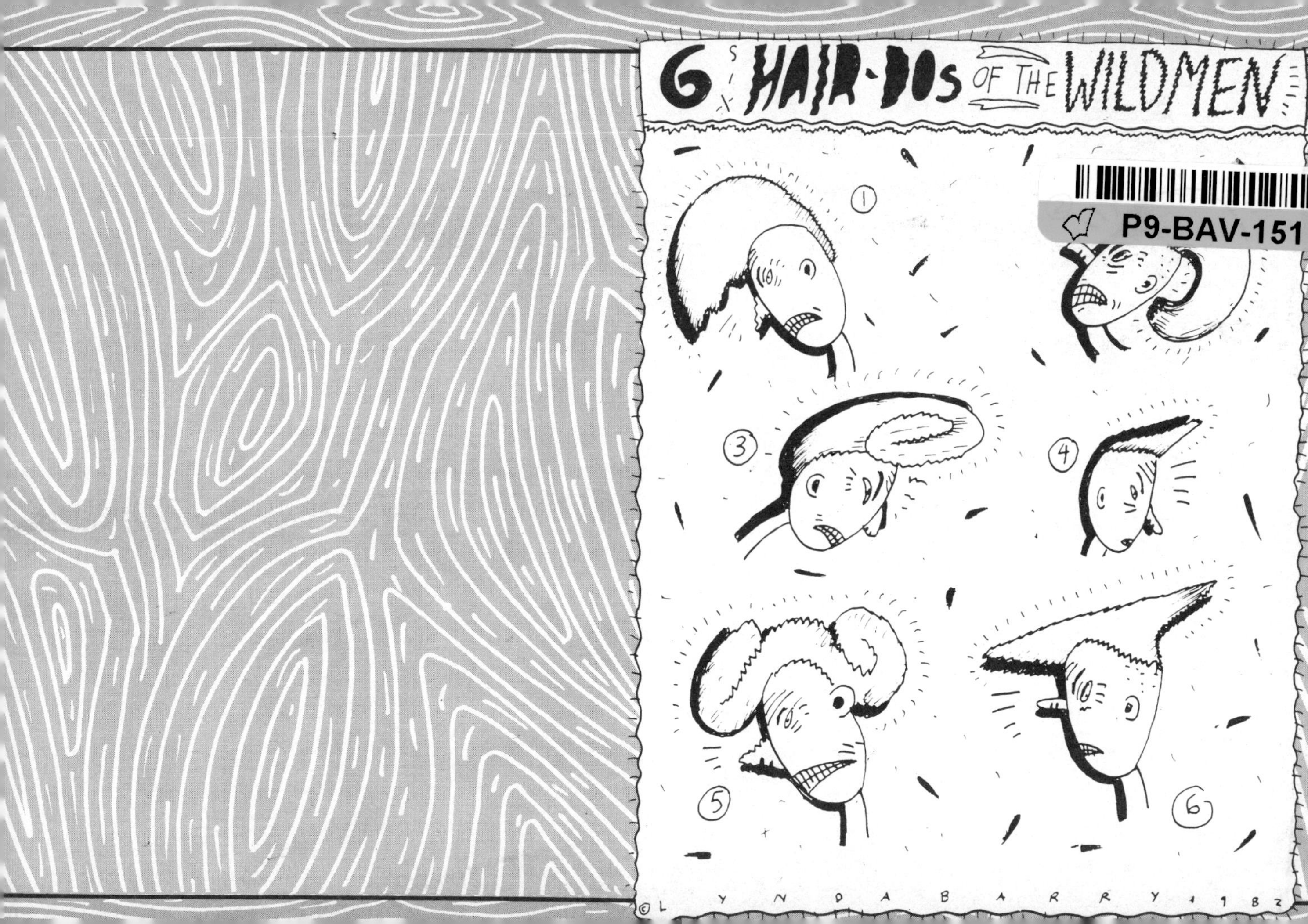
6 HAIR-DOs OF THE WILDMEN
1
3
4
5
6
© L Y N D A B A R R Y 1 9 8 2

Now it can be told...

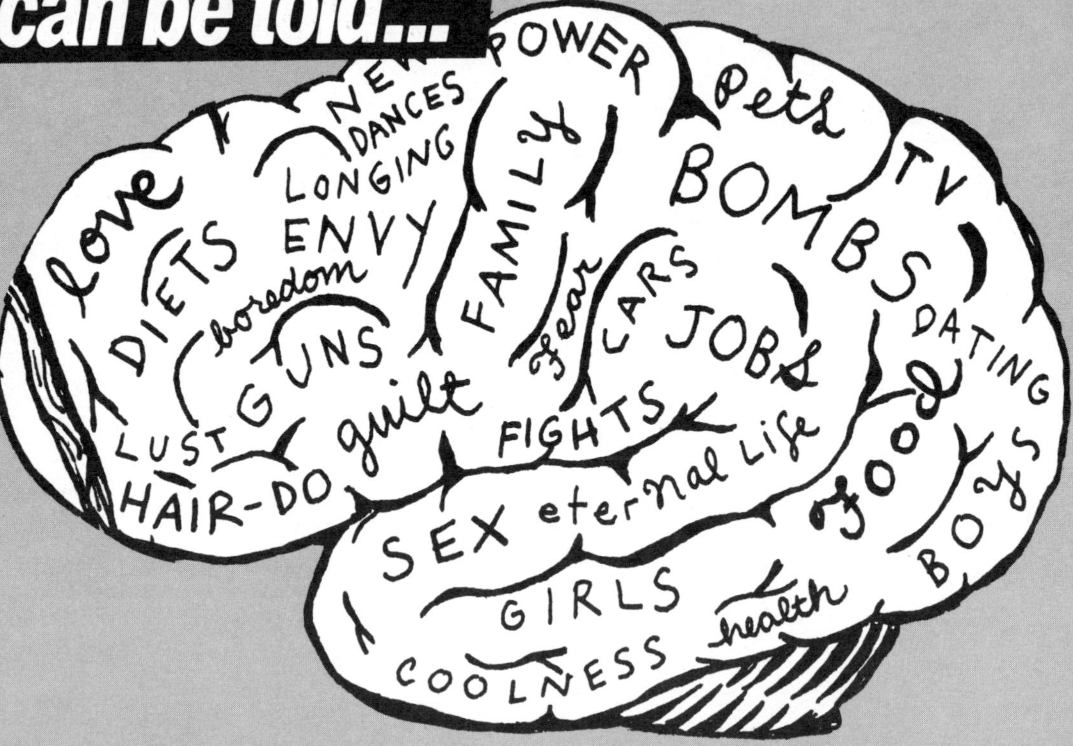
love
NEW DANCES
POWER
Pets
LONGING
DIETS
ENVY
boredom
FAMILY
BOMBS
TV
fear
CARS
JOBS
DATING
GUNS
guilt
LUST
FIGHTS
HAIR-DO
eternal life
food
SEX
BOYS
GIRLS
health
COOLNESS

BIG IDEAS

by LYNDA BARRY

HEY! WAIT A SECOND!
HELL HOLE

THE REAL COMET PRESS • SEATTLE • 1983

PUBLISHED BY ARRANGEMENT WITH THE AUTHOR.
BIG IDEAS IS AN ORIGINAL PUBLICATION OF

THE REAL COMET PRESS

A DIVISION OF SUCH A DEAL CORPORATION

FOR INFORMATION:
932-18TH AVENUE EAST, SEATTLE, WASHINGTON, 98112.

FIRST PRINTING: 1983

DESIGN BY:
WES ANDERSON / SQUARE STUDIO

MANUFACTURED IN THE UNITED STATES OF AMERICA

SPECIAL THANKS TO BERGMAN LOCK AND KEY
MATT GROENING IS FUNKLORD OF USA

ISBN: 0-941104-07-9
LIBRARY OF CONGRESS CATALOG CARD NUMBER: 83-61229

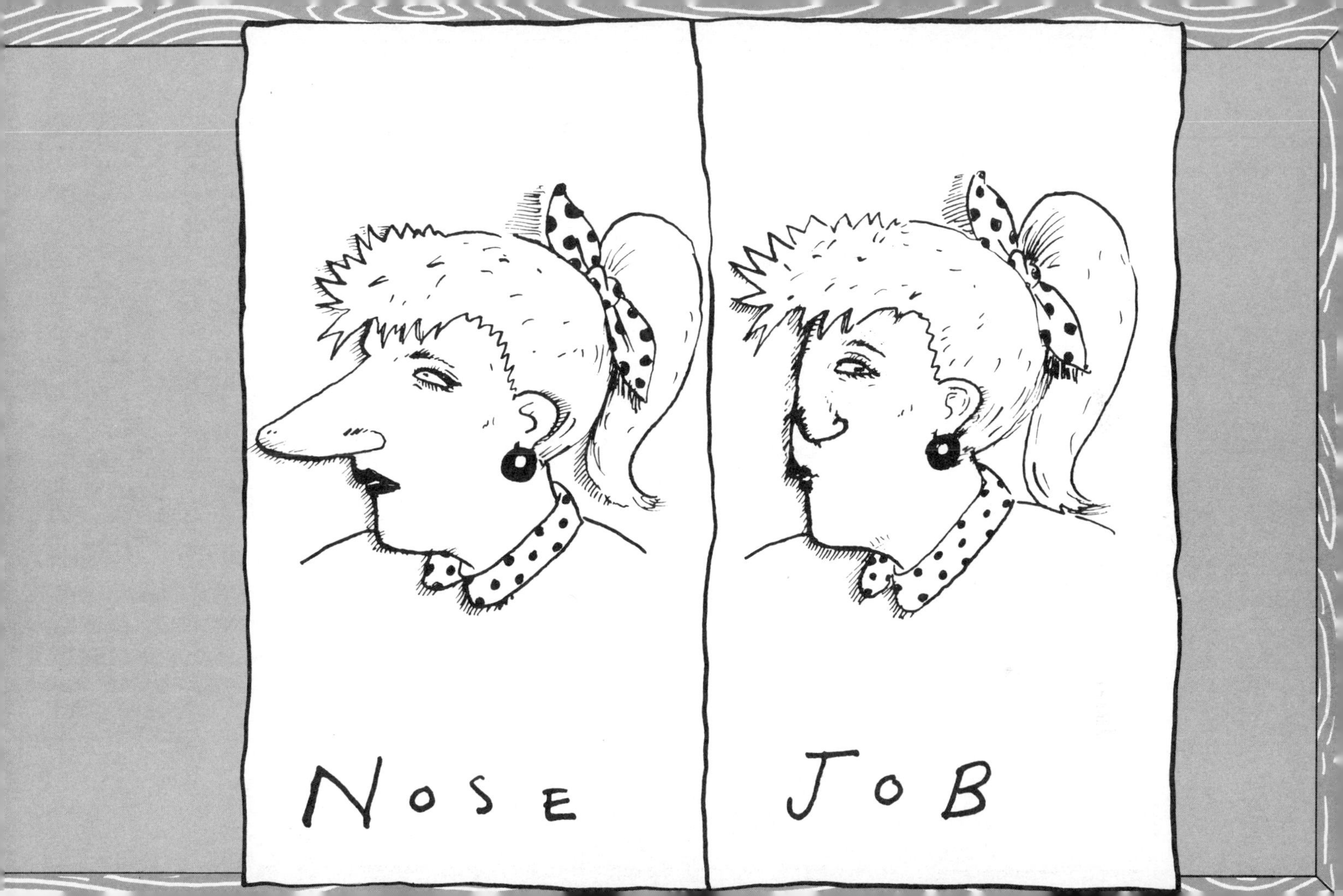
NOSE
JOB

The World Explained

Home Sweet Home

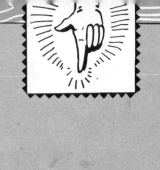

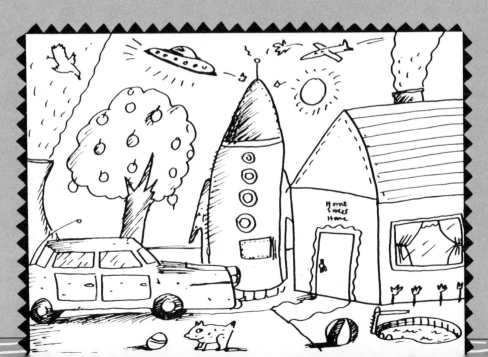

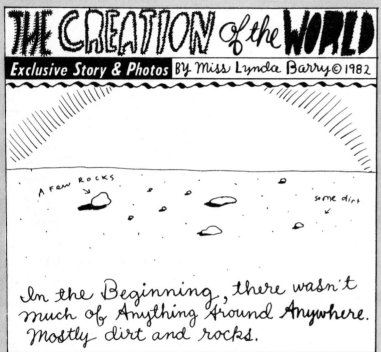

THE CREATION of the WORLD

Exclusive Story & Photos By Miss Lynda Barry © 1982

A Few ROCKS

some dirt

In the Beginning, there wasn't much of Anything Around Anywhere. Mostly dirt and rocks.

Pretty soon there were some other things but still not Alot. For sure not as many as there are now. One of the things that came out was a woman and a man came out

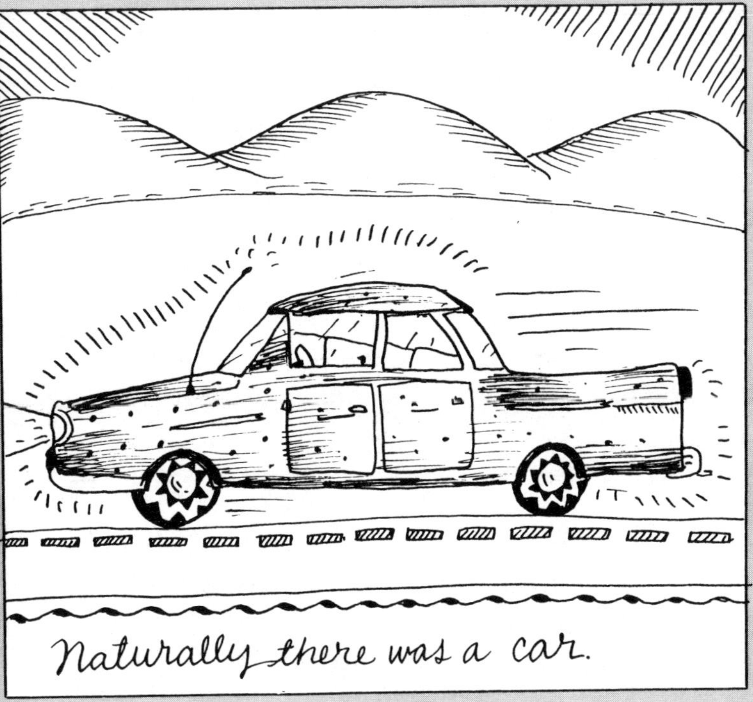
Naturally there was a car.

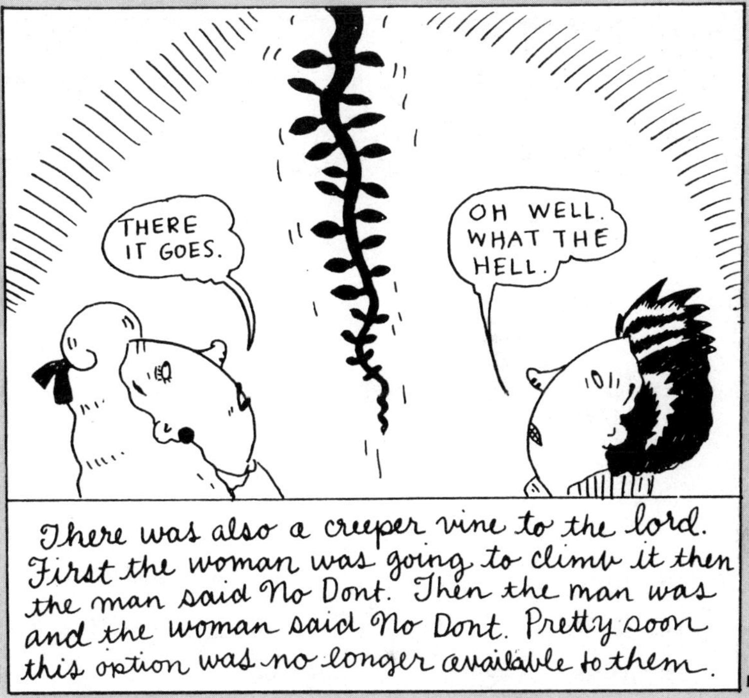
THERE IT GOES.
OH WELL. WHAT THE HELL.
There was also a creeper vine to the lord. First the woman was going to climb it then the man said No Dont. Then the man was and the woman said No Dont. Pretty soon this option was no longer available to them.

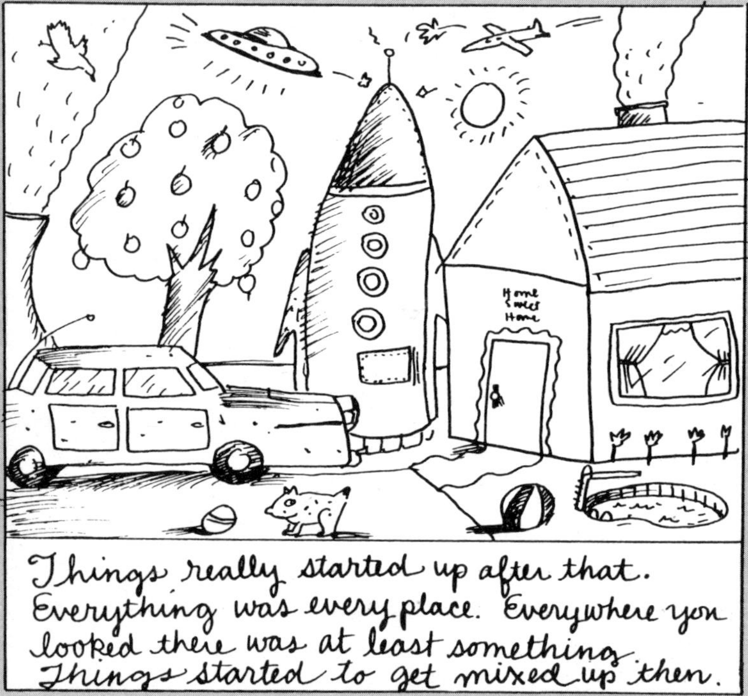
Home Sweet Home
Things really started up after that. Everything was every place. Everywhere you looked there was at least something. Things started to get mixed up then.

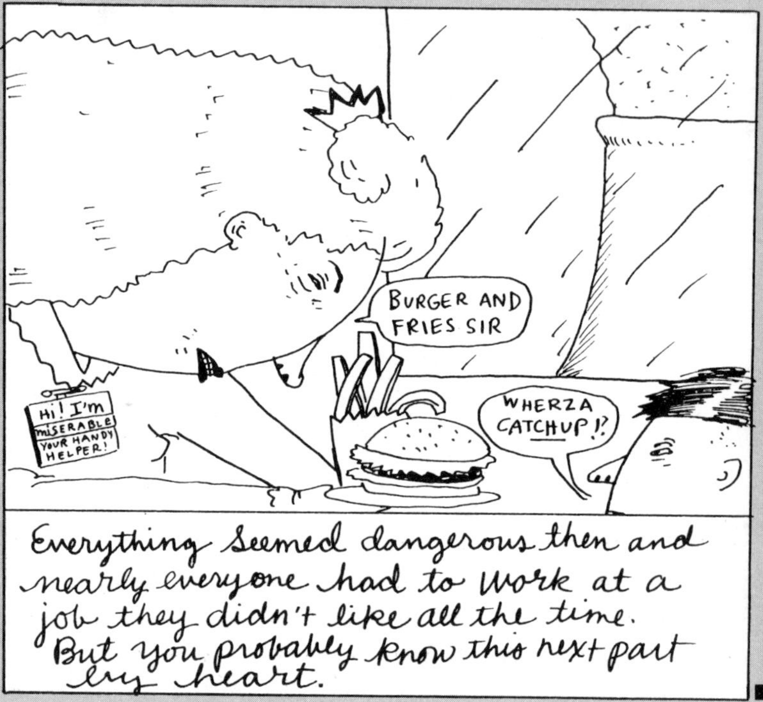
BURGER AND FRIES SIR
Hi! I'm MISERABLE YOUR HANDY HELPER!
WHERZA CATCHUP!?
Everything Seemed dangerous then and nearly everyone had to Work at a job they didn't like all the time. But you probably know this next part by heart.

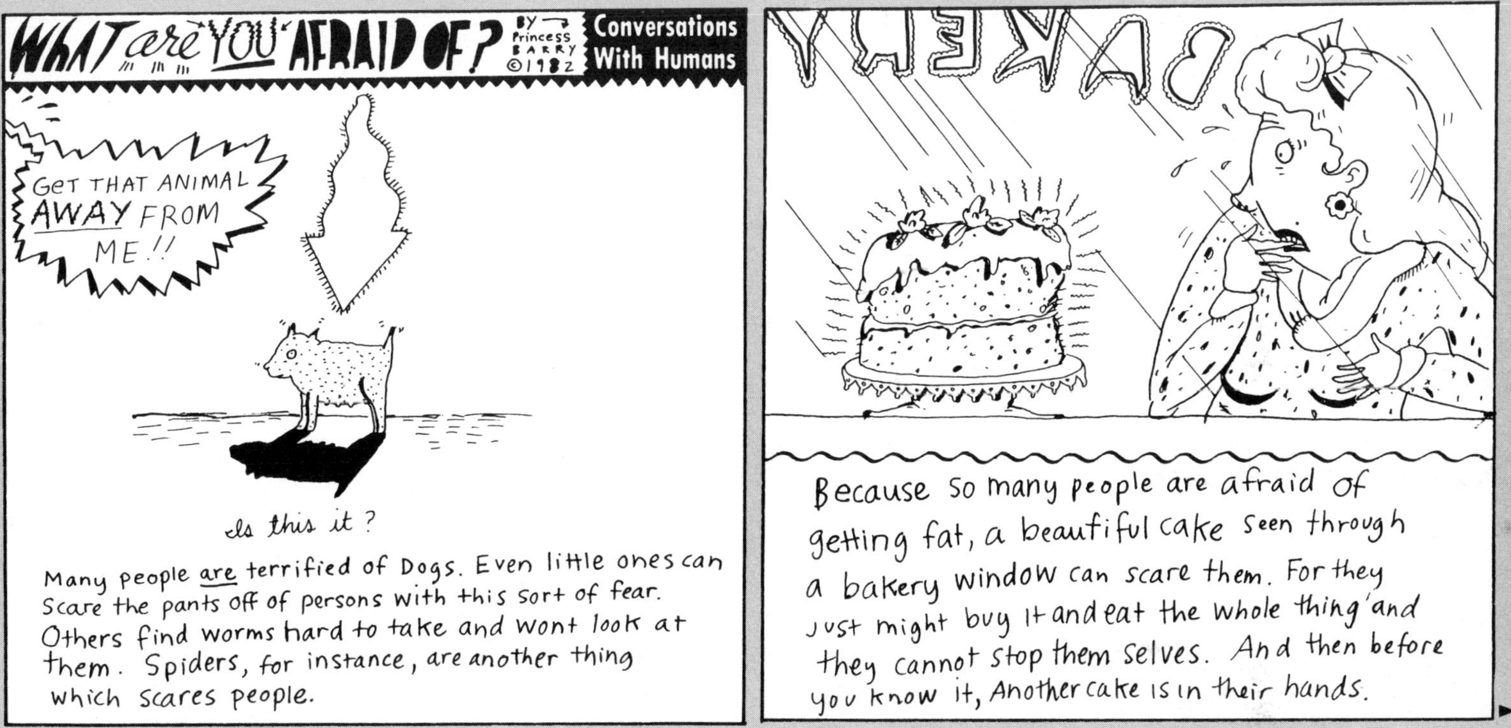
WHAT are YOU AFRAID OF?
BY Princess BARRY ©1982
Conversations With Humans
GET THAT ANIMAL AWAY FROM ME!!
Is this it?
Many people are terrified of Dogs. Even little ones can scare the pants off of persons with this sort of fear. Others find worms hard to take and wont look at them. Spiders, for instance, are another thing which scares people.
Because so many people are afraid of getting fat, a beautiful cake seen through a bakery window can scare them. For they just might buy it and eat the whole thing and they cannot stop them selves. And then before you know it, Another cake is in their hands.

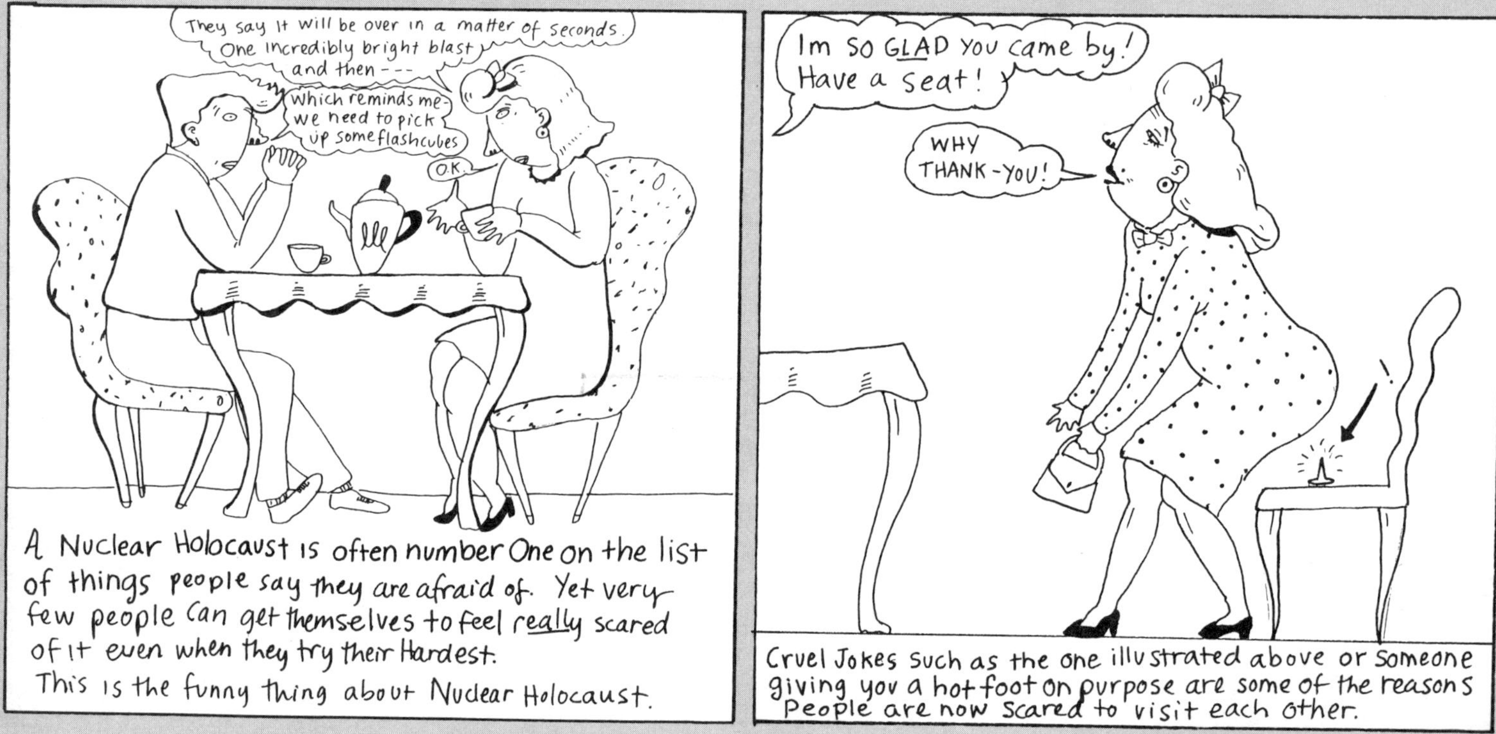
They say It will be over in a matter of seconds. One incredibly bright blast and then ---
Which reminds me- we need to pick up some flashcubes
O.K.
A Nuclear Holocaust is often number One on the list of things people say they are afraid of. Yet very few people can get themselves to feel really scared of it even when they try their Hardest.
This is the funny thing about Nuclear Holocaust.
Im SO GLAD you came by! Have a seat!
WHY THANK-YOU!
Cruel Jokes such as the one illustrated above or someone giving you a hot foot on purpose are some of the reasons People are now scared to visit each other.

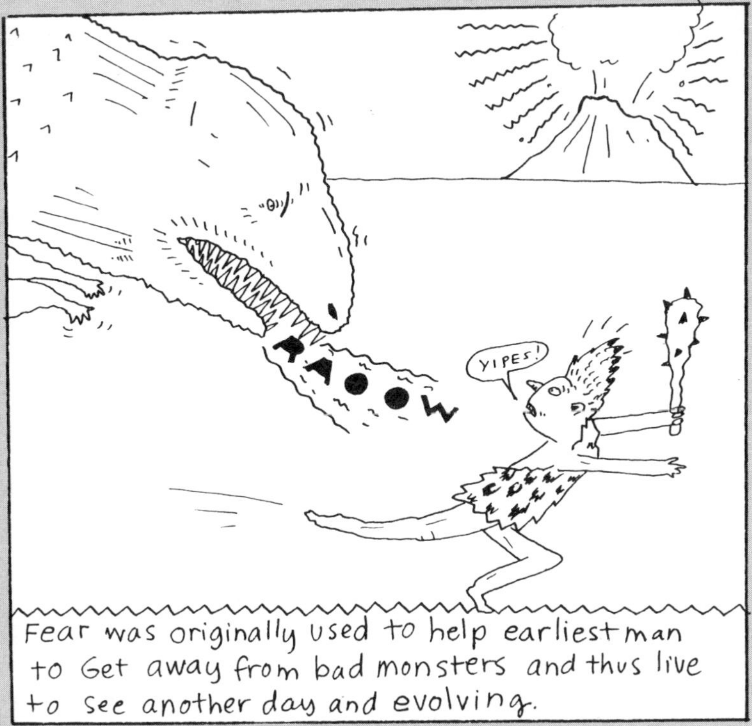
RAOOW
YIPES!
Fear was originally used to help earliest man to Get away from bad monsters and thus live to see another day and evolving.

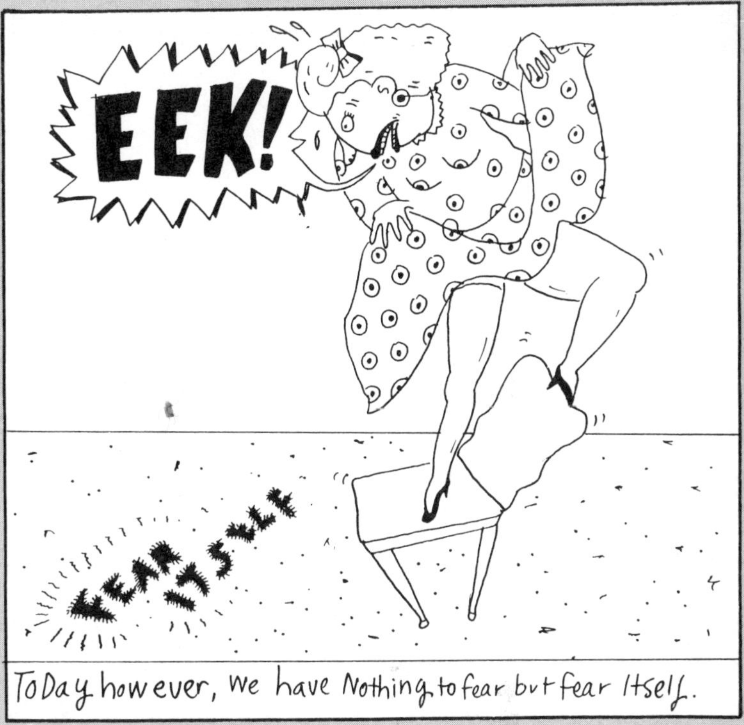
EEK!
FEAR ITSELF
ToDay however, We have Nothing to fear but fear Itself.

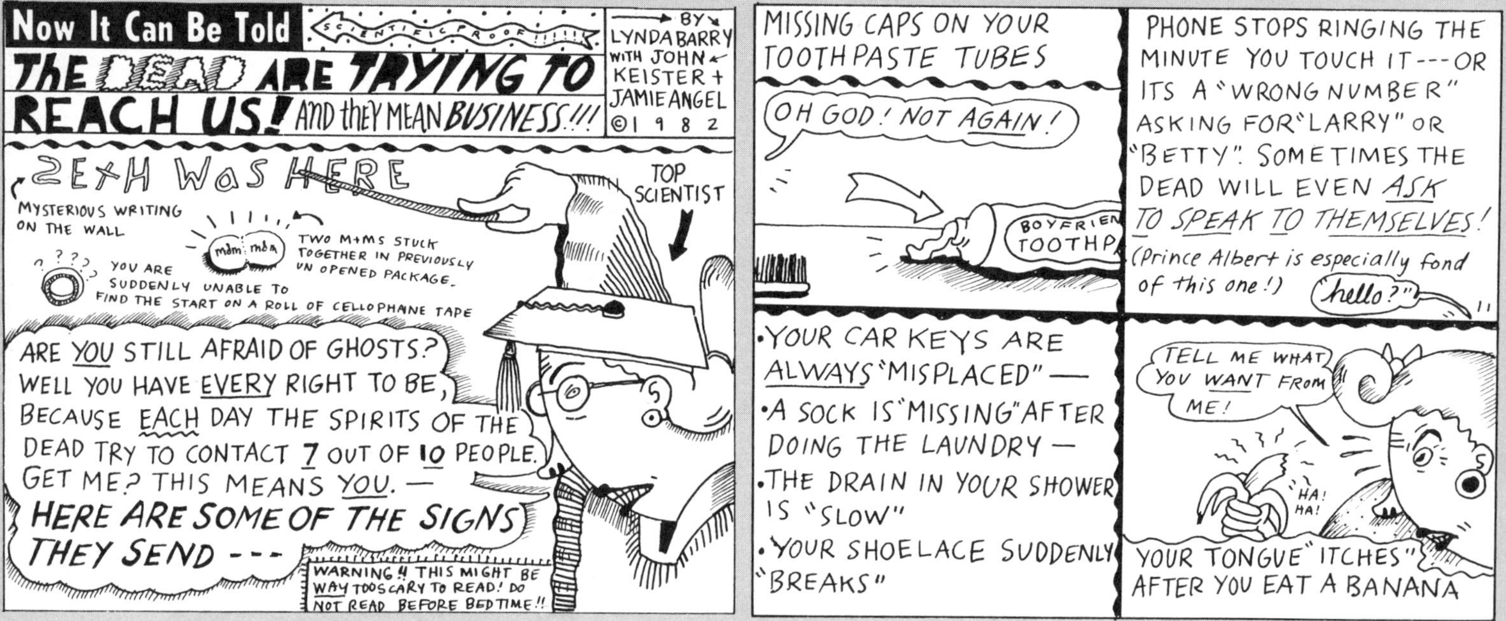
Now It Can Be Told
SCIENTIFIC PROOF!!!!!!
THE DEAD ARE TRYING TO REACH US! AND THEY MEAN BUSINESS!!!
BY LYNDA BARRY WITH JOHN KEISTER + JAMIE ANGEL ©1982
ZETH WAS HERE
MYSTERIOUS WRITING ON THE WALL
TOP SCIENTIST
TWO M+MS STUCK TOGETHER IN PREVIOUSLY UN OPENED PACKAGE.
YOU ARE SUDDENLY UNABLE TO FIND THE START ON A ROLL OF CELLOPHANE TAPE
ARE YOU STILL AFRAID OF GHOSTS? WELL YOU HAVE EVERY RIGHT TO BE, BECAUSE EACH DAY THE SPIRITS OF THE DEAD TRY TO CONTACT 7 OUT OF 10 PEOPLE. GET ME? THIS MEANS YOU. —
HERE ARE SOME OF THE SIGNS THEY SEND ---
WARNING!! THIS MIGHT BE WAY TOO SCARY TO READ! DO NOT READ BEFORE BEDTIME!!
MISSING CAPS ON YOUR TOOTHPASTE TUBES
OH GOD! NOT AGAIN!
BOYFRIEN TOOTHP
PHONE STOPS RINGING THE MINUTE YOU TOUCH IT---OR ITS A "WRONG NUMBER" ASKING FOR "LARRY" OR "BETTY". SOMETIMES THE DEAD WILL EVEN ASK TO SPEAK TO THEMSELVES!
(Prince Albert is especially fond of this one!)
"hello?"
•YOUR CAR KEYS ARE ALWAYS "MISPLACED" —
•A SOCK IS "MISSING" AFTER DOING THE LAUNDRY —
•THE DRAIN IN YOUR SHOWER IS "SLOW"
•YOUR SHOELACE SUDDENLY "BREAKS"
TELL ME WHAT YOU WANT FROM ME!
HA! HA!
YOUR TONGUE "ITCHES" AFTER YOU EAT A BANANA

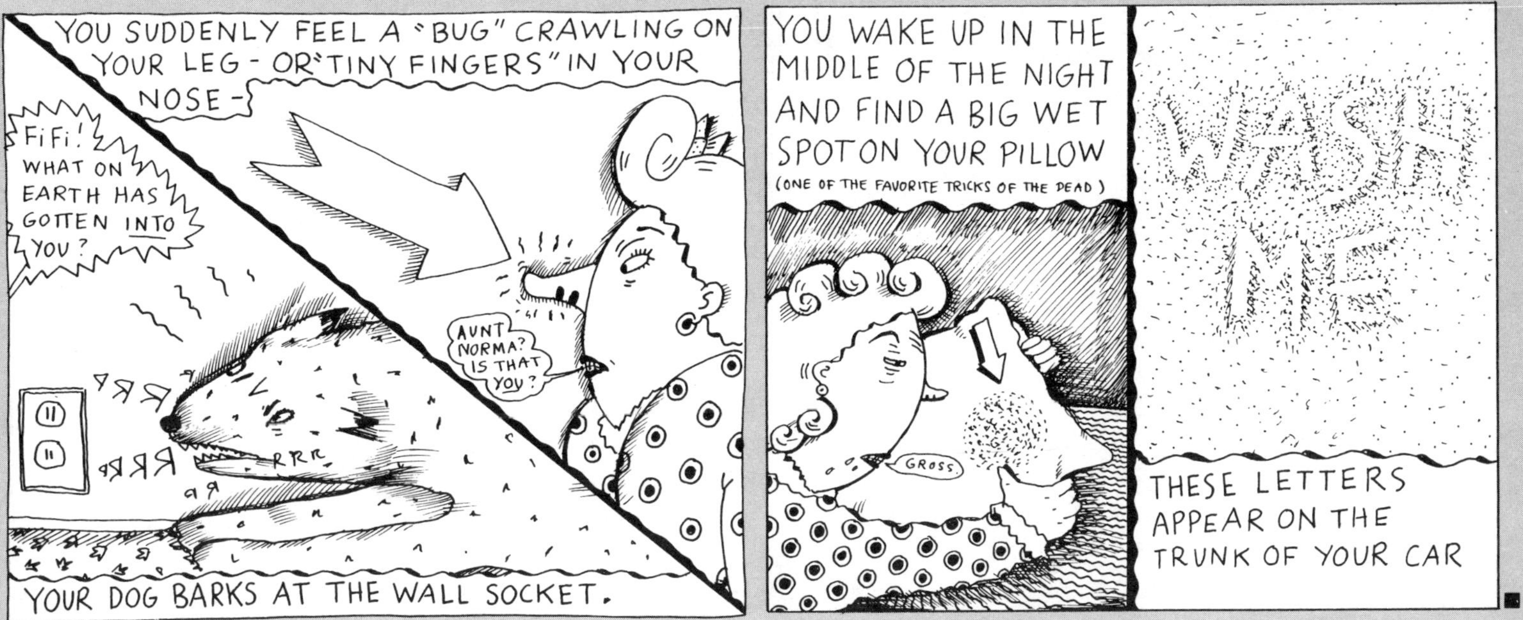
YOU SUDDENLY FEEL A "BUG" CRAWLING ON YOUR LEG - OR "TINY FINGERS" IN YOUR NOSE -
FiFi! WHAT ON EARTH HAS GOTTEN INTO YOU?
AUNT NORMA? IS THAT YOU?
RRR
YOUR DOG BARKS AT THE WALL SOCKET.
YOU WAKE UP IN THE MIDDLE OF THE NIGHT AND FIND A BIG WET SPOT ON YOUR PILLOW
(ONE OF THE FAVORITE TRICKS OF THE DEAD)
GROSS
WASH ME
THESE LETTERS APPEAR ON THE TRUNK OF YOUR CAR

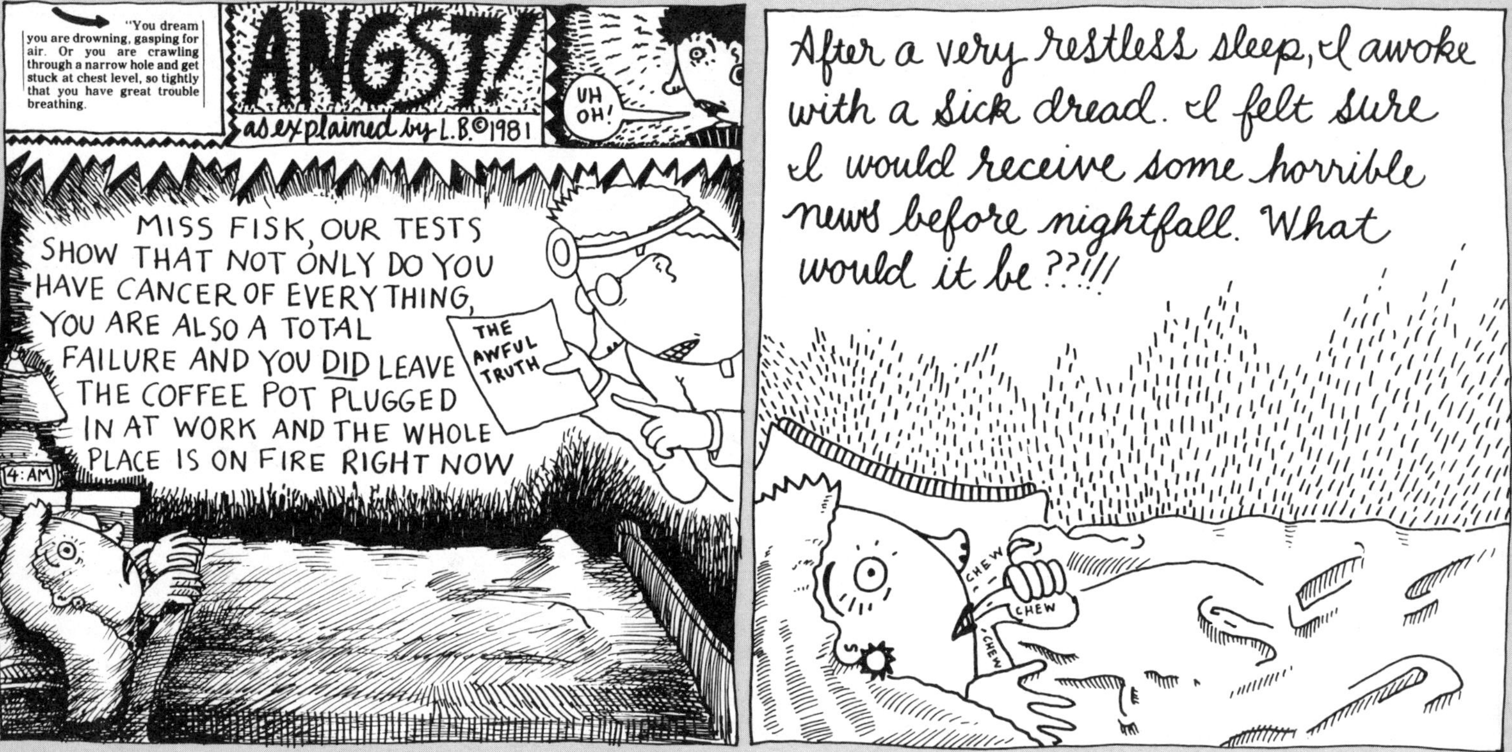
"You dream you are drowning, gasping for air. Or you are crawling through a narrow hole and get stuck at chest level, so tightly that you have great trouble breathing.
ANGST!
as explained by L.B.©1981
UH OH!
MISS FISK, OUR TESTS SHOW THAT NOT ONLY DO YOU HAVE CANCER OF EVERYTHING, YOU ARE ALSO A TOTAL FAILURE AND YOU DID LEAVE THE COFFEE POT PLUGGED IN AT WORK AND THE WHOLE PLACE IS ON FIRE RIGHT NOW
THE AWFUL TRUTH
4:AM
After a very restless sleep, I awoke with a sick dread. I felt sure I would receive some horrible news before nightfall. What would it be??!!!
CHEW
CHEW
CHEW

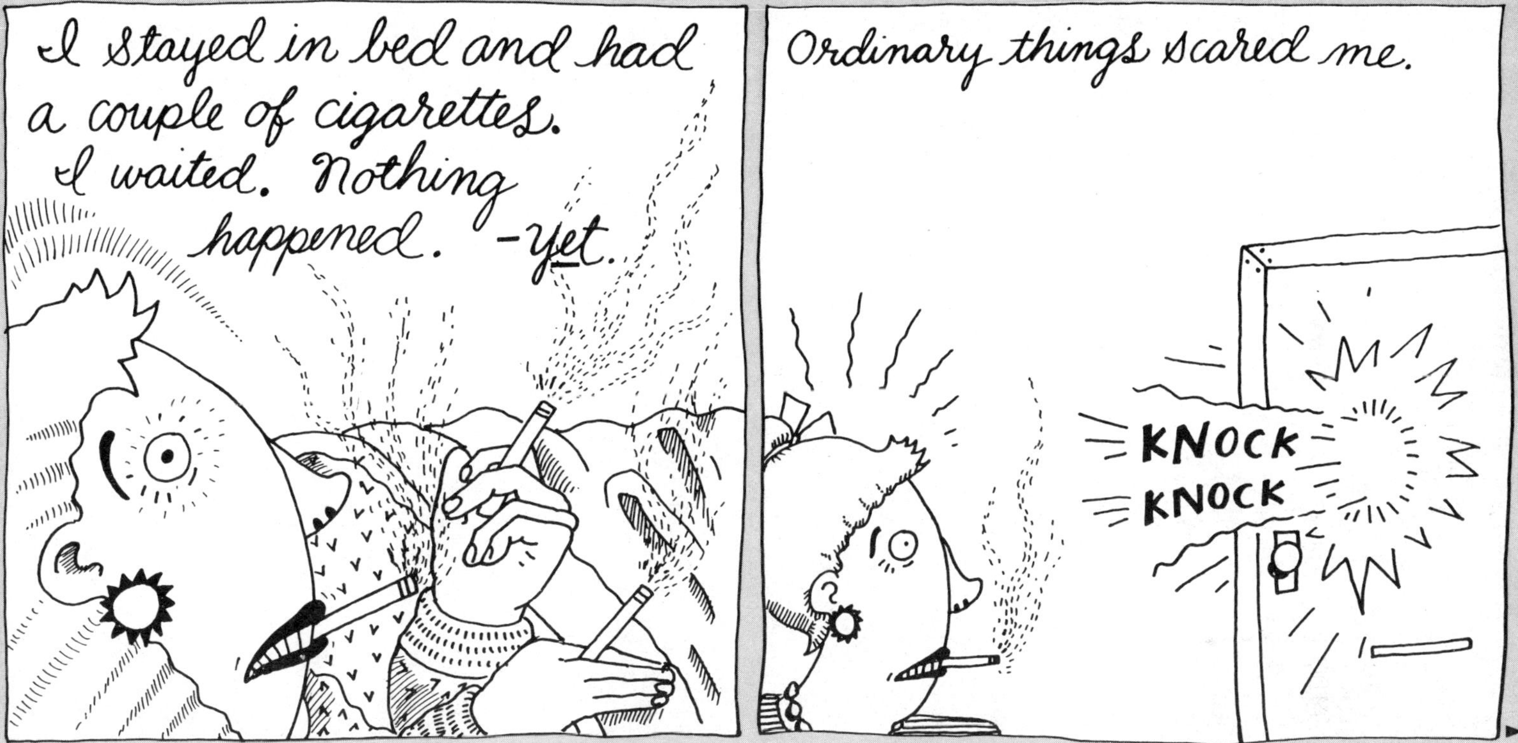
I stayed in bed and had a couple of cigarettes. I waited. Nothing happened. -yet.
Ordinary things scared me.
KNOCK
KNOCK

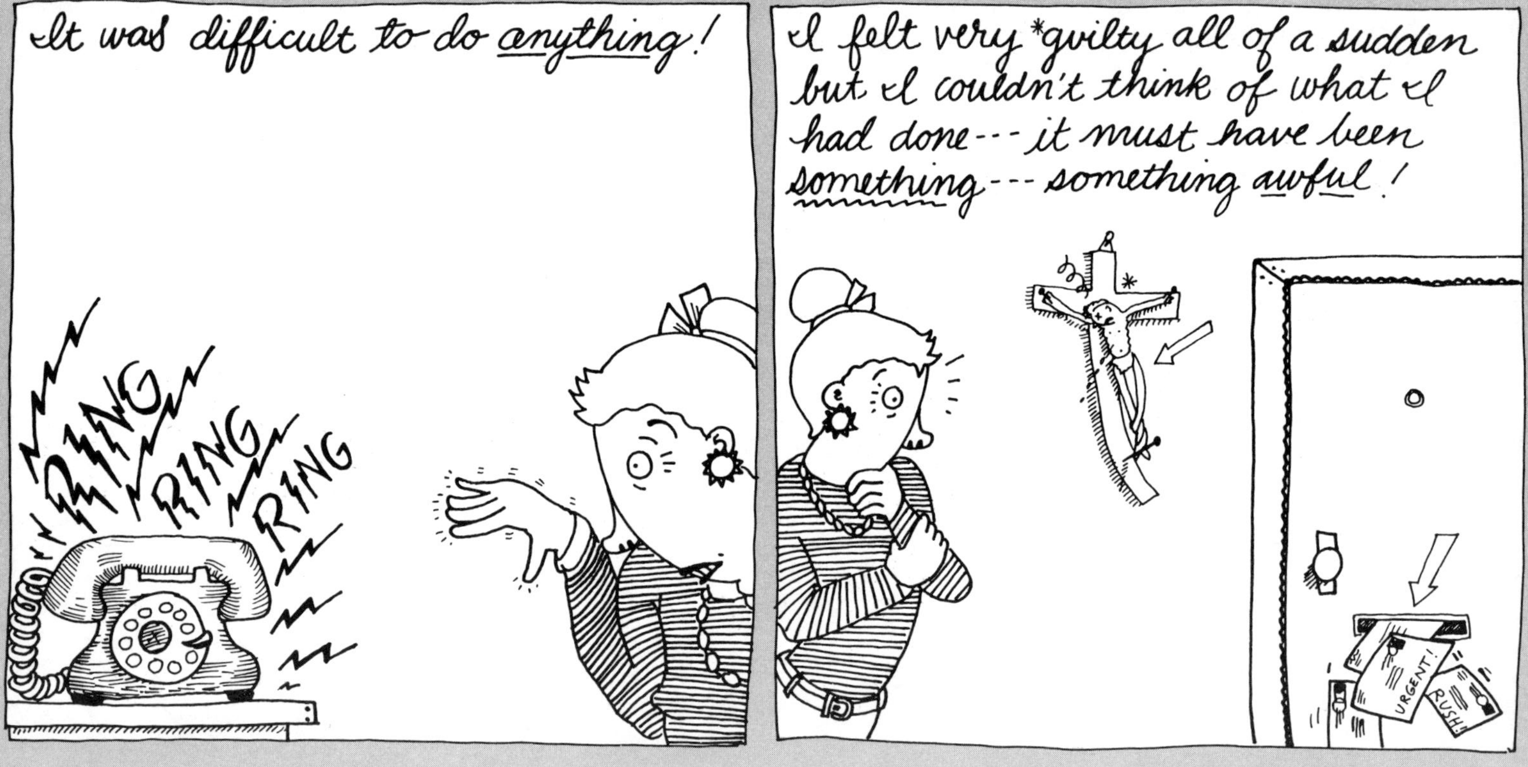
It was difficult to do anything!
RING
RING
RING
I felt very *guilty all of a sudden but I couldn't think of what I had done--- it must have been something--- something awful!
URGENT!
RUSH!

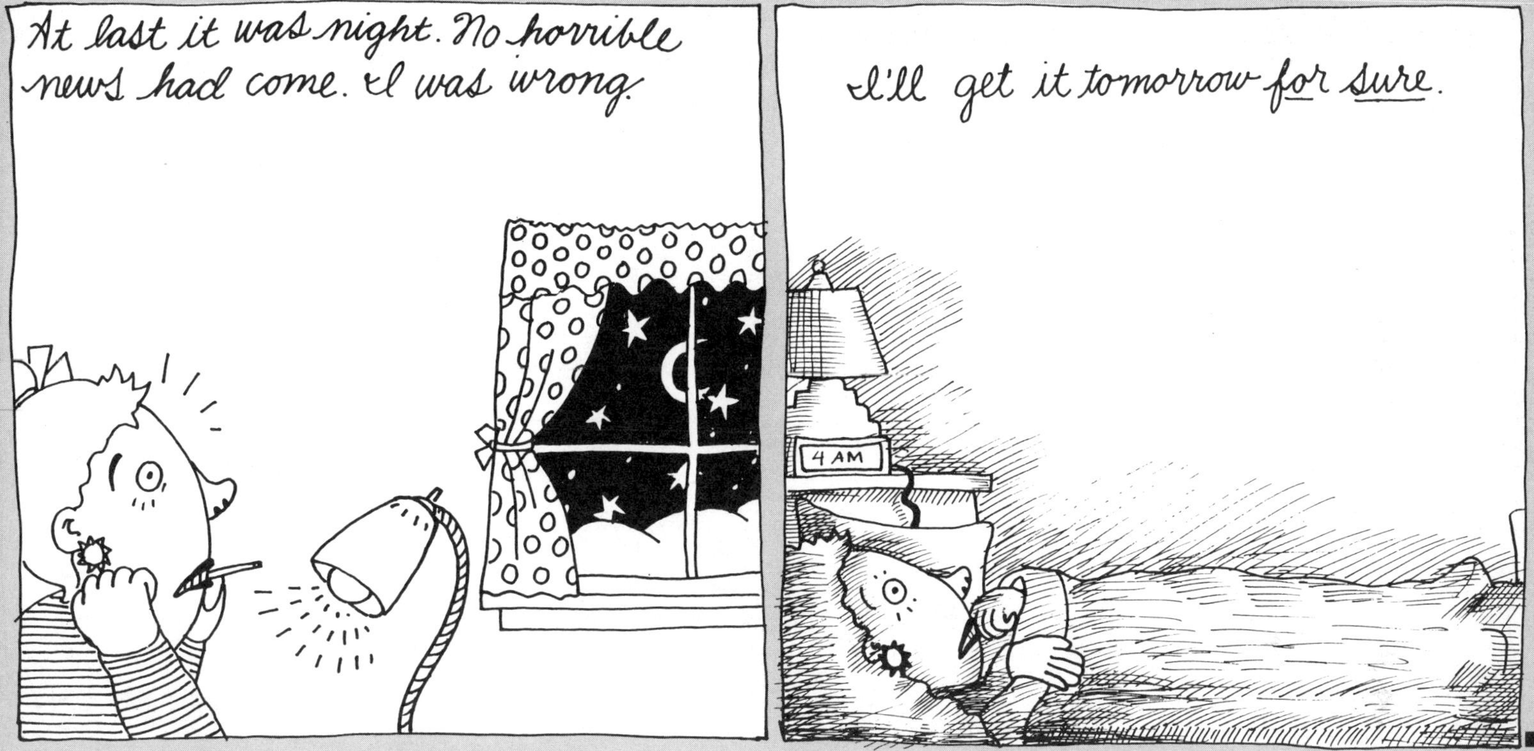
At last it was night. No horrible news had come. I was wrong.
4 AM
I'll get it tomorrow for sure.

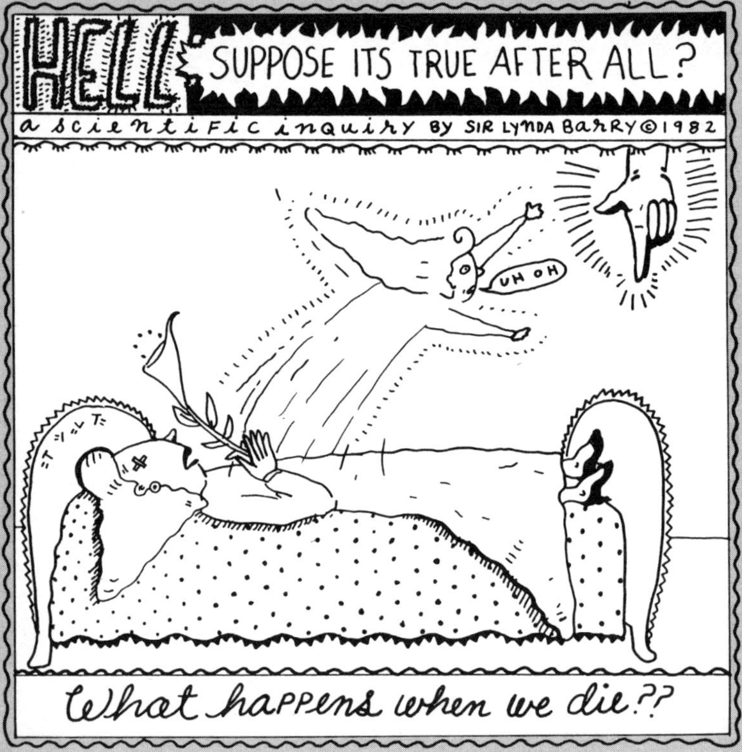
HELL: SUPPOSE ITS TRUE AFTER ALL?
a scientific inquiry BY SIR LYNDA BARRY © 1982
UH OH
What happens when we die??

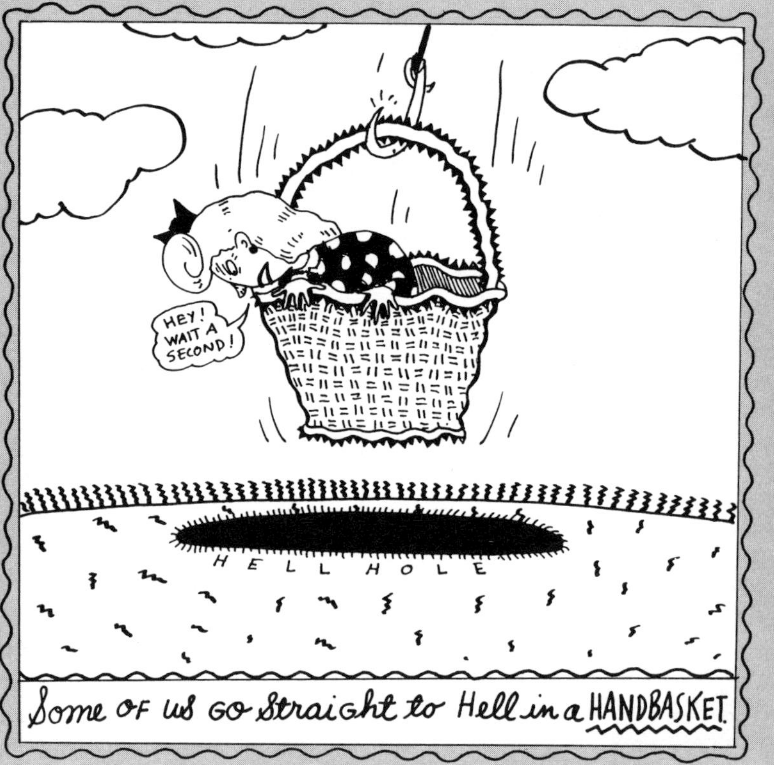
HEY! WAIT A SECOND!
HELL HOLE
Some OF US GO Straight to Hell in a HANDBASKET.

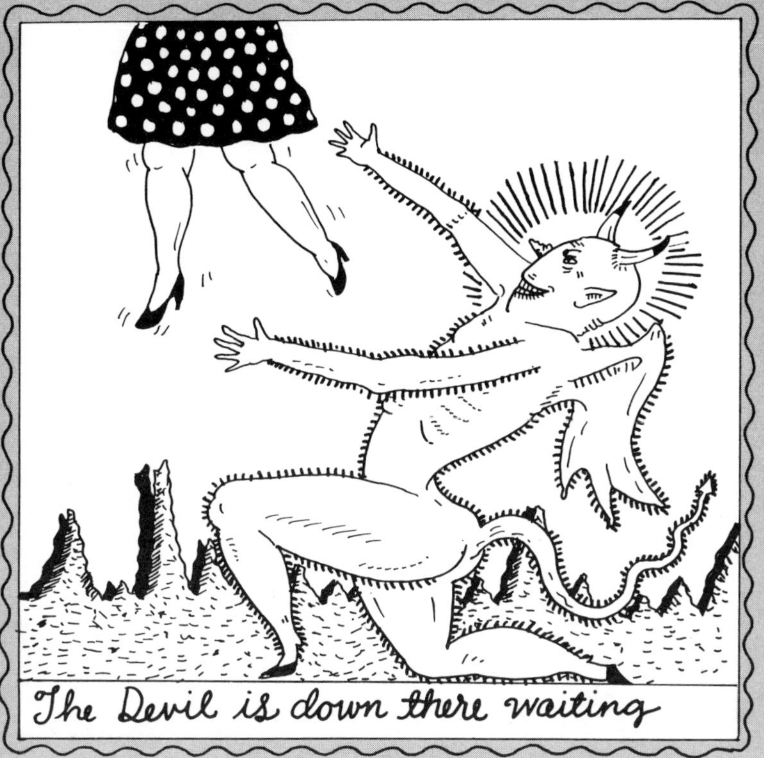
The Devil is down there waiting

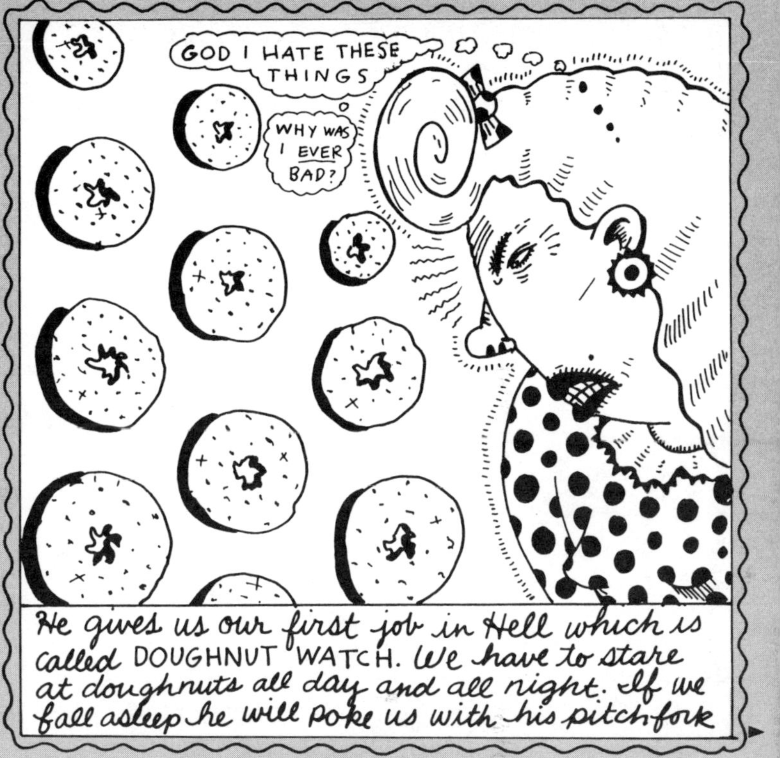
GOD I HATE THESE THINGS
WHY WAS I EVER BAD?
He gives us our first job in Hell which is called DOUGHNUT WATCH. We have to stare at doughnuts all day and all night. If we fall asleep he will poke us with his pitchfork

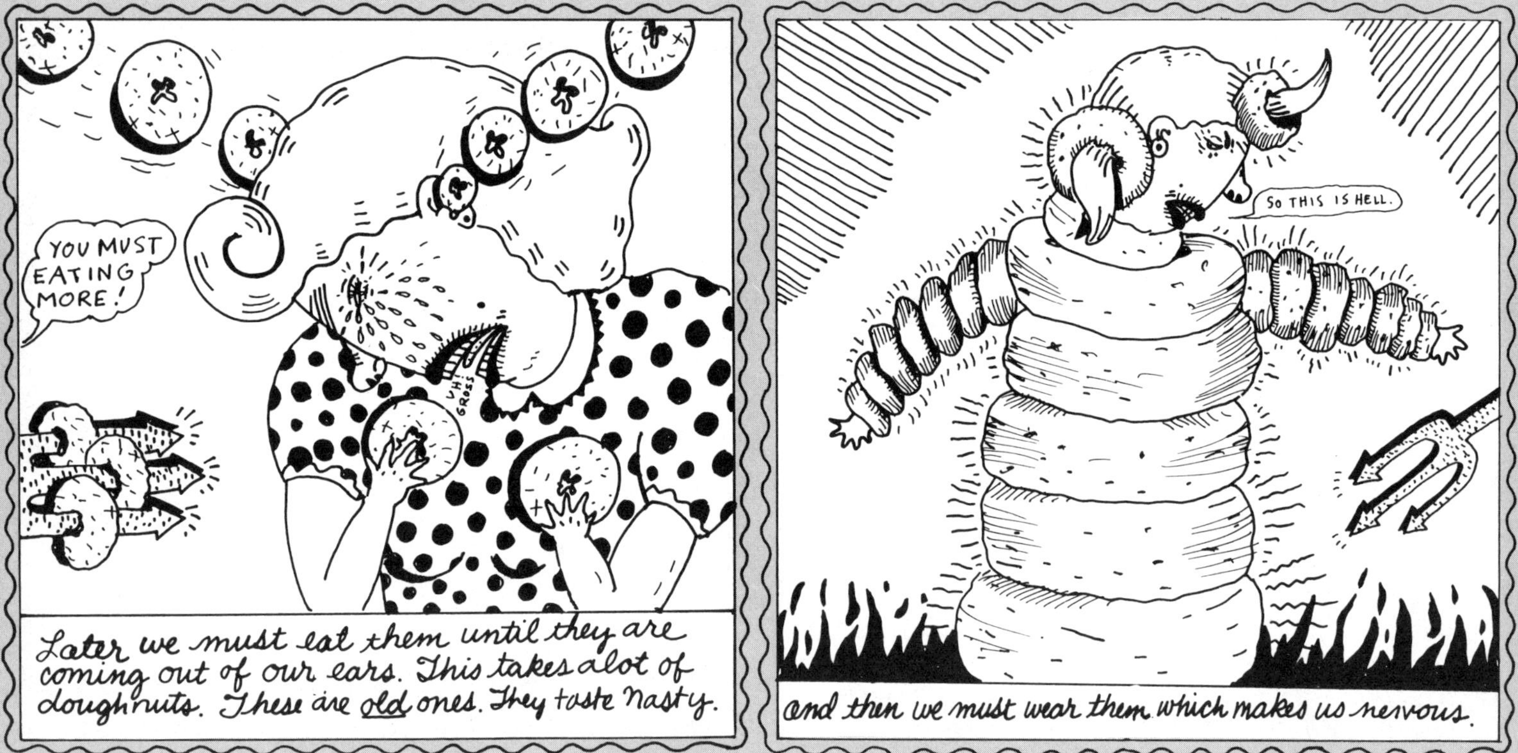
YOU MUST EATING MORE!
UH! GROSS
Later we must eat them until they are coming out of our ears. This takes alot of doughnuts. These are old ones. They taste nasty.
SO THIS IS HELL.
and then we must wear them which makes us nervous.

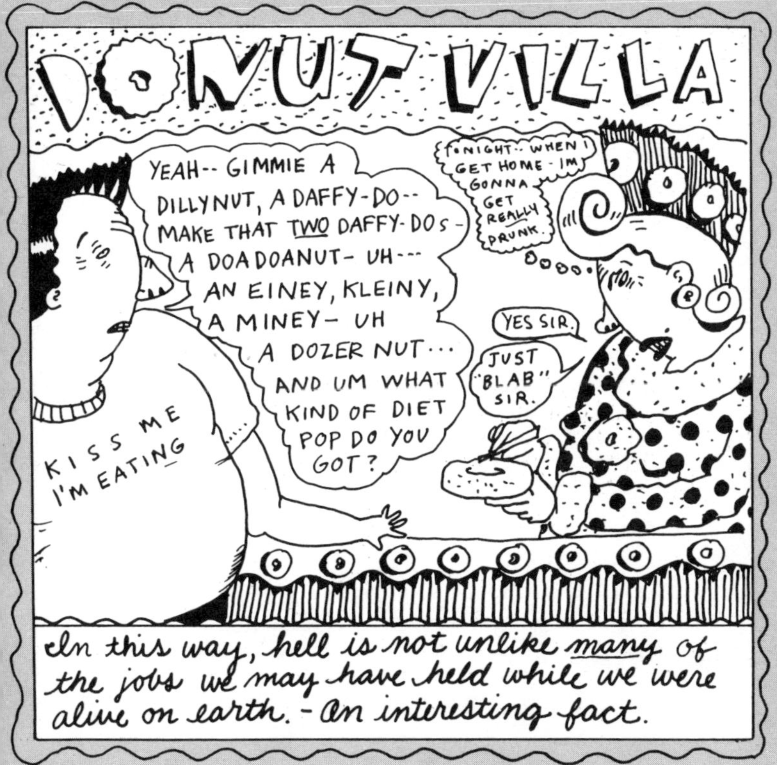
DONUT VILLA
YEAH-- GIMMIE A DILLYNUT, A DAFFY-DO-- MAKE THAT TWO DAFFY-DOS - A DOADOANUT- UH--- AN EINEY, KLEINY, A MINEY- UH A DOZER NUT... AND UM WHAT KIND OF DIET POP DO YOU GOT?
TONIGHT-- WHEN I GET HOME - IM GONNA GET REALLY DRUNK.
YES SIR.
JUST "BLAB" SIR.
KISS ME I'M EATING
In this way, hell is not unlike many of the jobs we may have held while we were alive on earth. - An interesting fact.

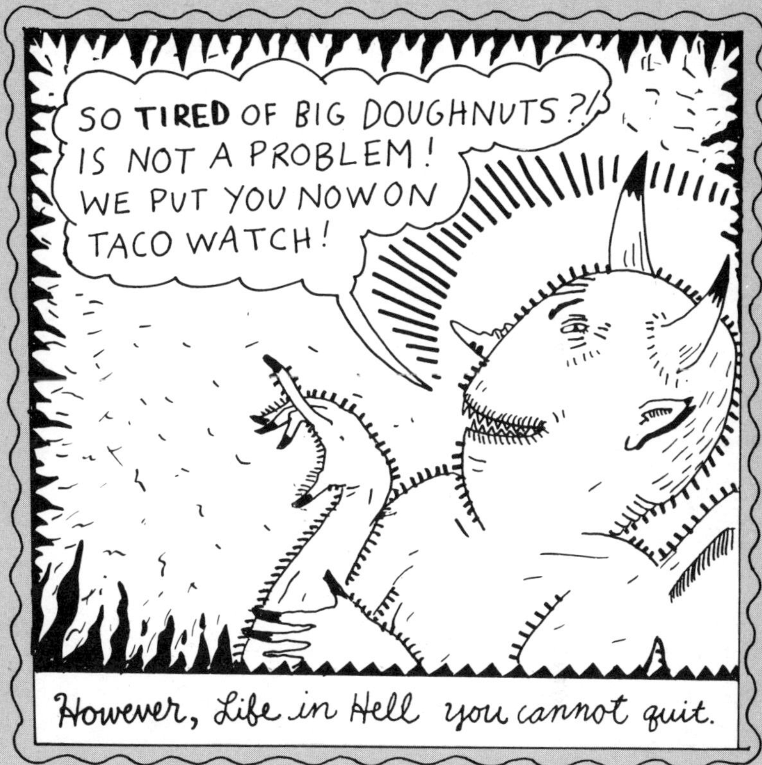
SO TIRED OF BIG DOUGHNUTS?/ IS NOT A PROBLEM! WE PUT YOU NOWON TACO WATCH!
However, Life in Hell you cannot quit.

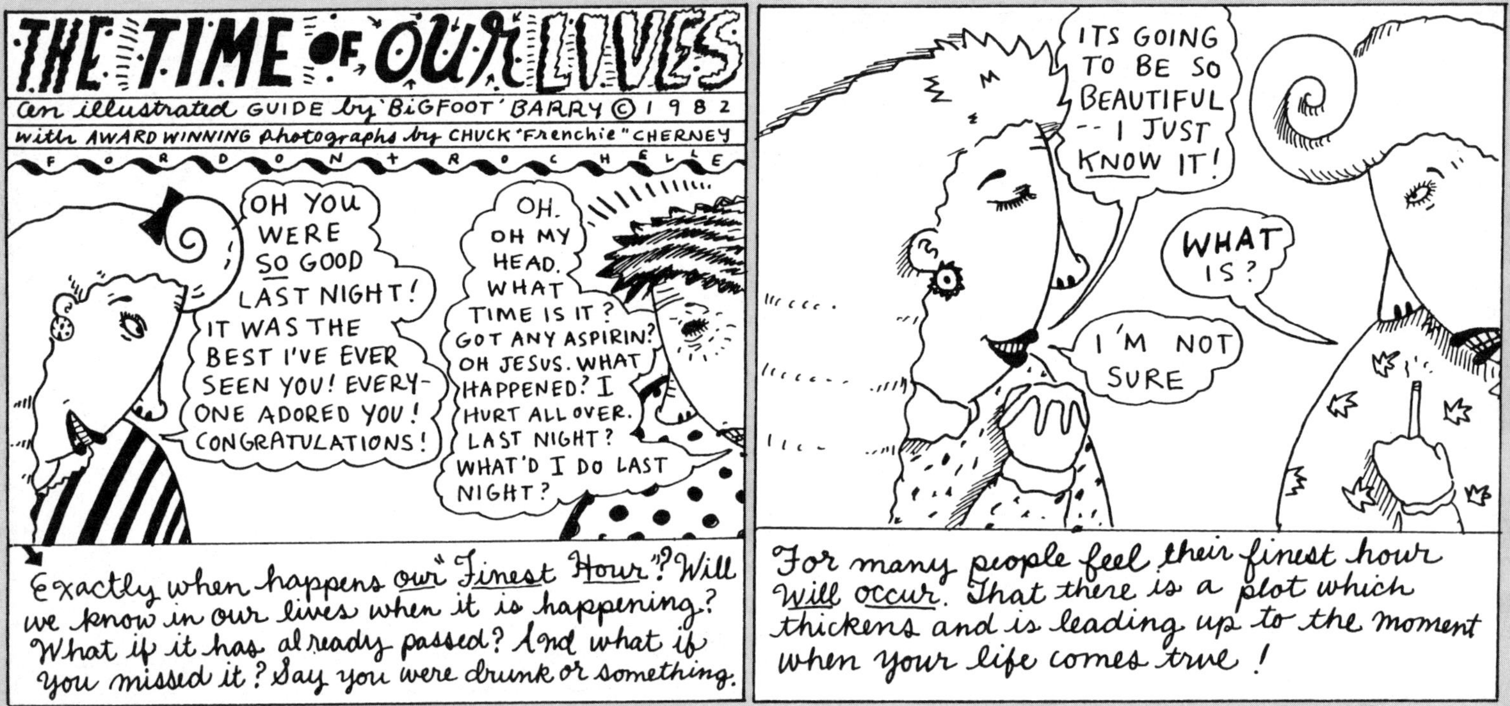
THE TIME OF OUR LIVES
an illustrated GUIDE by 'BIGFOOT' BARRY © 1982
with AWARD WINNING photographs by CHUCK "Frenchie" CHERNEY
FOR DON + ROCHELLE
OH YOU WERE SO GOOD LAST NIGHT! IT WAS THE BEST I'VE EVER SEEN YOU! EVERY-ONE ADORED YOU! CONGRATULATIONS!
OH. OH MY HEAD. WHAT TIME IS IT? GOT ANY ASPIRIN? OH JESUS. WHAT HAPPENED? I HURT ALL OVER. LAST NIGHT? WHAT'D I DO LAST NIGHT?
Exactly when happens our "Finest Hour"? Will we know in our lives when it is happening? What if it has already passed? And what if you missed it? Say you were drunk or something.
ITS GOING TO BE SO BEAUTIFUL -- I JUST KNOW IT!
WHAT IS?
I'M NOT SURE
For many people feel their finest hour will occur. That there is a plot which thickens and is leading up to the moment when your life comes true!

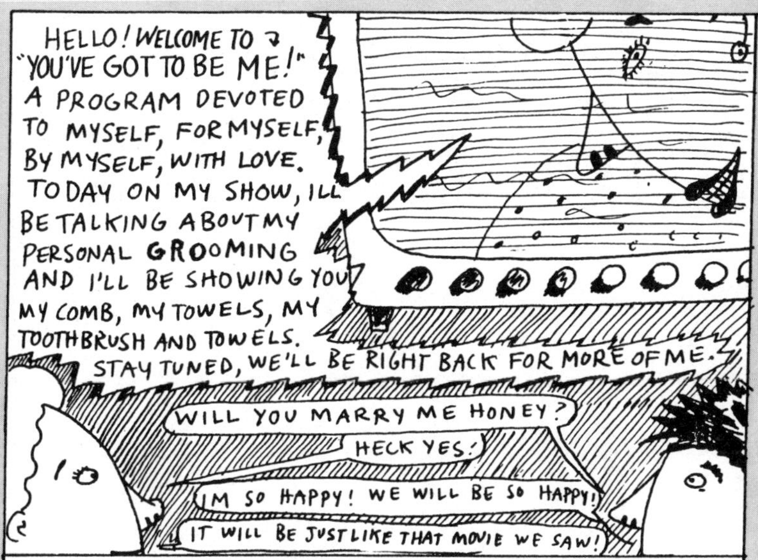
HELLO! WELCOME TO "YOU'VE GOT TO BE ME!" A PROGRAM DEVOTED TO MYSELF, FOR MYSELF, BY MYSELF, WITH LOVE. TODAY ON MY SHOW, ILL BE TALKING ABOUT MY PERSONAL GROOMING AND I'LL BE SHOWING YOU MY COMB, MY TOWELS, MY TOOTHBRUSH AND TOWELS.
STAY TUNED, WE'LL BE RIGHT BACK FOR MORE OF ME.
WILL YOU MARRY ME HONEY?
HECK YES!
IM SO HAPPY! WE WILL BE SO HAPPY!
IT WILL BE JUST LIKE THAT MOVIE WE SAW!

Some people think it is the moment they are man and wife. Others think it is when they have their own T.V. Show.

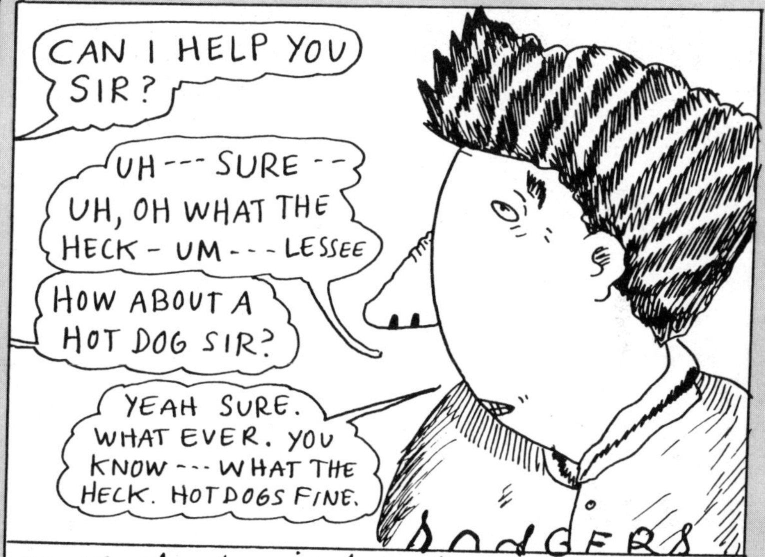
CAN I HELP YOU SIR?
UH --- SURE -- UH, OH WHAT THE HECK - UM --- LESSEE
HOW ABOUT A HOT DOG SIR?
YEAH SURE. WHAT EVER. YOU KNOW --- WHAT THE HECK. HOTDOGS FINE.
DODGERS

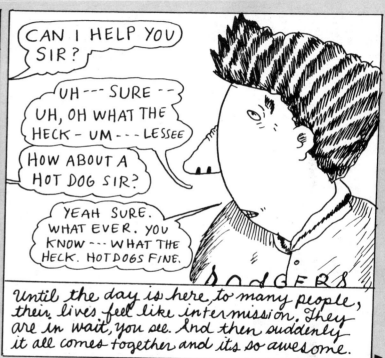

Until the day is here, to many people, their lives feel like intermission. They are in wait, you see. And then suddenly it all comes together and its so awesome.

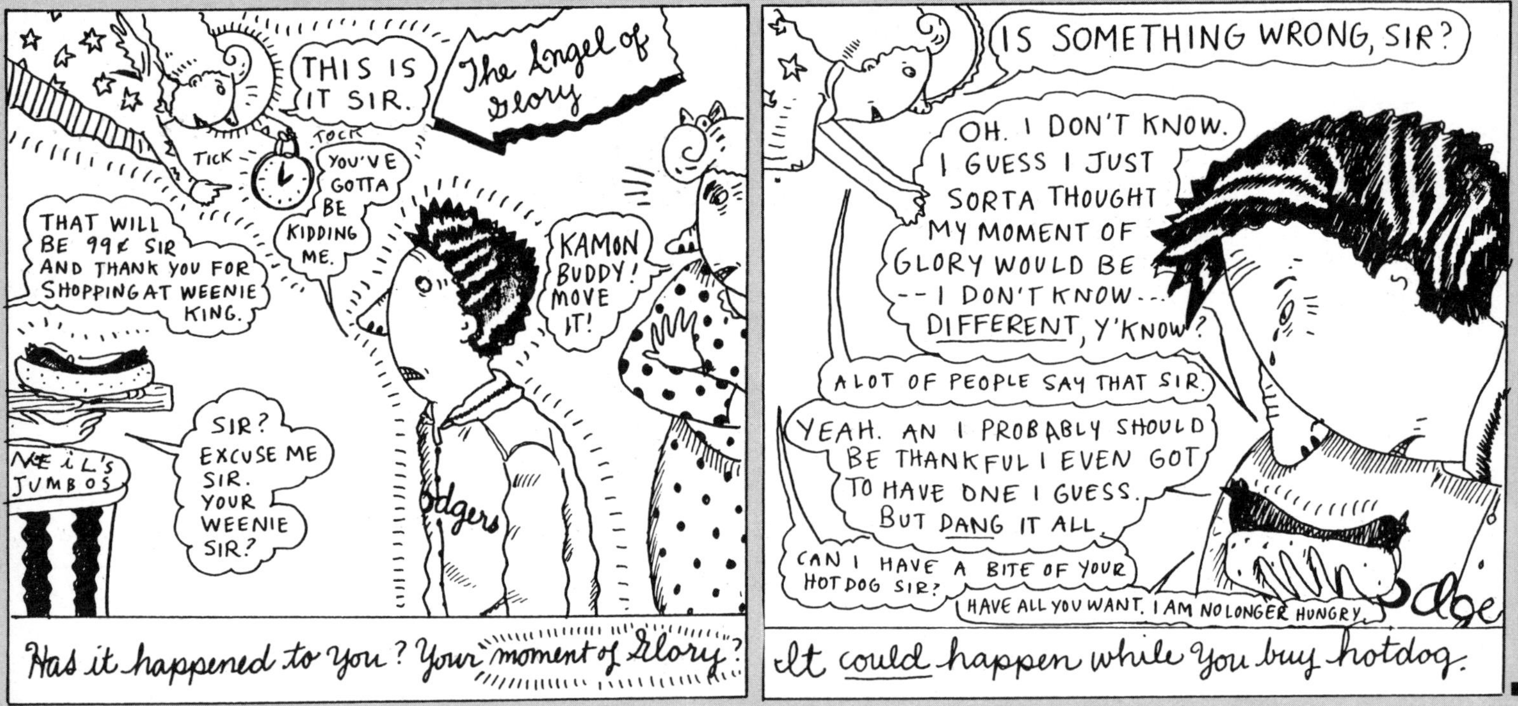

The Angel of Glory
THIS IS IT SIR.
TICK
TOCK
YOU'VE GOTTA BE KIDDING ME.
THAT WILL BE 99¢ SIR AND THANK YOU FOR SHOPPING AT WEENIE KING.
KAMON BUDDY! MOVE IT!
SIR? EXCUSE ME SIR. YOUR WEENIE SIR?
NEIL'S JUMBOS
odgers
Has it happened to you? Your moment of Glory?
IS SOMETHING WRONG, SIR?
OH. I DON'T KNOW. I GUESS I JUST SORTA THOUGHT MY MOMENT OF GLORY WOULD BE --I DON'T KNOW... DIFFERENT, Y'KNOW?
A LOT OF PEOPLE SAY THAT SIR.
YEAH. AN I PROBABLY SHOULD BE THANKFUL I EVEN GOT TO HAVE ONE I GUESS. BUT DANG IT ALL.
CAN I HAVE A BITE OF YOUR HOTDOG SIR?
HAVE ALL YOU WANT. I AM NO LONGER HUNGRY.
It could happen while You buy hotdog.

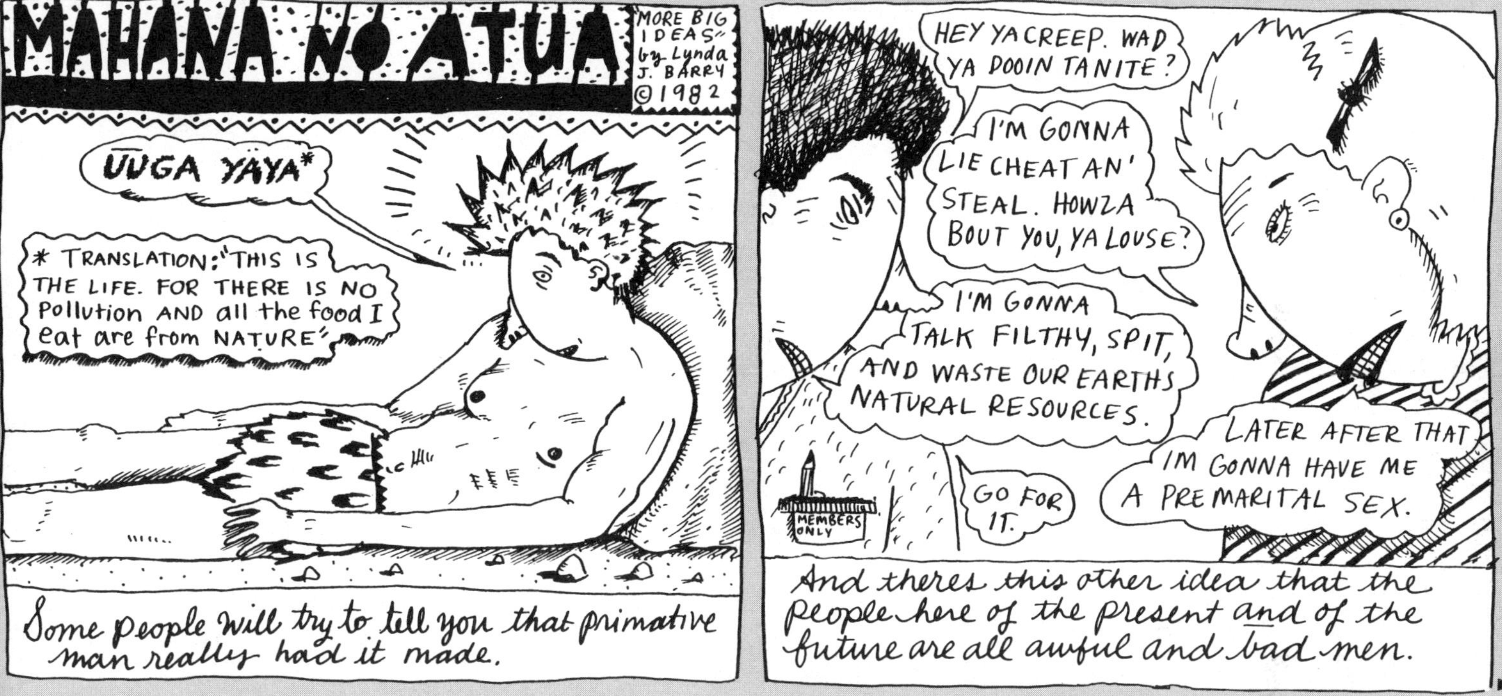
MAHANA NO ATUA
MORE BIG IDEAS" by Lynda J. BARRY ©1982
UUGA YAYA*
* TRANSLATION: "THIS IS THE LIFE. FOR THERE IS NO Pollution AND all the food I eat are from NATURE"
Some people will try to tell you that primative man really had it made.
HEY YA CREEP. WAD YA DOOIN TANITE?
I'M GONNA LIE CHEAT AN' STEAL. HOWZA BOUT YOU, YA LOUSE?
I'M GONNA TALK FILTHY, SPIT, AND WASTE OUR EARTHS NATURAL RESOURCES.
LATER AFTER THAT IM GONNA HAVE ME A PREMARITAL SEX.
GO FOR IT.
MEMBERS ONLY
And theres this other idea that the people here of the present and of the future are all awful and bad men.

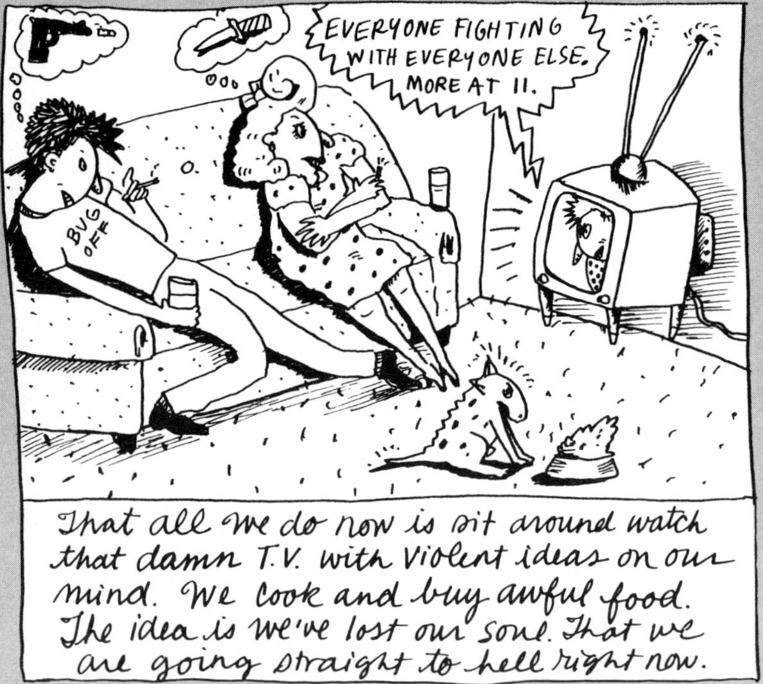
EVERYONE FIGHTING WITH EVERYONE ELSE. MORE AT 11.
BUG OFF
That all we do now is sit around watch that damn T.V. with violent ideas on our mind. We cook and buy awful food. The idea is we've lost our soul. That we are going straight to hell right now.

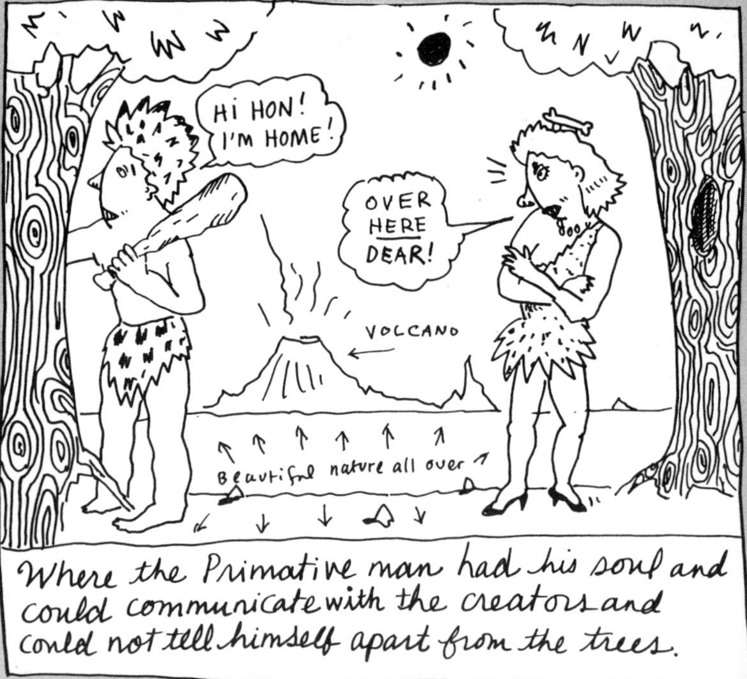
Hi HON! I'M HOME!
OVER HERE DEAR!
VOLCANO
Beautiful nature all over
Where the Primative man had his soul and could communicate with the creators and could not tell himself apart from the trees.

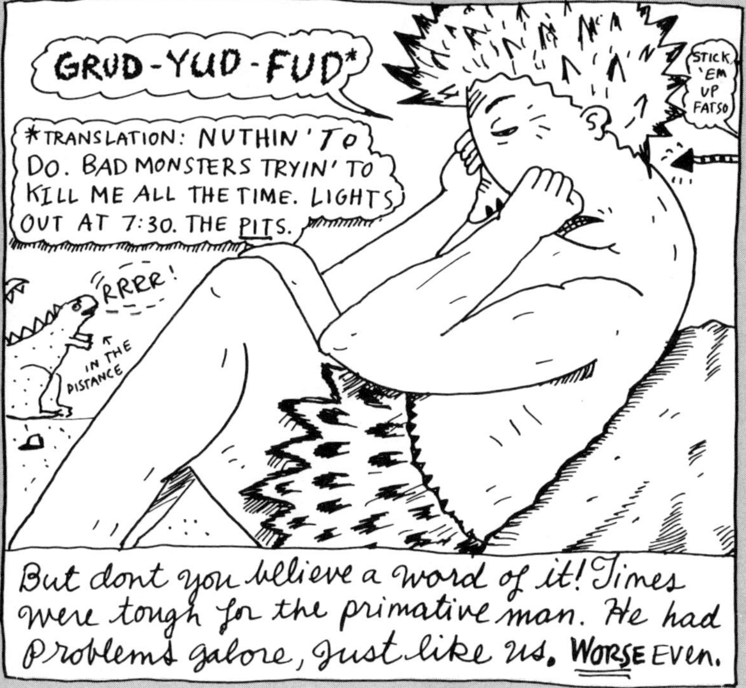
GRUD-YUD-FUD*
*TRANSLATION: NUTHIN' TO DO. BAD MONSTERS TRYIN' TO KILL ME ALL THE TIME. LIGHTS OUT AT 7:30. THE PITS.
STICK 'EM UP FATSO
RRRR!
IN THE DISTANCE
But dont you believe a word of it! Times were tough for the primative man. He had problems galore, just like us. WORSE EVEN.

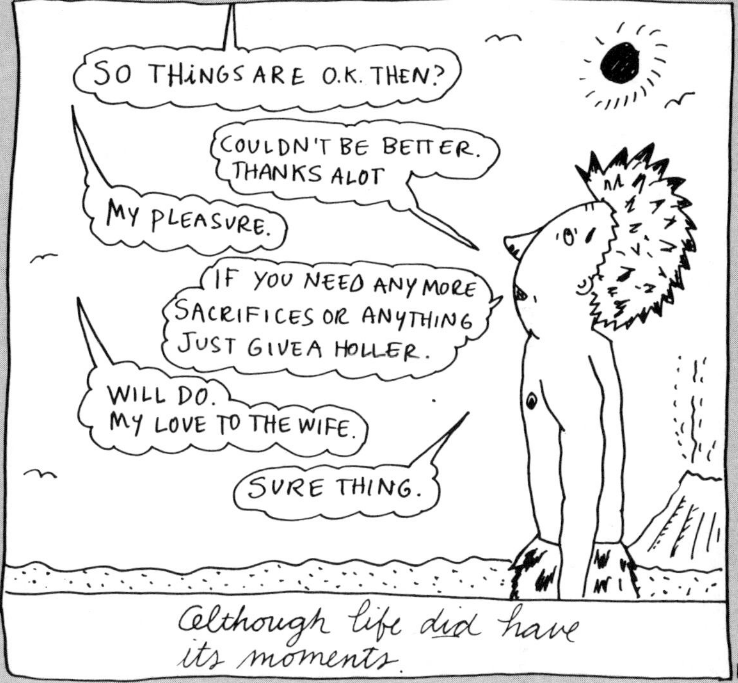
SO THINGS ARE O.K. THEN?
COULDN'T BE BETTER. THANKS ALOT
MY PLEASURE.
IF YOU NEED ANY MORE SACRIFICES OR ANYTHING JUST GIVE A HOLLER.
WILL DO. MY LOVE TO THE WIFE.
SURE THING.
Although life did have its moments.

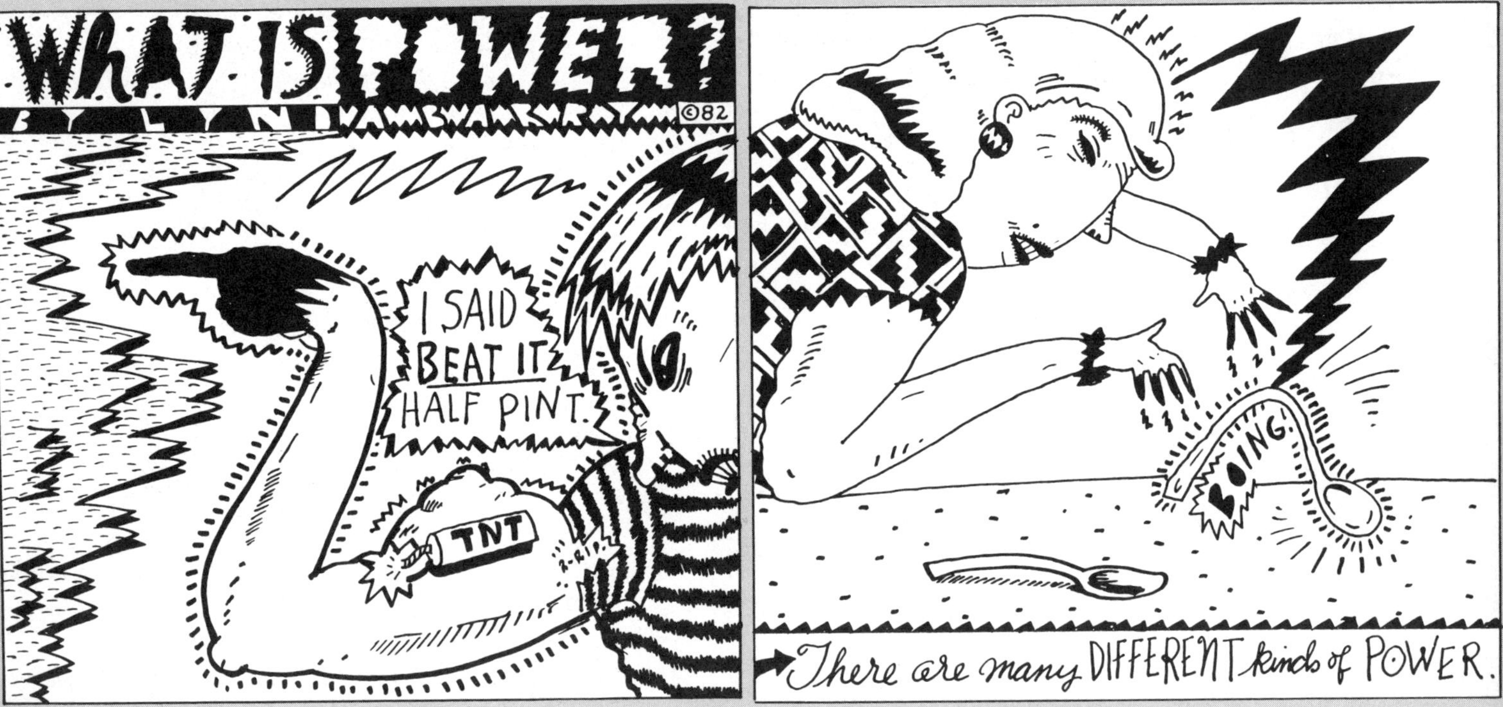
WHAT IS POWER?
©82
I SAID BEAT IT HALF PINT.
TNT
R-RIP
BOING!
There are many DIFFERENT kinds of POWER.

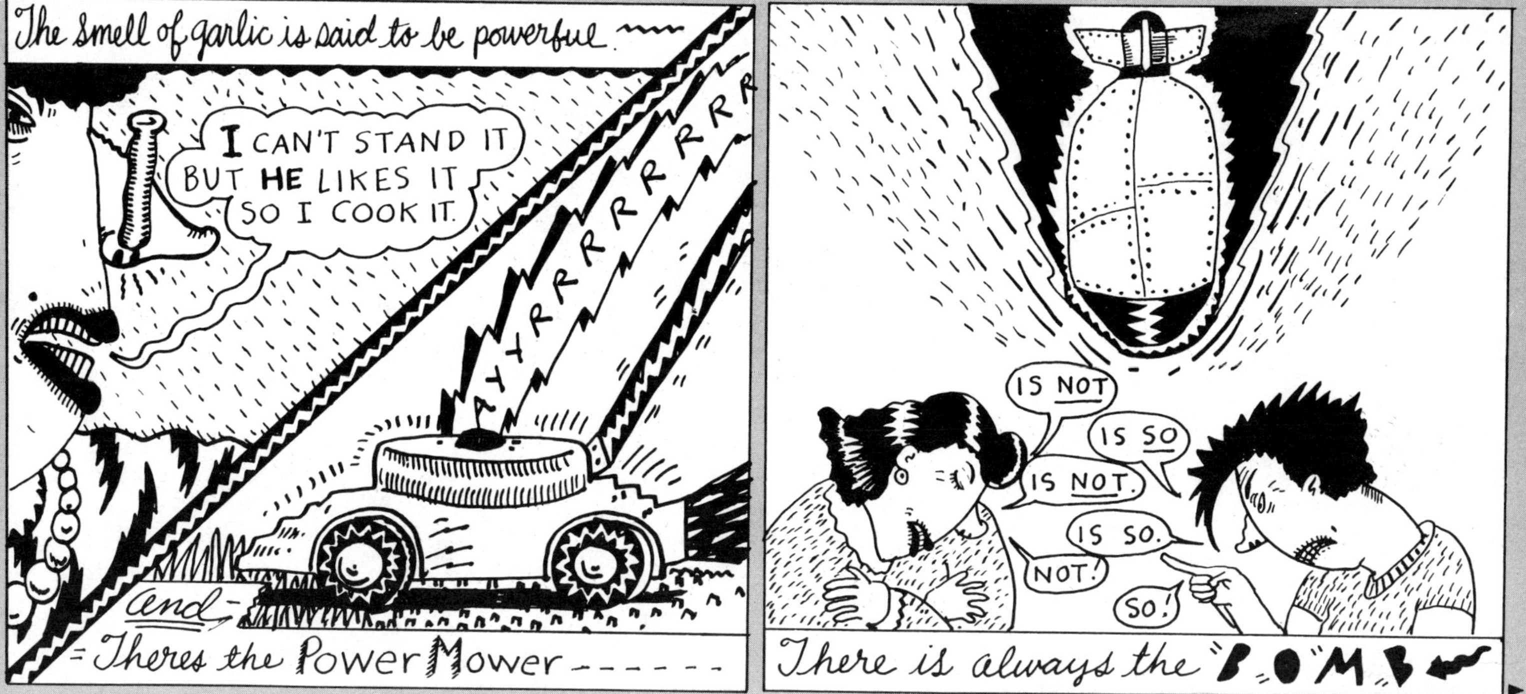
The Smell of garlic is said to be powerful
I CAN'T STAND IT BUT HE LIKES IT SO I COOK IT.
AYYRRRRRRRRRR
and
Theres the Power Mower
There is always the BOMB
IS NOT
IS SO
IS NOT.
IS SO.
NOT!
SO!

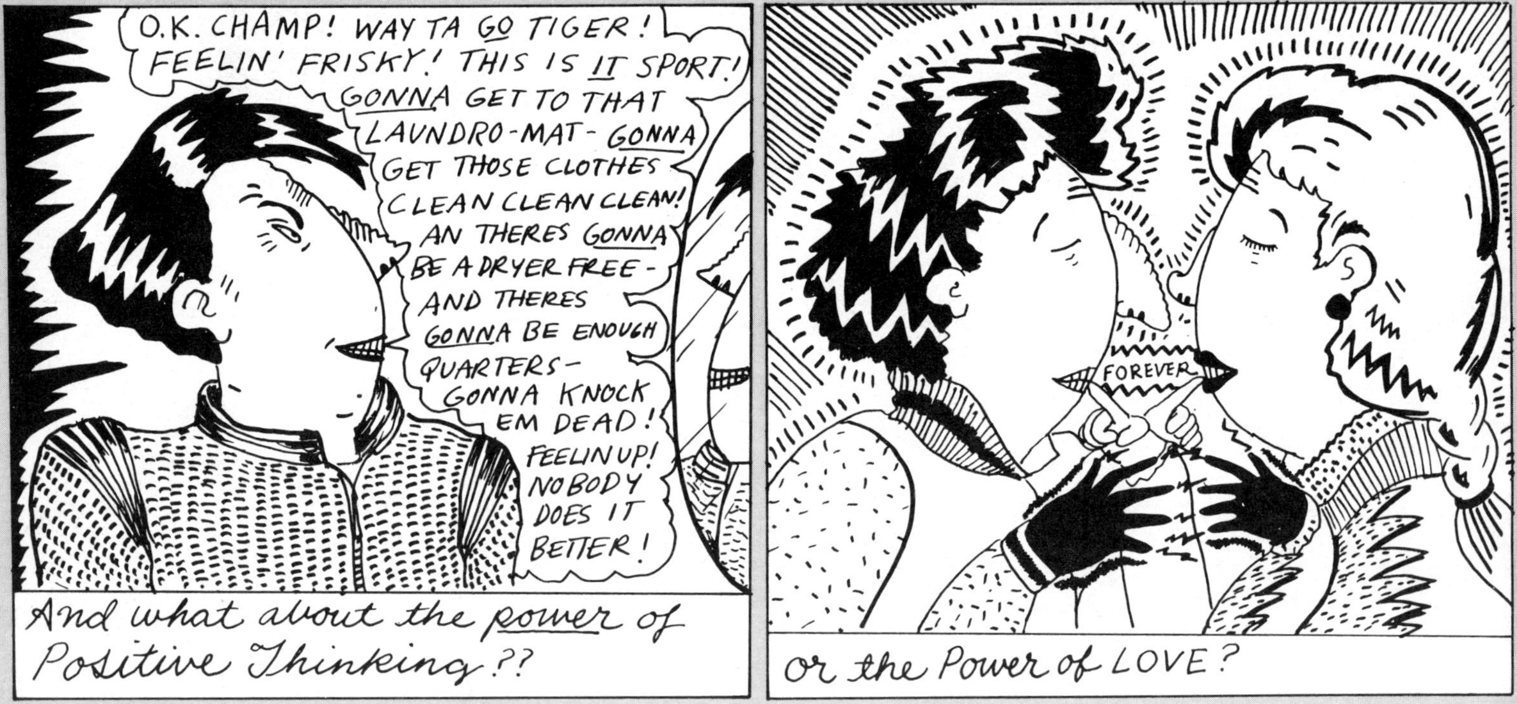
O.K. CHAMP! WAY TA GO TIGER! FEELIN' FRISKY! THIS IS IT SPORT! GONNA GET TO THAT LAUNDRO-MAT - GONNA GET THOSE CLOTHES CLEAN CLEAN CLEAN! AN THERES GONNA BE A DRYER FREE - AND THERES GONNA BE ENOUGH QUARTERS - GONNA KNOCK EM DEAD! FEELIN UP! NOBODY DOES IT BETTER!
And what about the power of Positive Thinking??
FOREVER
Or the Power of LOVE?

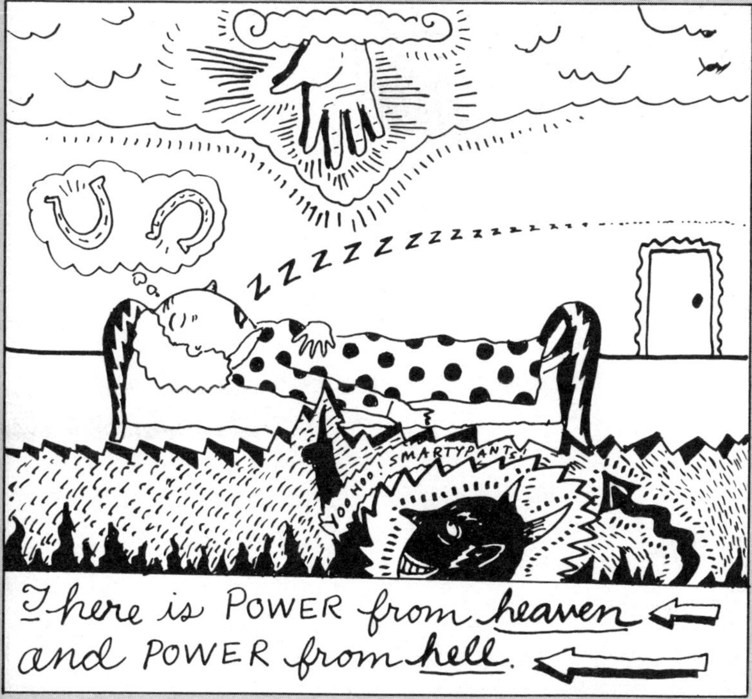
Z Z Z Z Z Z Z Z Z Z Z
YOO HOO! SMARTYPANTS!
There is POWER from heaven
and POWER from hell.

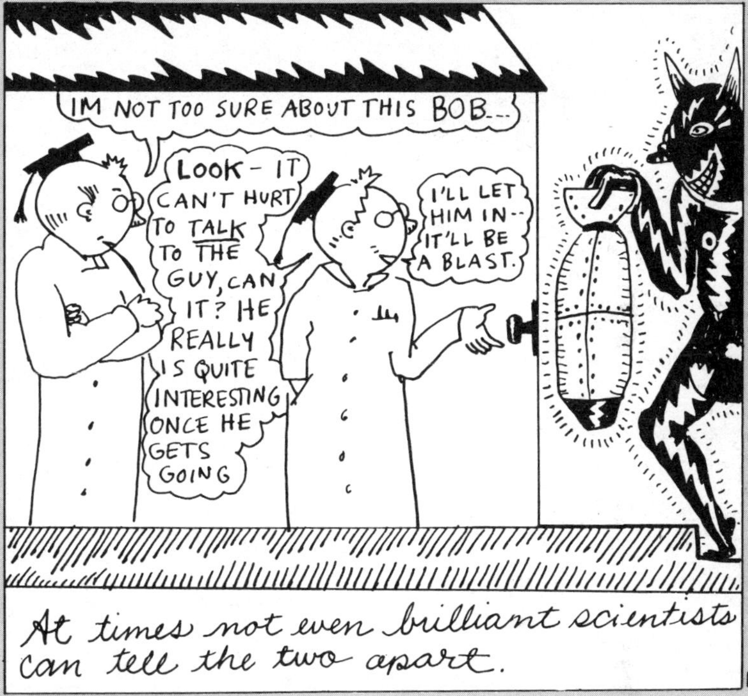
IM NOT TOO SURE ABOUT THIS BOB...
LOOK - IT CAN'T HURT TO TALK TO THE GUY, CAN IT? HE REALLY IS QUITE INTERESTING ONCE HE GETS GOING
I'LL LET HIM IN-- IT'LL BE A BLAST.
At times not even brilliant scientists can tell the two apart.

True Stories

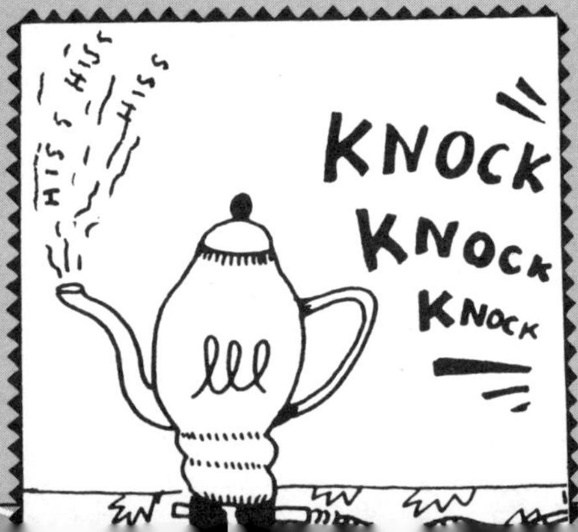
HISS HISS HISS
KNOCK
KNOCK
KNOCK

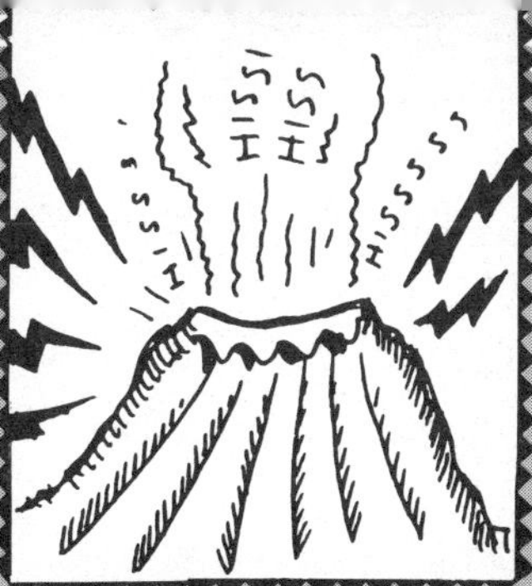
HISSS!
HISS
HISS
HISSSSSS

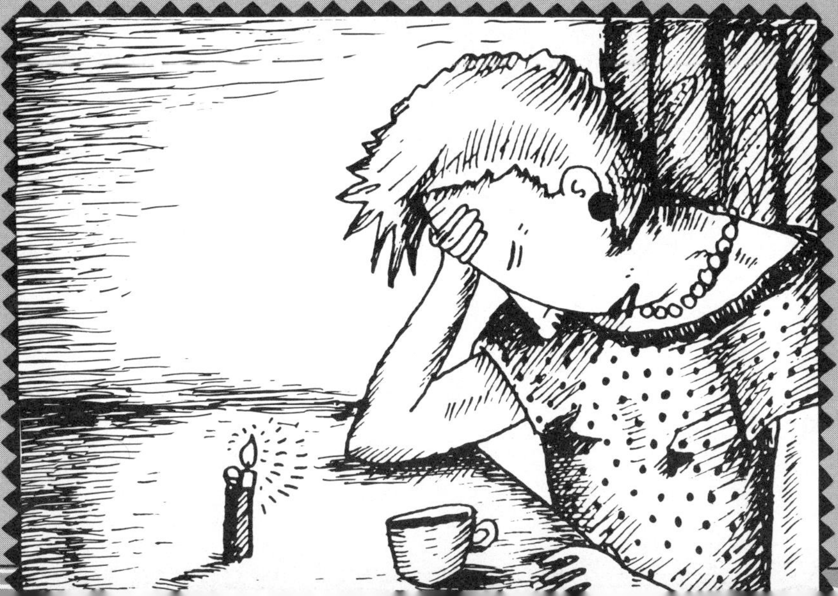

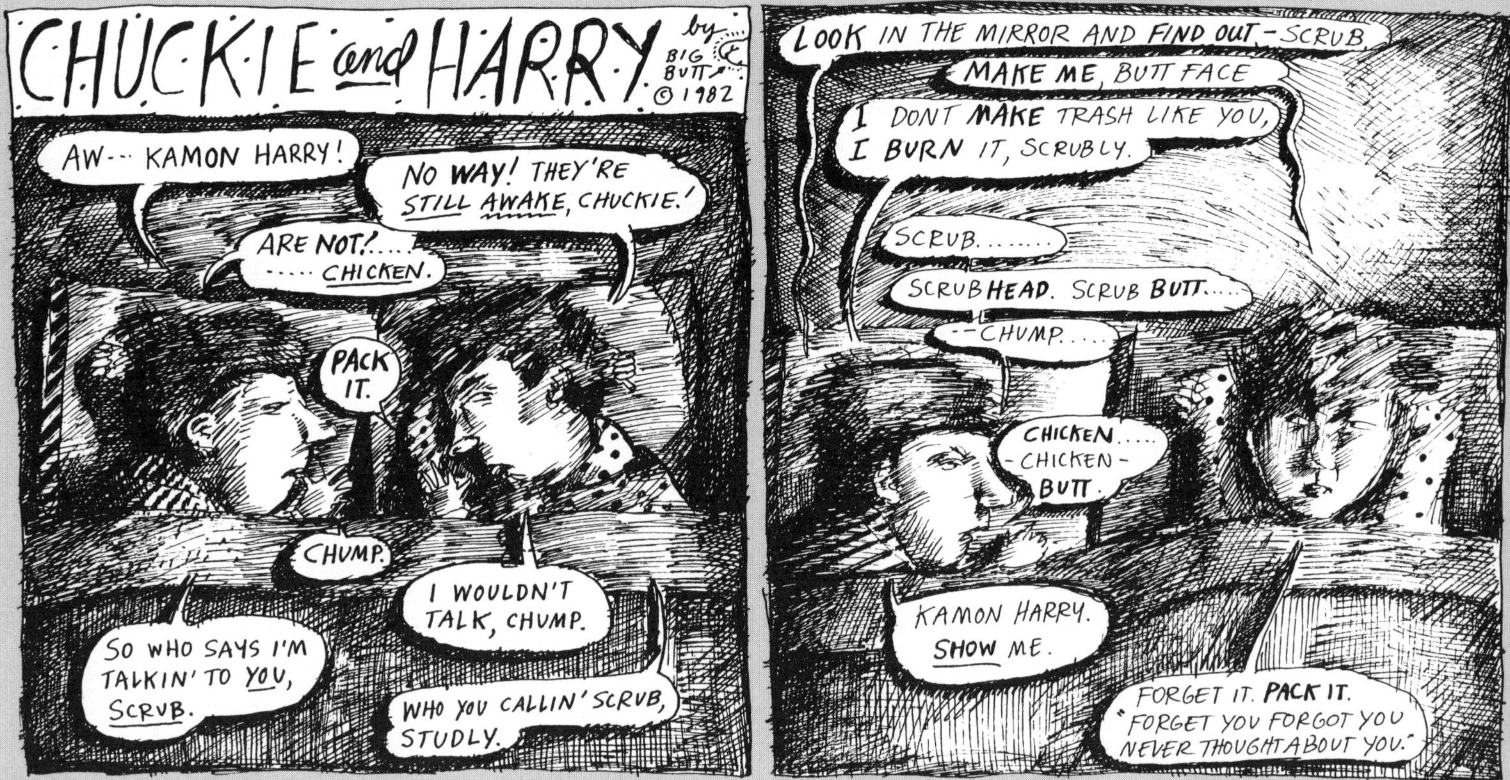
CHUCKIE and HARRY
by BIG BUTT © 1982
AW-- KAMON HARRY!
NO WAY! THEY'RE STILL AWAKE, CHUCKIE!
ARE NOT!..... ----- CHICKEN.
PACK IT.
CHUMP.
I WOULDN'T TALK, CHUMP.
SO WHO SAYS I'M TALKIN' TO YOU, SCRUB.
WHO YOU CALLIN' SCRUB, STUDLY.
LOOK IN THE MIRROR AND FIND OUT - SCRUB.
MAKE ME, BUTT FACE
I DONT MAKE TRASH LIKE YOU, I BURN IT, SCRUBLY.
SCRUB.......
SCRUBHEAD. SCRUB BUTT.....
--CHUMP.....
CHICKEN..... -CHICKEN- BUTT.
KAMON HARRY. SHOW ME.
FORGET IT. PACK IT. "FORGET YOU FORGOT YOU NEVER THOUGHT ABOUT YOU."

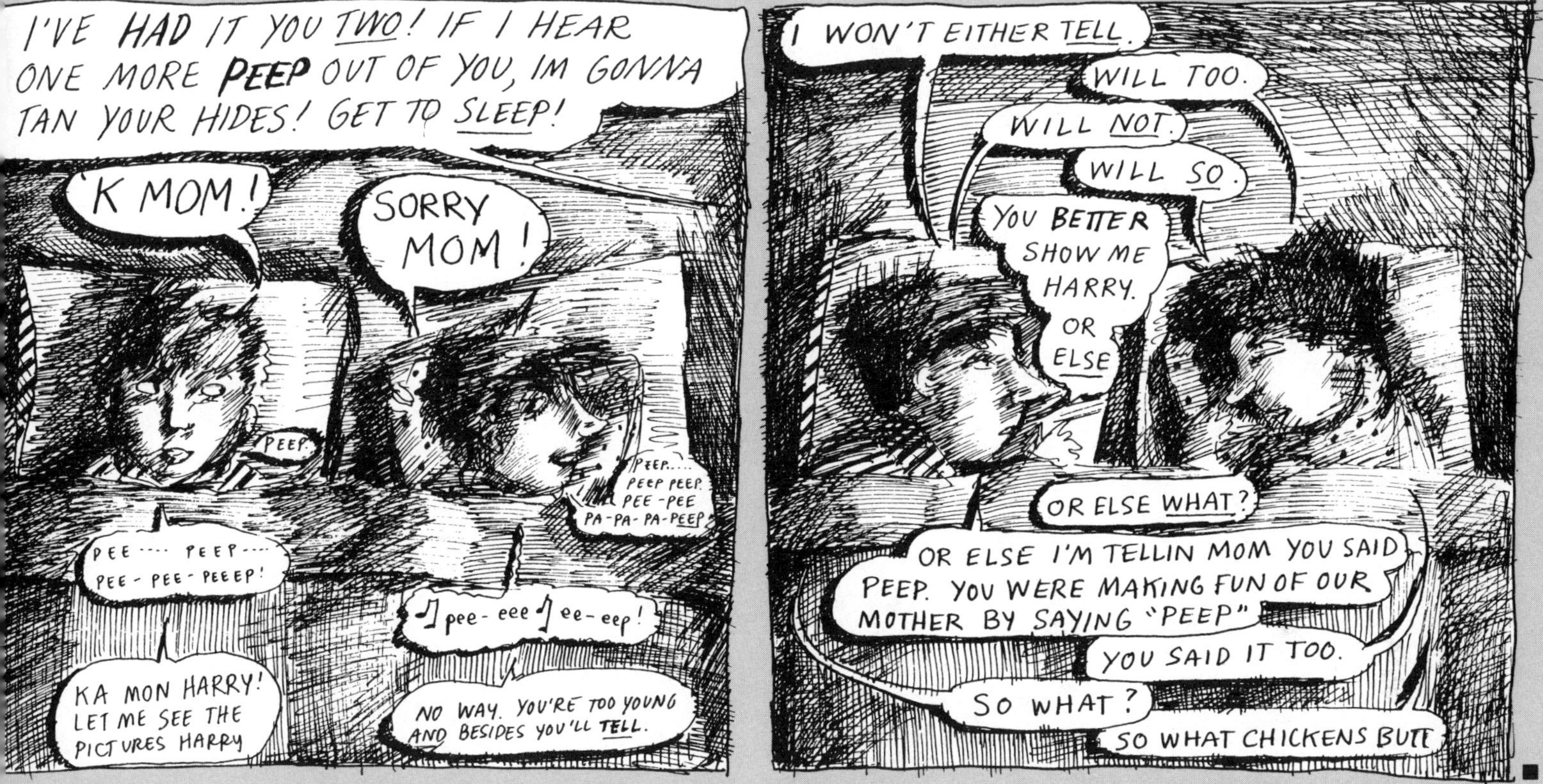
I'VE HAD IT YOU TWO! IF I HEAR ONE MORE PEEP OUT OF YOU, IM GONNA TAN YOUR HIDES! GET TO SLEEP!
K MOM!
SORRY MOM!
PEEP.
PEEP.... PEEP PEEP. PEE-PEE PA-PA-PA-PEEP
PEE.... PEEP.... PEE-PEE-PEEEP!
pee-eee ee-eep!
KA MON HARRY! LET ME SEE THE PICTURES HARRY
NO WAY. YOU'RE TOO YOUNG AND BESIDES YOU'LL TELL.
I WON'T EITHER TELL.
WILL TOO.
WILL NOT.
WILL SO.
YOU BETTER SHOW ME HARRY. OR ELSE
OR ELSE WHAT?
OR ELSE I'M TELLIN MOM YOU SAID PEEP. YOU WERE MAKING FUN OF OUR MOTHER BY SAYING "PEEP"
YOU SAID IT TOO.
SO WHAT?
SO WHAT CHICKENS BUTT

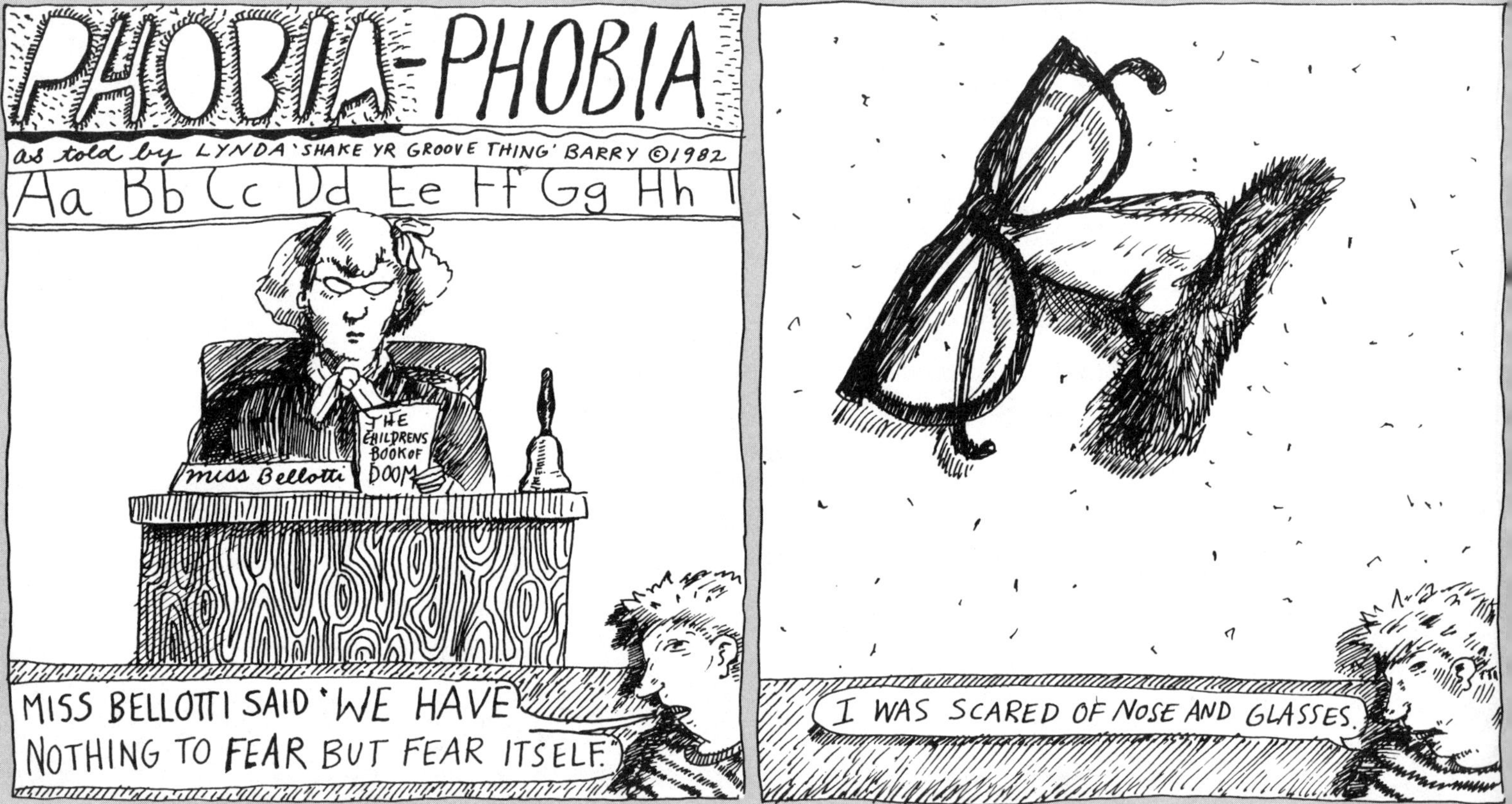
PHOBIA-PHOBIA
as told by LYNDA 'SHAKE YR GROOVE THING' BARRY ©1982
Aa Bb Cc Dd Ee Ff Gg Hh I
miss Bellotti
THE CHILDRENS BOOK OF DOOM
MISS BELLOTTI SAID "WE HAVE NOTHING TO FEAR BUT FEAR ITSELF."
I WAS SCARED OF NOSE AND GLASSES.

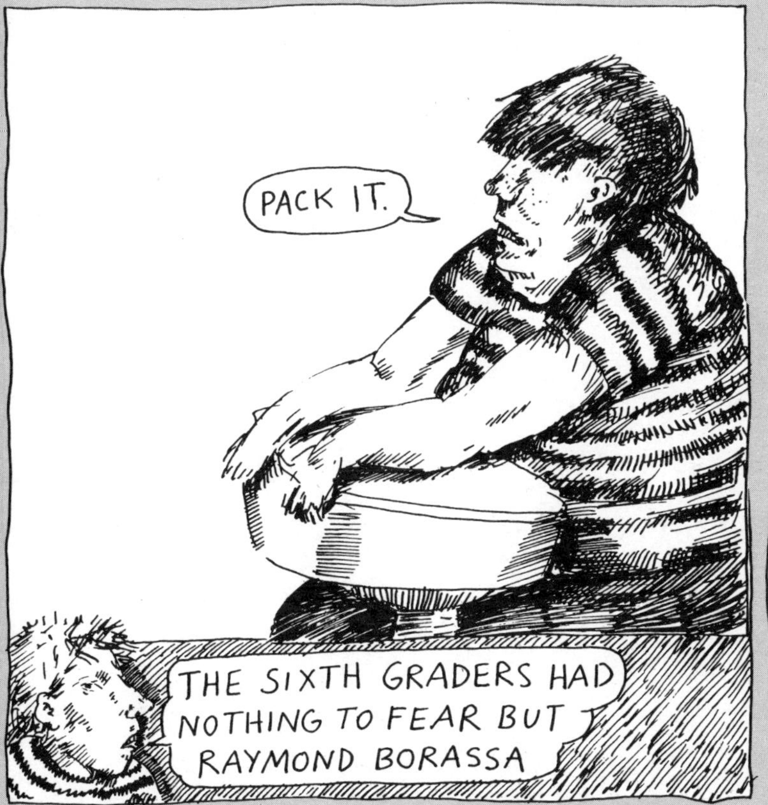
PACK IT.
THE SIXTH GRADERS HAD NOTHING TO FEAR BUT RAYMOND BORASSA

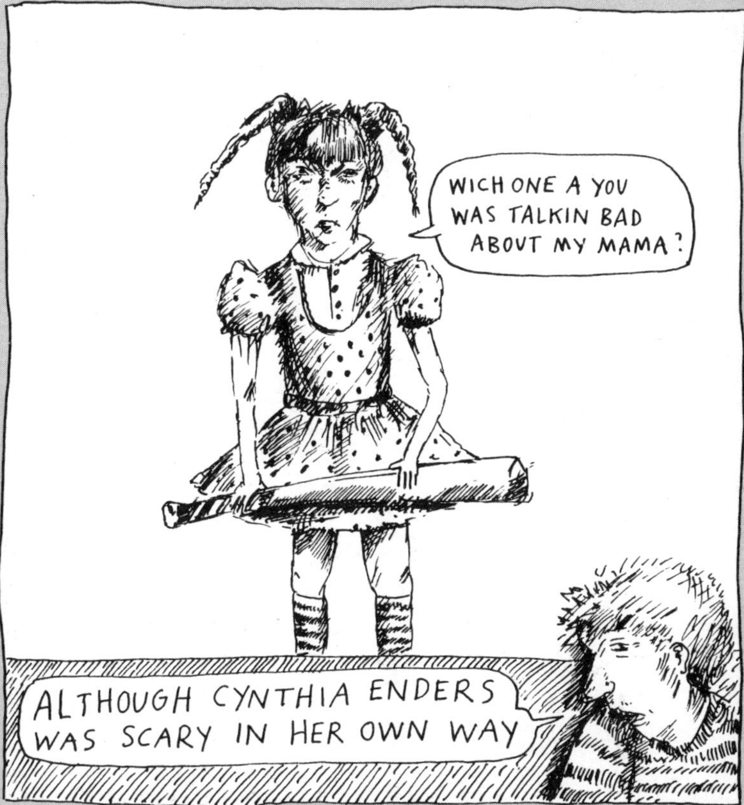
WICH ONE A YOU WAS TALKIN BAD ABOUT MY MAMA?
ALTHOUGH CYNTHIA ENDERS WAS SCARY IN HER OWN WAY

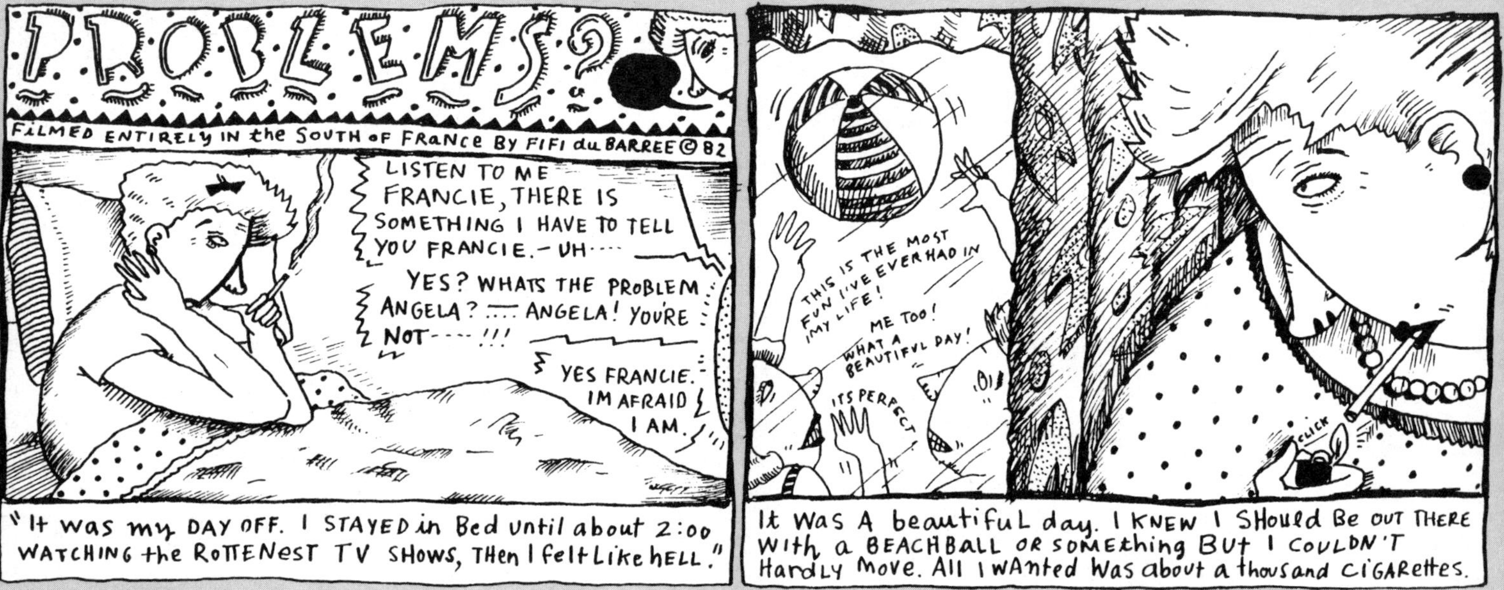
PROBLEMS?
FILMED ENTIRELY IN THE SOUTH OF FRANCE BY FIFI du BARREE © 82
LISTEN TO ME FRANCIE, THERE IS SOMETHING I HAVE TO TELL YOU FRANCIE. - UH ···
YES? WHATS THE PROBLEM ANGELA? ···· ANGELA! YOU'RE NOT ···· !!!
YES FRANCIE. IM AFRAID I AM.
"It was my DAY OFF. I STAYED in Bed until about 2:00 WATCHING the ROTTENEST TV SHOWS, THen I felt Like hELL."
THIS IS THE MOST FUN I'VE EVER HAD IN MY LIFE!
ME TOO!
WHAT A BEAUTIFUL DAY!
ITS PERFECT
CLICK
It Was A beautiful day. I KNEW I SHould Be OUT THERE With a BEACHBALL OR SOMEthing But I COULDN'T Hardly Move. All I WAnted Was about a thousand CiGARettes.

"EDNA. WE'VE GOT TO HAVE AN IMPORTANT MEETING.

THATS FUNNY... I WAS SURE I TURNED THAT THING OFF.

DIRECTLY AFter I closed The DRAPES to SHUT OUT The LIGHT, MY SOUL SPOKE to me. IT WAS the first time my SOUL EVER SPOKE to ME AND I THOUGHT IT WAS the T.V.

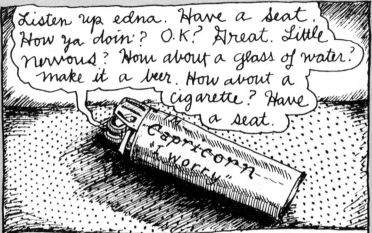

Listen up edna. Have a seat. How ya doin'? O.K.? Great. Little nervous? How about a glass of water? make it a beer. How about a cigarette? Have a seat.

"Capricorn" "I worry"

The Voice of my SOUL SOUNDED a little bit like the Voice of Peter Sellers AND It WAS Coming out of this cigarette lighter I had bought the day Before FOR 69¢. IMAGINE MY SURPRISE.

you're in trouble deep girl,
and you know it. This is
not a drill. Everything
in the world and
everything else in the
world and you and
everything you do. Every
second counts. You can't
get blood from a turnip.
It's better to light one candle
than to curse the darkness.
Your Father, your mother,
you're skating on thin ice.
Buck up Billy boy.
How many roads
must a man
walk down?

Sweat was pouring all over me and all over Hell.
I knew I was in for it........ What could I do but
PULL UP A CHAIR? MY SOUL WAS A TALKATIVE Little
DEVIL. I LISTENED AND MY SOUL TALKED MY EAR OFF.

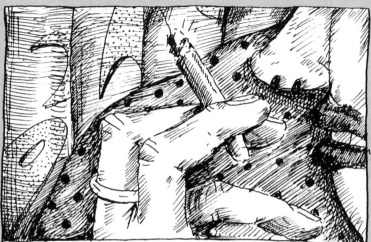

IT WAS WELL PAST MIDNIGHT WHEN I NOTICED MY
SOUL HADN'T SPOKEN FOR AWHILE. I LIT A CIGARETTE
AND TRIED TO GET RIGHT WITH MYSELF. BUT I DIDN'T
KNOW HOW TO START OR WHERE. I WAS **ALL SHOOK UP.**

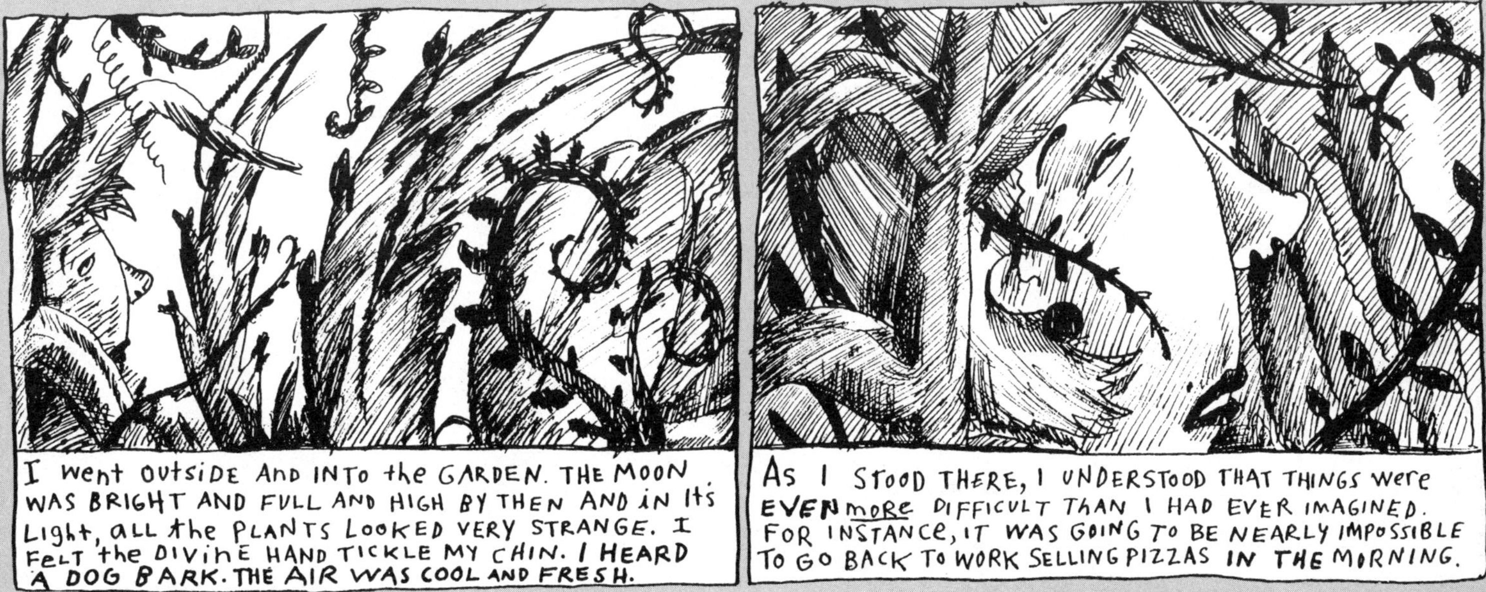
I went outside and into the garden. The moon was bright and full and high by then and in it's light, all the plants looked very strange. I felt the divine hand tickle my chin. I heard a dog bark. The air was cool and fresh.
As I stood there, I understood that things were even more difficult than I had ever imagined. For instance, it was going to be nearly impossible to go back to work selling pizzas in the morning.

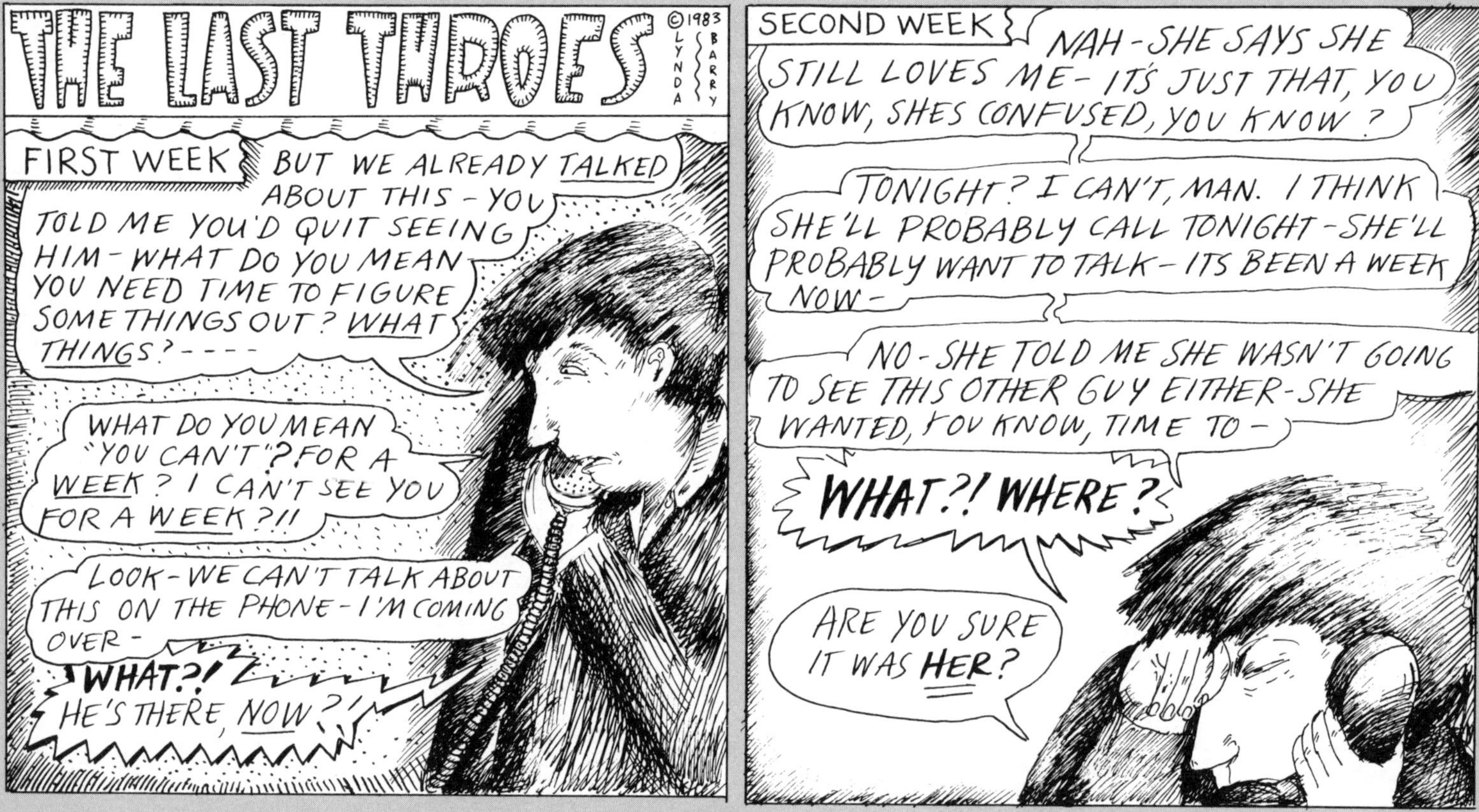
THE LAST THROES
©1983 LYNDA BARRY
FIRST WEEK
BUT WE ALREADY TALKED ABOUT THIS - YOU TOLD ME YOU'D QUIT SEEING HIM - WHAT DO YOU MEAN YOU NEED TIME TO FIGURE SOME THINGS OUT? WHAT THINGS? ----
WHAT DO YOU MEAN "YOU CAN'T"? FOR A WEEK? I CAN'T SEE YOU FOR A WEEK?!!
LOOK - WE CAN'T TALK ABOUT THIS ON THE PHONE - I'M COMING OVER -
WHAT?! HE'S THERE, NOW?!
SECOND WEEK
NAH - SHE SAYS SHE STILL LOVES ME - IT'S JUST THAT, YOU KNOW, SHES CONFUSED, YOU KNOW?
TONIGHT? I CAN'T, MAN. I THINK SHE'LL PROBABLY CALL TONIGHT - SHE'LL PROBABLY WANT TO TALK - ITS BEEN A WEEK NOW -
NO - SHE TOLD ME SHE WASN'T GOING TO SEE THIS OTHER GUY EITHER - SHE WANTED, YOU KNOW, TIME TO -
WHAT?! WHERE?
ARE YOU SURE IT WAS HER?

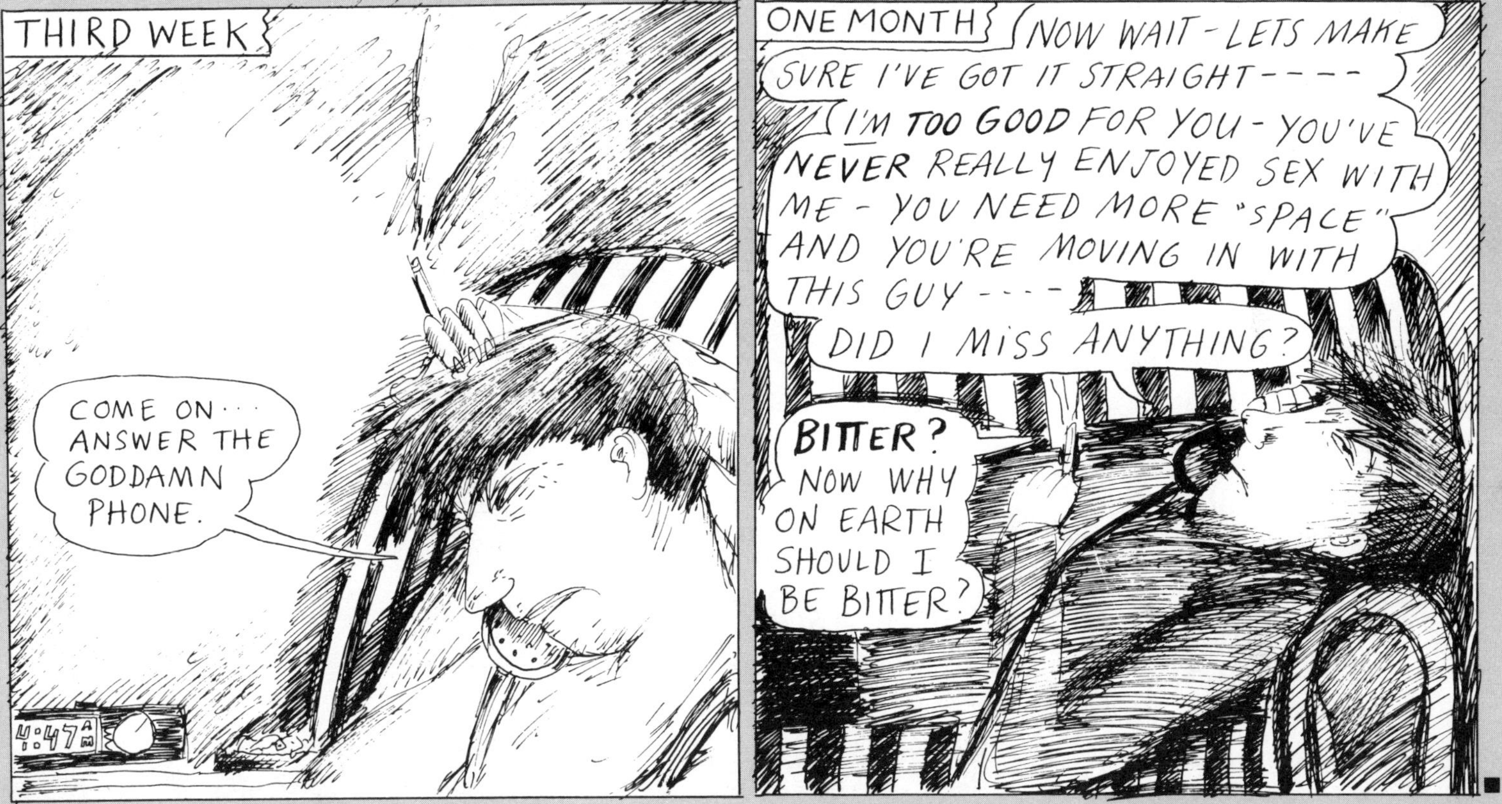
THIRD WEEK
COME ON··· ANSWER THE GODDAMN PHONE.
4:47 AM
ONE MONTH
NOW WAIT - LETS MAKE SURE I'VE GOT IT STRAIGHT----
I'M **TOO GOOD** FOR YOU - YOU'VE **NEVER** REALLY ENJOYED SEX WITH ME - YOU NEED MORE "SPACE" AND YOU'RE MOVING IN WITH THIS GUY----
DID I MISS ANYTHING?
BITTER? NOW WHY ON EARTH SHOULD I BE BITTER?

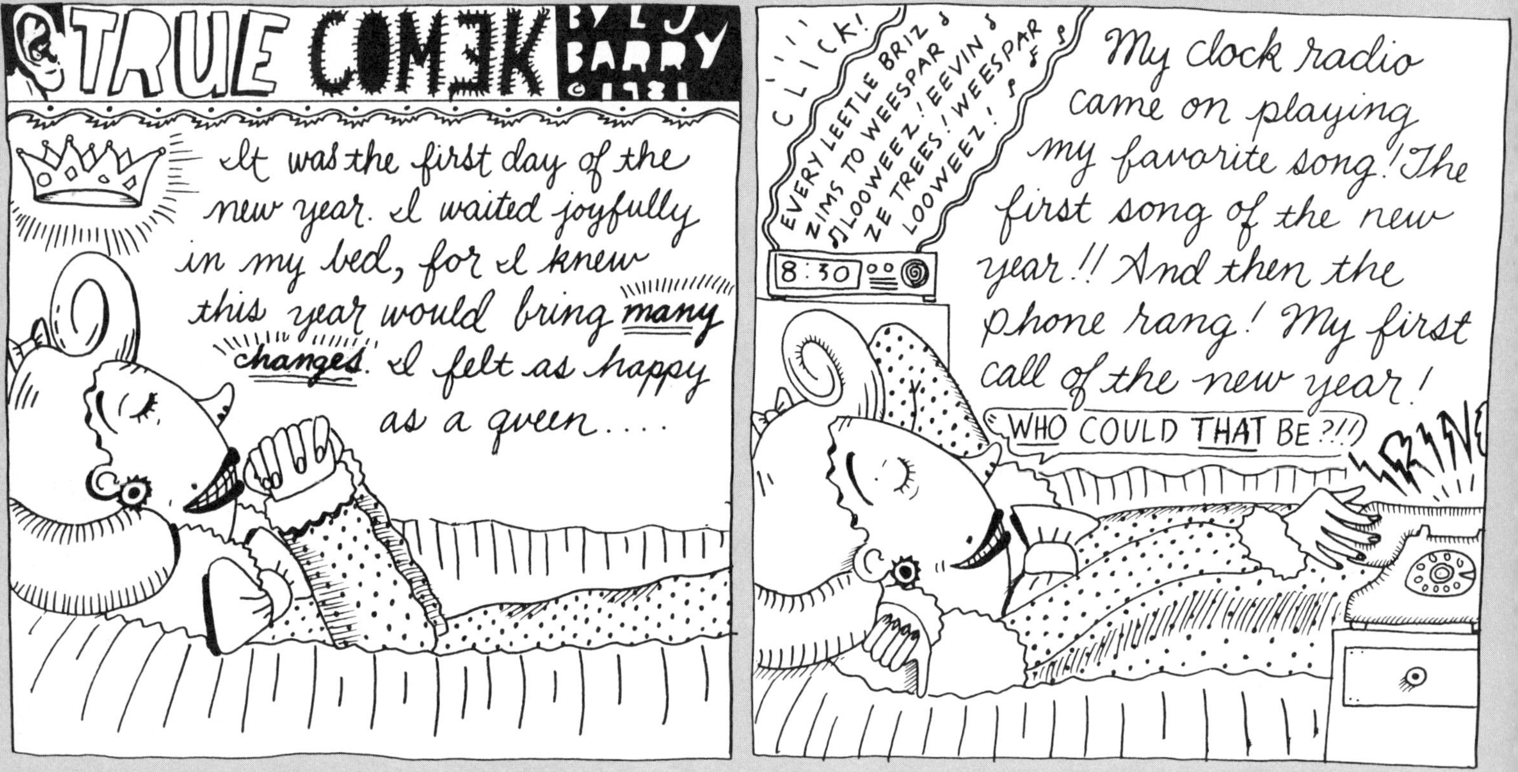

TRUE COMEK
BY L J BARRY ©1981
It was the first day of the new year. I waited joyfully in my bed, for I knew this year would bring many changes. I felt as happy as a queen....
CLICK!
EVERY LEETLE BRIZ ZIMS TO WEESPAR LOOWEEZ! EEVIN ZE TREES! WEESPAR LOOWEEZ!
8:30
My clock radio came on playing my favorite song! The first song of the new year!! And then the phone rang! My first call of the new year!
WHO COULD THAT BE?!!

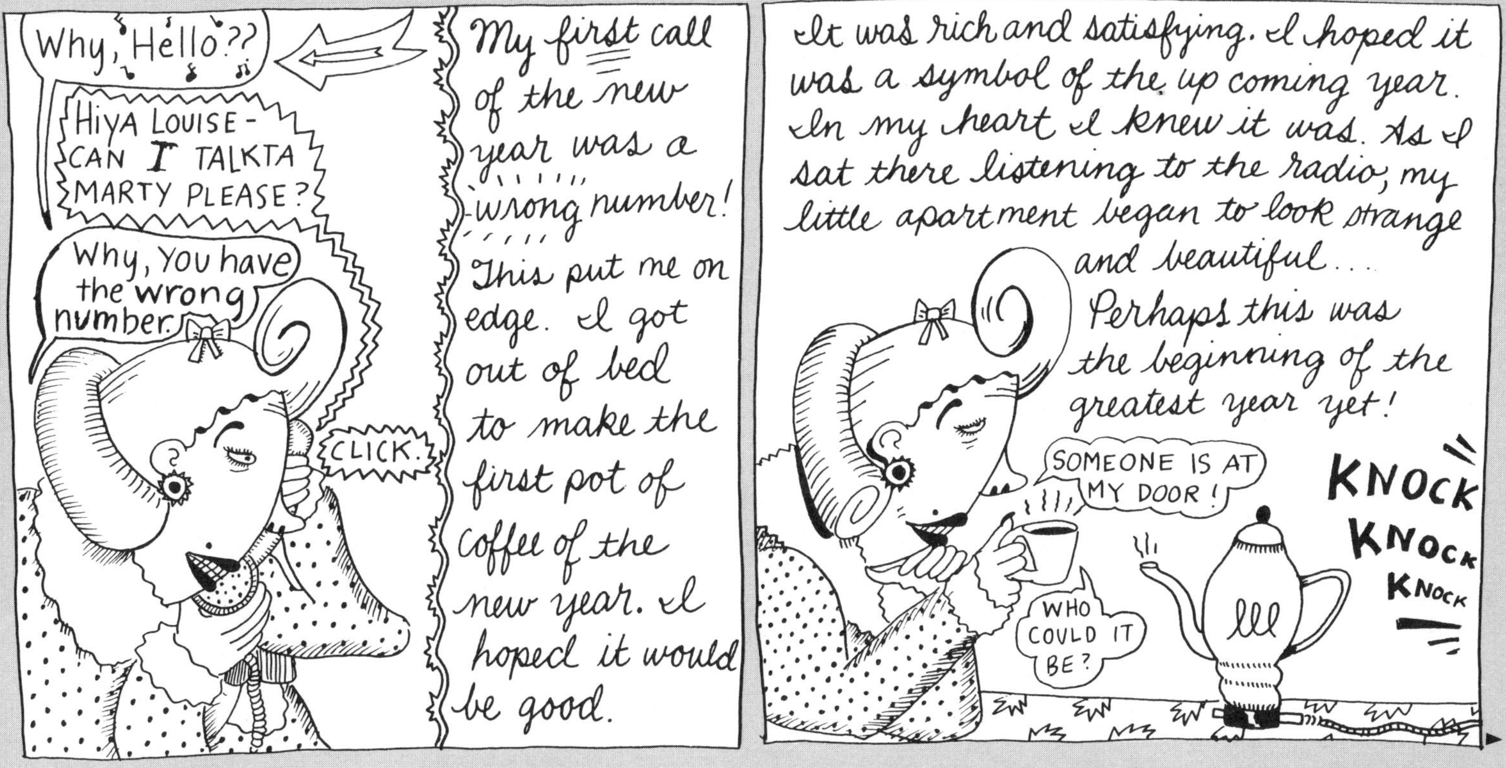
Why, Hello??
HiyA LOUISE - CAN I TALKTA MARTY PLEASE?
Why, You have the wrong number.
CLICK.
My first call of the new year was a wrong number! This put me on edge. I got out of bed to make the first pot of coffee of the new year. I hoped it would be good.
It was rich and satisfying. I hoped it was a symbol of the up coming year. In my heart I knew it was. As I sat there listening to the radio, my little apartment began to look strange and beautiful...
Perhaps this was the beginning of the greatest year yet!
SOMEONE IS AT MY DOOR!
KNOCK
KNOCK
KNOCK
WHO COULD IT BE?

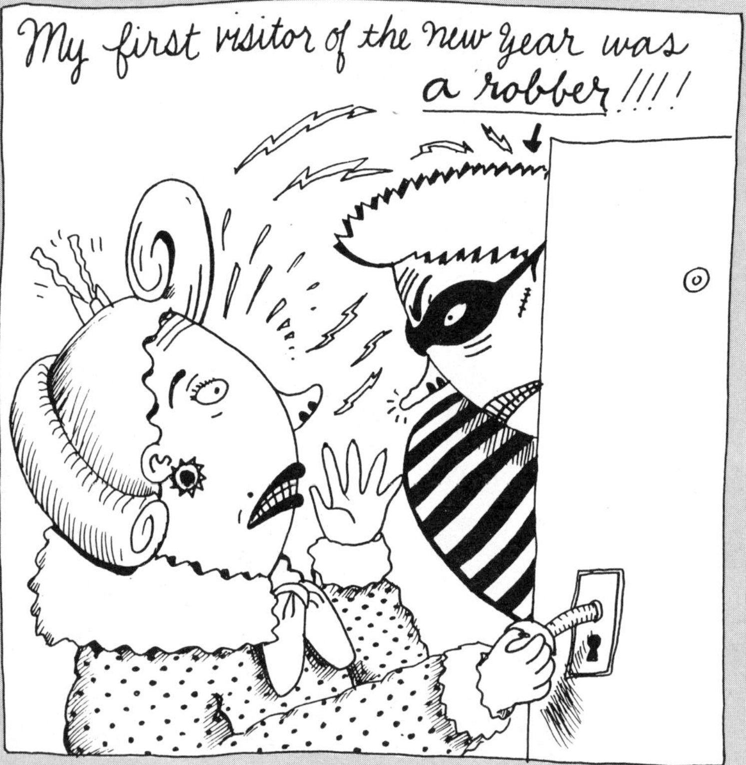
My first visitor of the new year was a robber!!!!

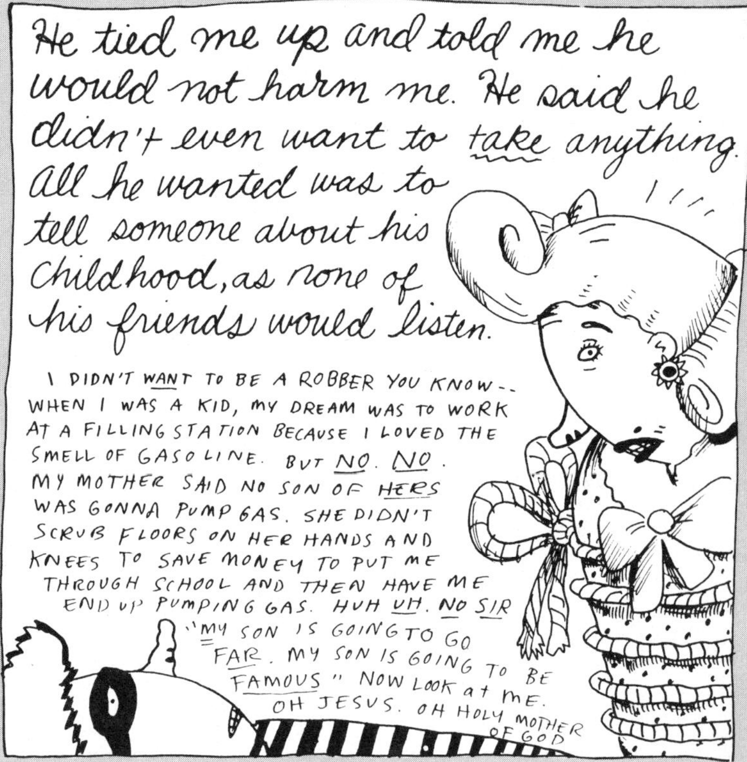
He tied me up and told me he would not harm me. He said he didn't even want to take anything. All he wanted was to tell someone about his childhood, as none of his friends would listen.
I DIDN'T WANT TO BE A ROBBER YOU KNOW-- WHEN I WAS A KID, MY DREAM WAS TO WORK AT A FILLING STATION BECAUSE I LOVED THE SMELL OF GASOLINE. BUT NO. NO. MY MOTHER SAID NO SON OF HERS WAS GONNA PUMP GAS. SHE DIDN'T SCRUB FLOORS ON HER HANDS AND KNEES TO SAVE MONEY TO PUT ME THROUGH SCHOOL AND THEN HAVE ME END UP PUMPING GAS. HUH UH. NO SIR "MY SON IS GOING TO GO FAR. MY SON IS GOING TO BE FAMOUS" NOW LOOK at ME. OH JESUS. OH HOLY MOTHER OF GOD

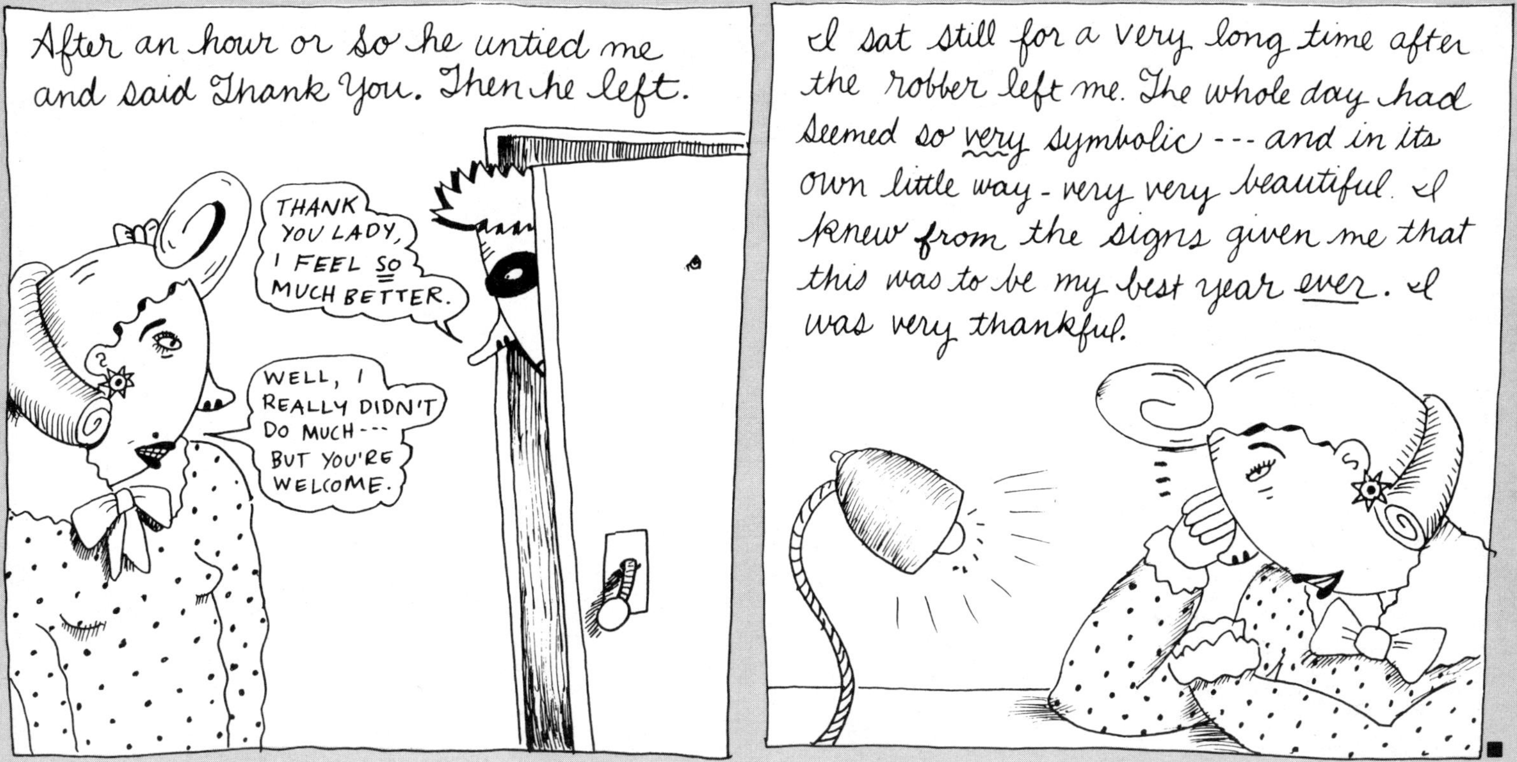
After an hour or so he untied me and said Thank You. Then he left.
THANK YOU LADY, I FEEL SO MUCH BETTER.
WELL, I REALLY DIDN'T DO MUCH --- BUT YOU'RE WELCOME.
I sat still for a very long time after the robber left me. The whole day had seemed so very symbolic --- and in its own little way - very very beautiful. I knew from the signs given me that this was to be my best year ever. I was very thankful.

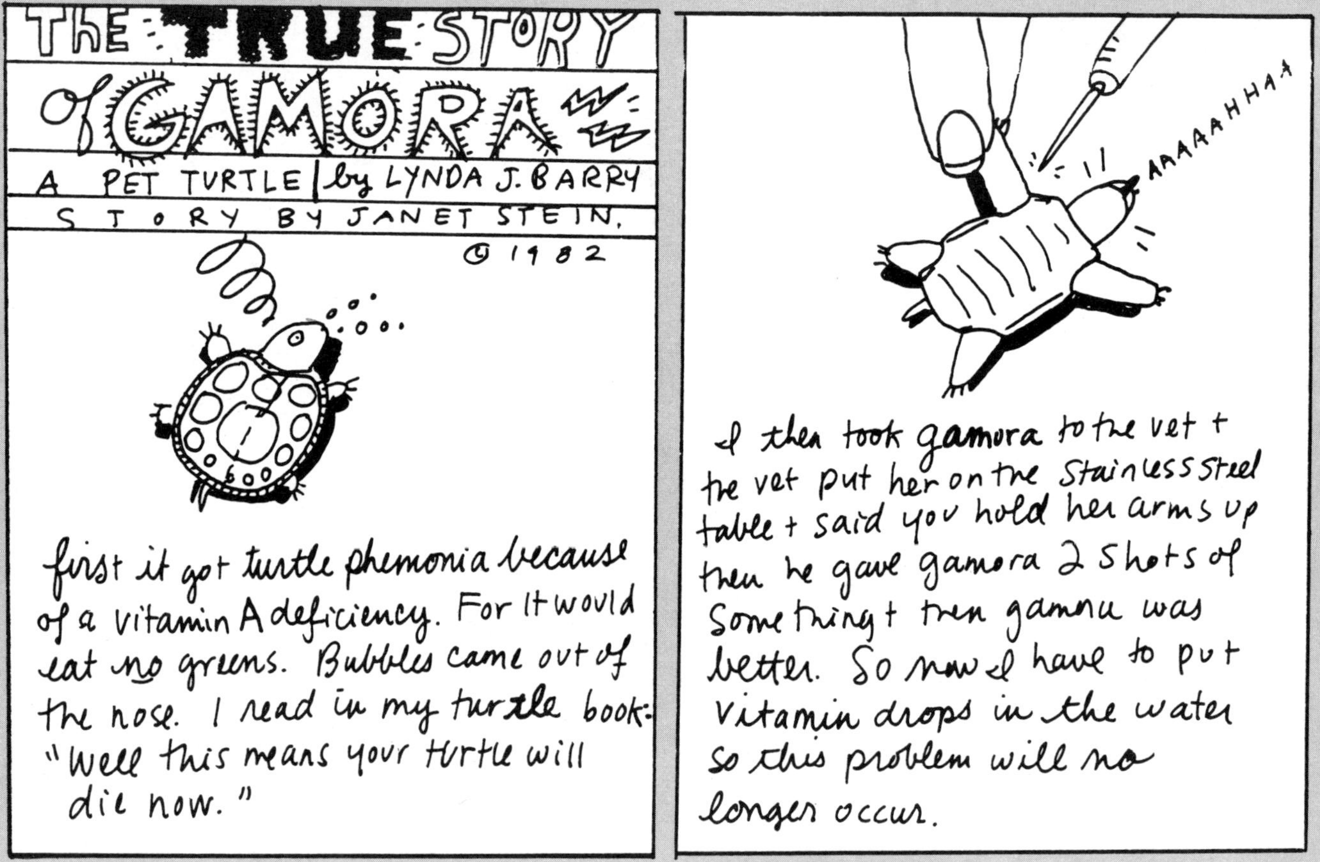
THE TRUE STORY
OF GAMORA
A PET TURTLE
by LYNDA J. BARRY
STORY BY JANET STEIN.
© 1982
first it got turtle phemonia because of a vitamin A deficiency. For It would eat no greens. Bubbles came out of the nose. I read in my turtle book: "Well this means your turtle will die now."
AAAAAAHHAA
I then took gamora to the vet + the vet put her on the stainless steel table + said you hold her arms up then he gave gamora 2 shots of something + then gamnu was better. So now I have to put vitamin drops in the water so this problem will no longer occur.

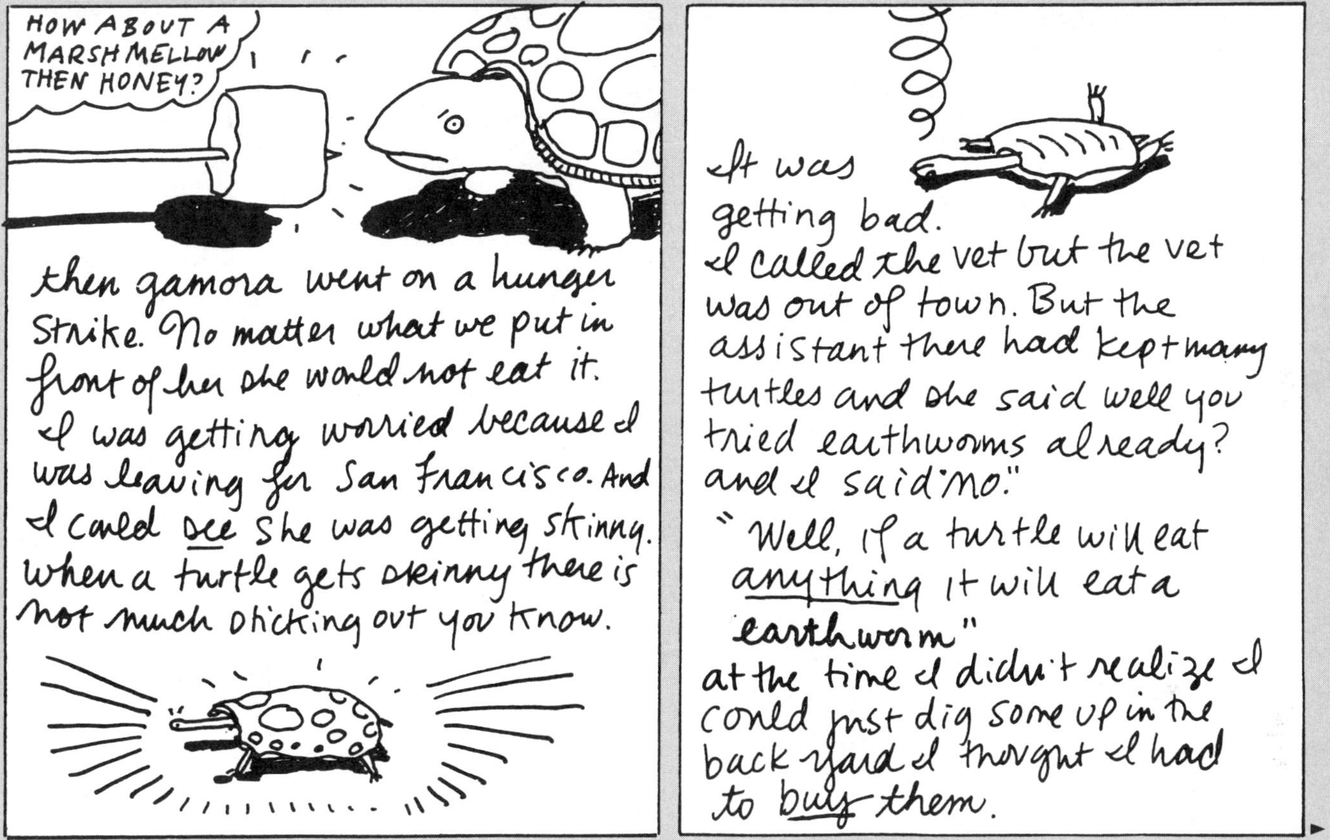
HOW ABOUT A MARSHMELLOW THEN HONEY?
then gamora went on a hunger strike. No matter what we put in front of her she would not eat it. I was getting worried because I was leaving for San Francisco. And I could see she was getting skinny. When a turtle gets skinny there is not much sticking out you know.
It was getting bad.
I called the vet but the vet was out of town. But the assistant there had kept many turtles and she said well you tried earthworms already? and I said "no."
"Well, if a turtle will eat anything it will eat a earthworm"
at the time I didn't realize I could just dig some up in the back yard I thought I had to buy them.

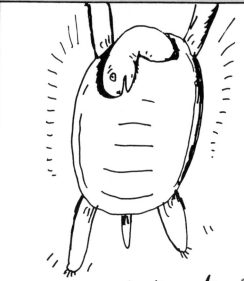

They (the earthworms) did the trick. Gamora ate like there was no tomorrow but just to make sure I took her along to San Francisco. It wasn't that hard to travel with her either.

After she started eating the worms she started hanging from the top of her cage then dropping suddenly. Especially at night. But this is the only side effect the worms had on her.

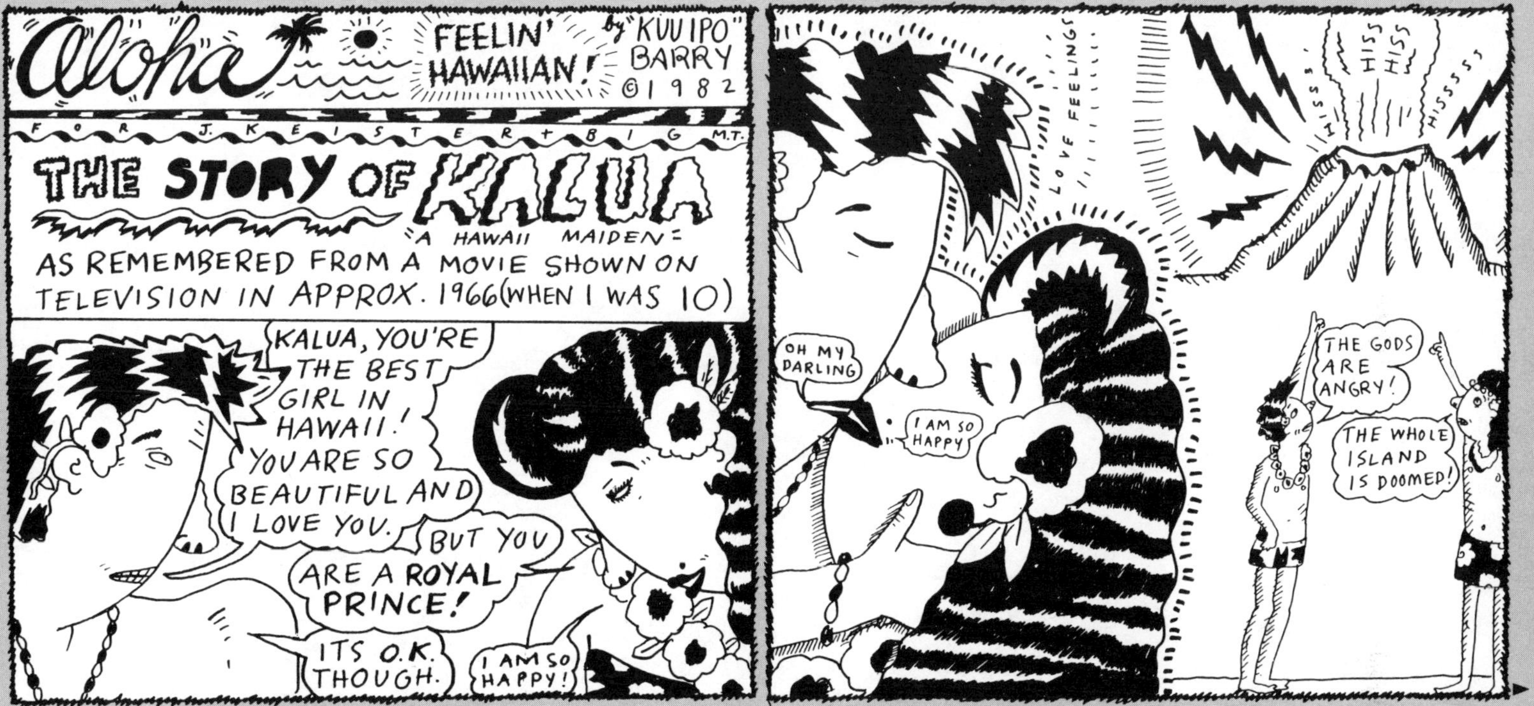
Aloha
FEELIN' HAWAIIAN!
by "KUUIPO" BARRY ©1982
FOR J. KEISTER + BIG M.T.
THE STORY OF KALUA
A HAWAII MAIDEN
AS REMEMBERED FROM A MOVIE SHOWN ON TELEVISION IN APPROX. 1966 (WHEN I WAS 10)
KALUA, YOU'RE THE BEST GIRL IN HAWAII! YOU ARE SO BEAUTIFUL AND I LOVE YOU.
BUT YOU ARE A ROYAL PRINCE!
ITS O.K. THOUGH.
I AM SO HAPPY!
LOVE FEELINGS
HISS HISS HISS HISSSSSS
OH MY DARLING
I AM SO HAPPY
THE GODS ARE ANGRY!
THE WHOLE ISLAND IS DOOMED!

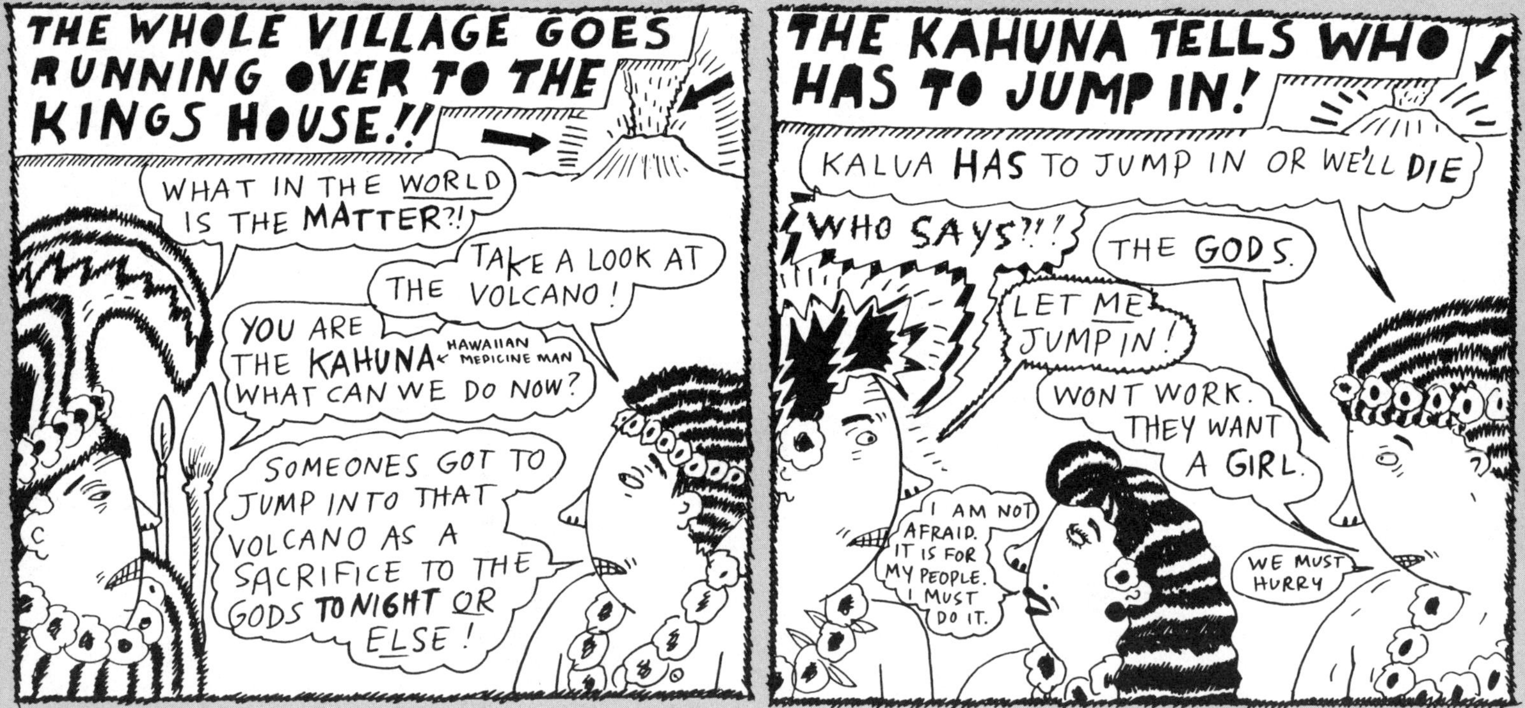
THE WHOLE VILLAGE GOES RUNNING OVER TO THE KINGS HOUSE!!
WHAT IN THE WORLD IS THE MATTER?!
TAKE A LOOK AT THE VOLCANO!
YOU ARE THE KAHUNA ← HAWAIIAN MEDICINE MAN WHAT CAN WE DO NOW?
SOMEONES GOT TO JUMP INTO THAT VOLCANO AS A SACRIFICE TO THE GODS TONIGHT OR ELSE!
THE KAHUNA TELLS WHO HAS TO JUMP IN!
KALUA HAS TO JUMP IN OR WE'LL DIE
WHO SAYS?!!
THE GODS.
LET ME JUMP IN!
WONT WORK. THEY WANT A GIRL.
I AM NOT AFRAID. IT IS FOR MY PEOPLE. I MUST DO IT.
WE MUST HURRY

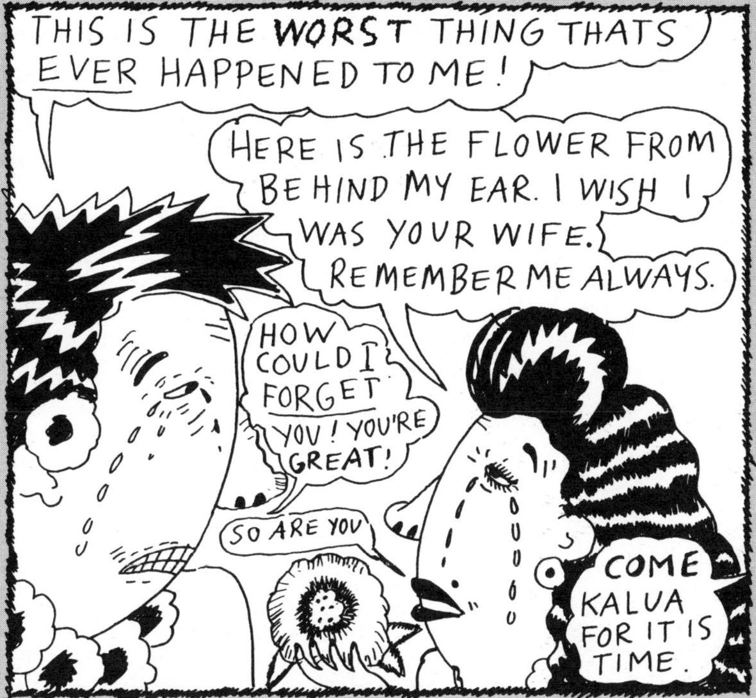
THIS IS THE WORST THING THATS EVER HAPPENED TO ME!
HERE IS THE FLOWER FROM BEHIND MY EAR. I WISH I WAS YOUR WIFE. REMEMBER ME ALWAYS.
HOW COULD I FORGET YOU! YOU'RE GREAT!
SO ARE YOU
COME KALUA FOR IT IS TIME.

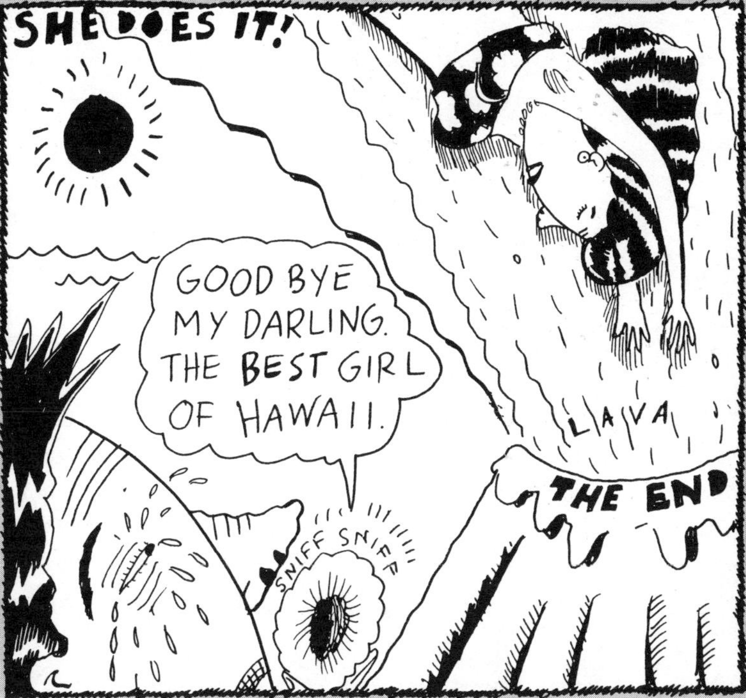
SHE DOES IT!
GOOD BYE MY DARLING. THE BEST GIRL OF HAWAII.
LAVA
THE END
SNIFF SNIFF

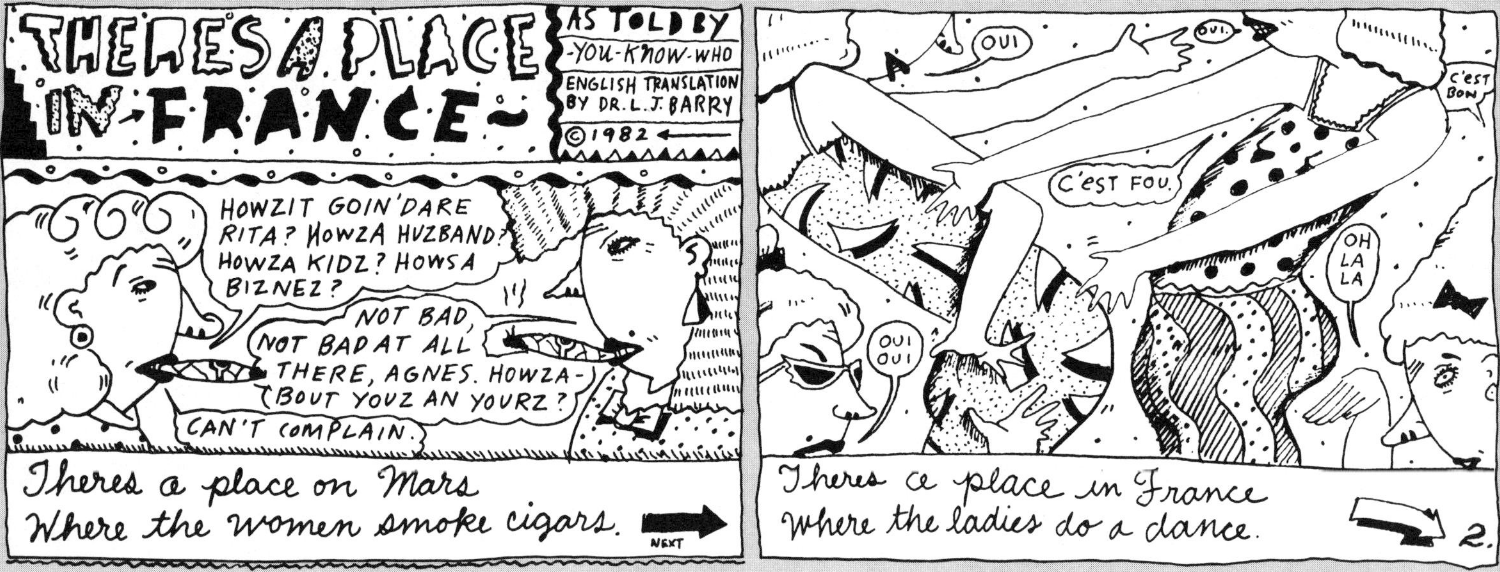
THERES A PLACE IN FRANCE
AS TOLD BY -YOU-KNOW-WHO
ENGLISH TRANSLATION BY DR. L. J. BARRY
©1982
HOWZIT GOIN' DARE RITA? HOWZA HUZBAND? HOWZA KIDZ? HOWS A BIZNEZ?
NOT BAD, NOT BAD AT ALL THERE, AGNES. HOWZA-BOUT YOUZ AN YOURZ?
CAN'T COMPLAIN.
Theres a place on Mars
Where the women smoke cigars.
NEXT
OUI
OUI.
C'EST BON
C'EST FOU.
OH LA LA
OUI OUI
Theres a place in France
Where the ladies do a dance.
2.

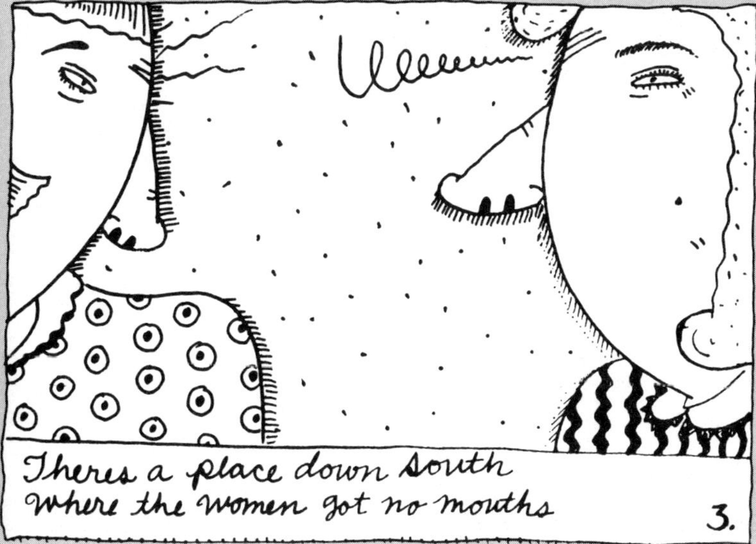
Ulleeeeee
Theres a place down South
Where the women got no mouths
3.

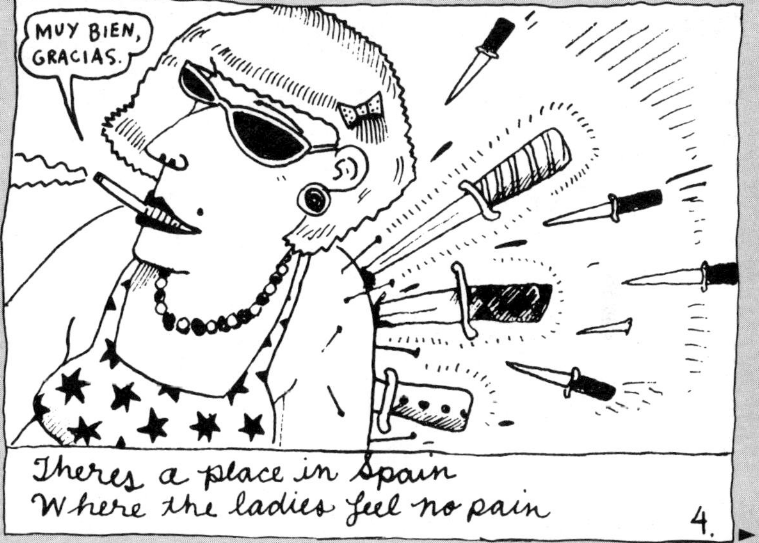
MUY BIEN, GRACIAS.
Theres a place in Spain
Where the ladies feel no pain
4.

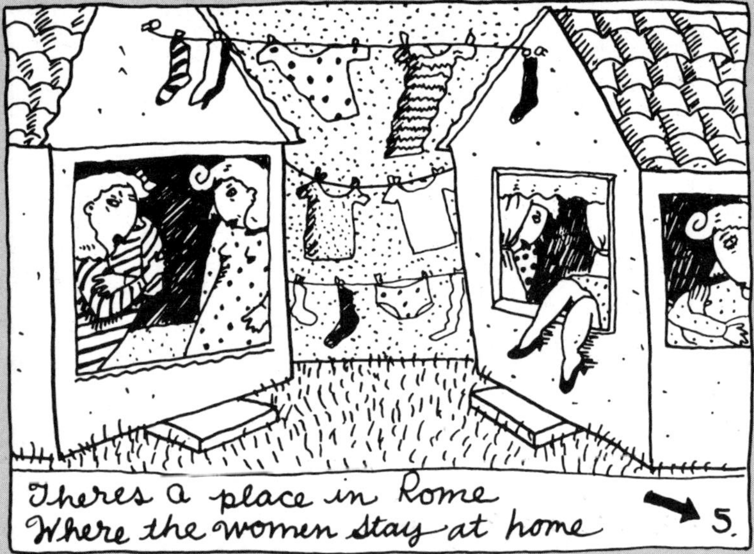
Theres a place in Rome
Where the women stay at home
5.

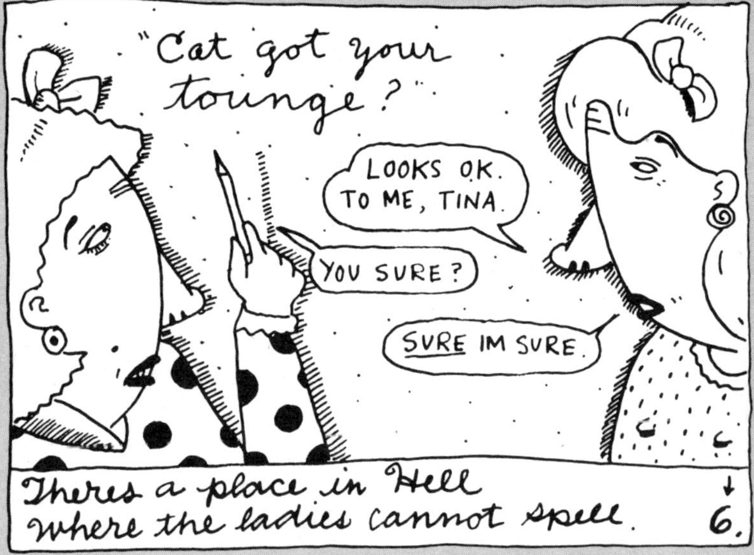
"Cat got your tounge?"
LOOKS OK. TO ME, TINA.
YOU SURE?
SURE IM SURE.
Theres a place in Hell
Where the ladies cannot spell
6.

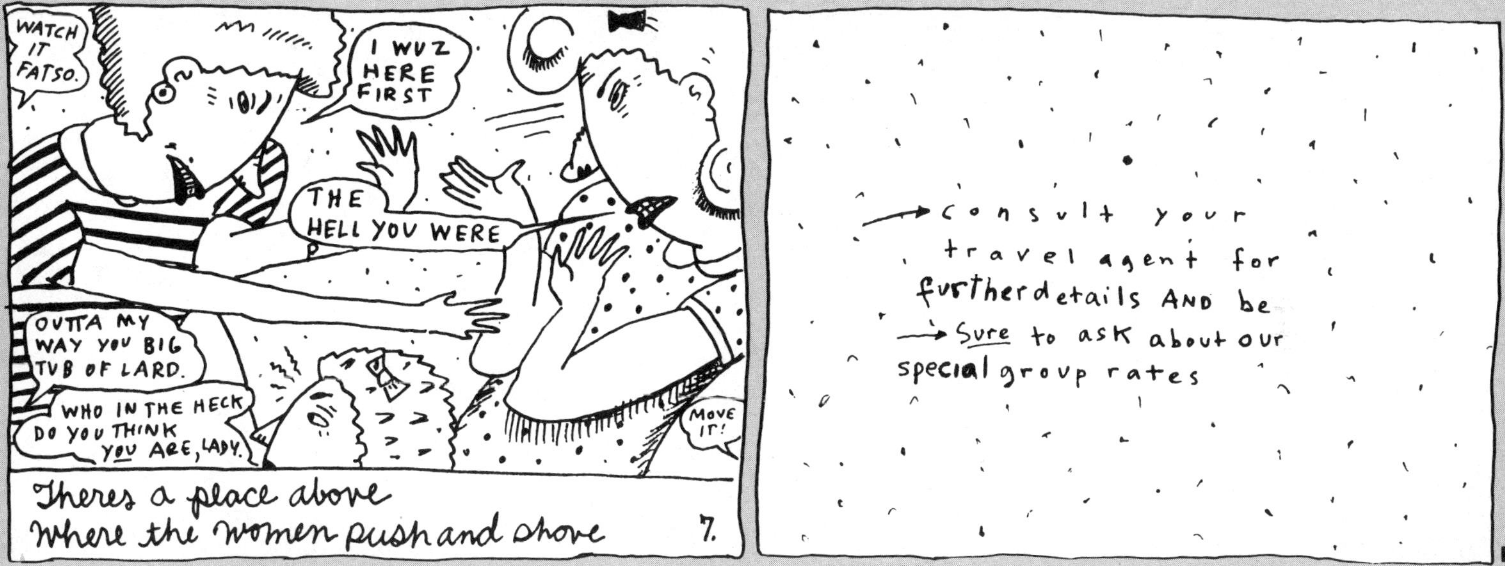
WATCH IT FATSO.
I WUZ HERE FIRST
THE HELL YOU WERE
OUTTA MY WAY YOU BIG TUB OF LARD.
WHO IN THE HECK DO YOU THINK YOU ARE, LADY.
MOVE IT!
Theres a place above
Where the women push and shove
7.
consult your travel agent for furtherdetails AND be Sure to ask about our special group rates

Love

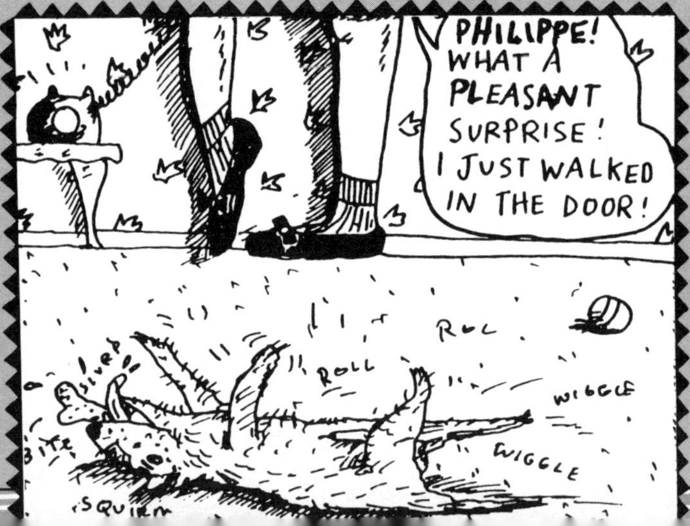
PHILIPPE! WHAT A PLEASANT SURPRISE! I JUST WALKED IN THE DOOR!
ROLL
ROLL
WIGGLE
WIGGLE
BITE
SQUIRM

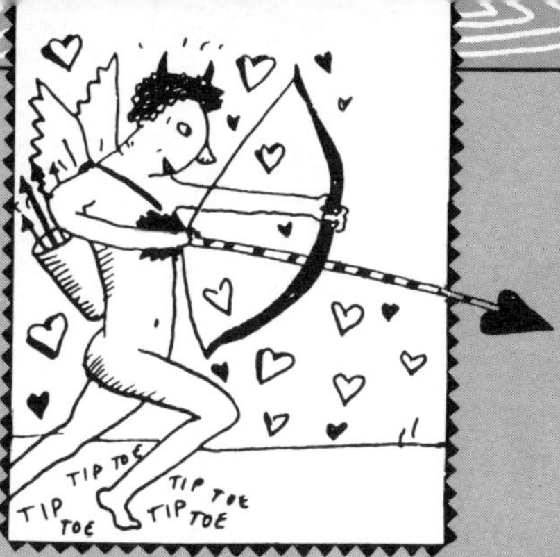
TIP TOE
TIP TOE
TIP TOE
TIP TOE
TIP TOE

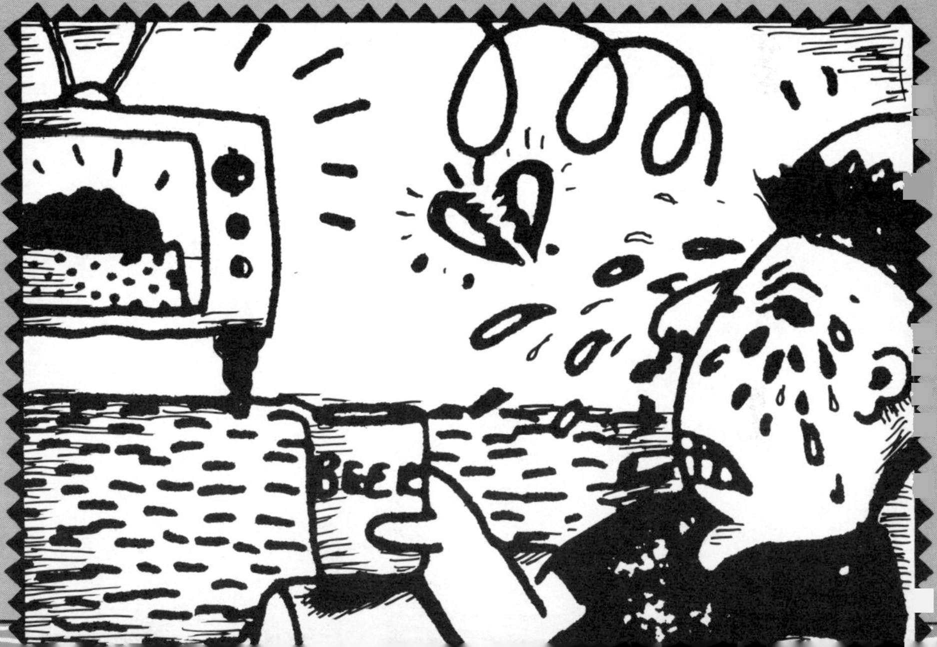
BEER

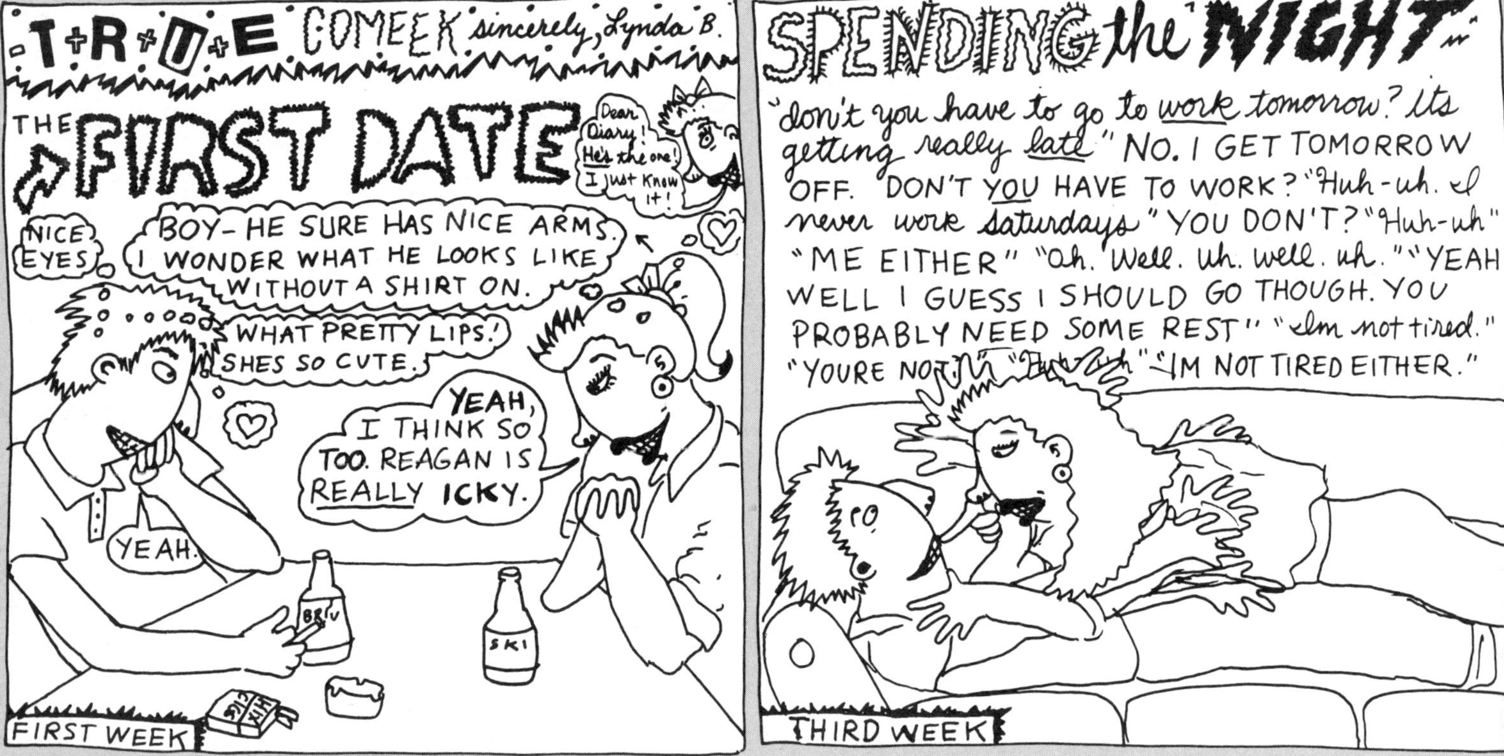
T R U E COMEEK sincerely, Lynda B.
THE FIRST DATE
Dear Diary! He's the one! I just know it!
NICE EYES
BOY- HE SURE HAS NICE ARMS. I WONDER WHAT HE LOOKS LIKE WITHOUT A SHIRT ON.
WHAT PRETTY LIPS! SHES SO CUTE.
YEAH, I THINK SO TOO. REAGAN IS REALLY ICKY.
YEAH.
BRU
SKI
FIRST WEEK
SPENDING the NIGHT
"don't you have to go to work tomorrow? its getting really late" NO. I GET TOMORROW OFF. DON'T YOU HAVE TO WORK?" "Huh-uh. I never work saturdays" "YOU DON'T?" "Huh-uh" "ME EITHER" "Oh. Well. Uh. well. uh." "YEAH WELL I GUESS I SHOULD GO THOUGH. YOU PROBABLY NEED SOME REST" "Im not tired." "YOURE NOT?" "IM NOT TIRED EITHER."
THIRD WEEK

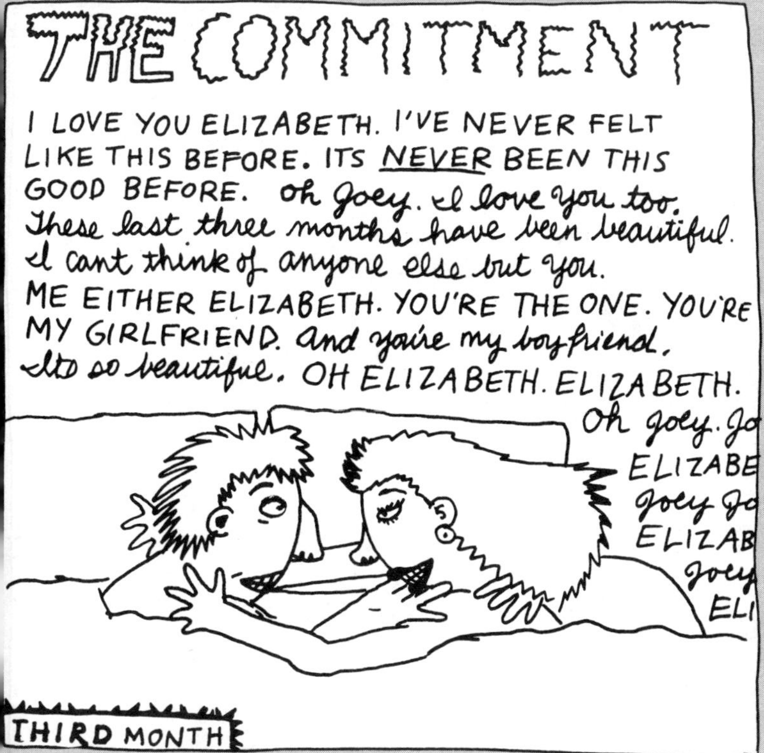
THE COMMITMENT
I LOVE YOU ELIZABETH. I'VE NEVER FELT LIKE THIS BEFORE. ITS NEVER BEEN THIS GOOD BEFORE.
Oh Joey. I love you too. These last three months have been beautiful. I cant think of anyone else but you.
ME EITHER ELIZABETH. YOU'RE THE ONE. YOU'RE MY GIRLFRIEND.
and you're my boyfriend. Its so beautiful.
OH ELIZABETH. ELIZABETH.
Oh Joey. Jo
ELIZABE
Joey Jo
ELIZAB
Joey
ELI
THIRD MONTH

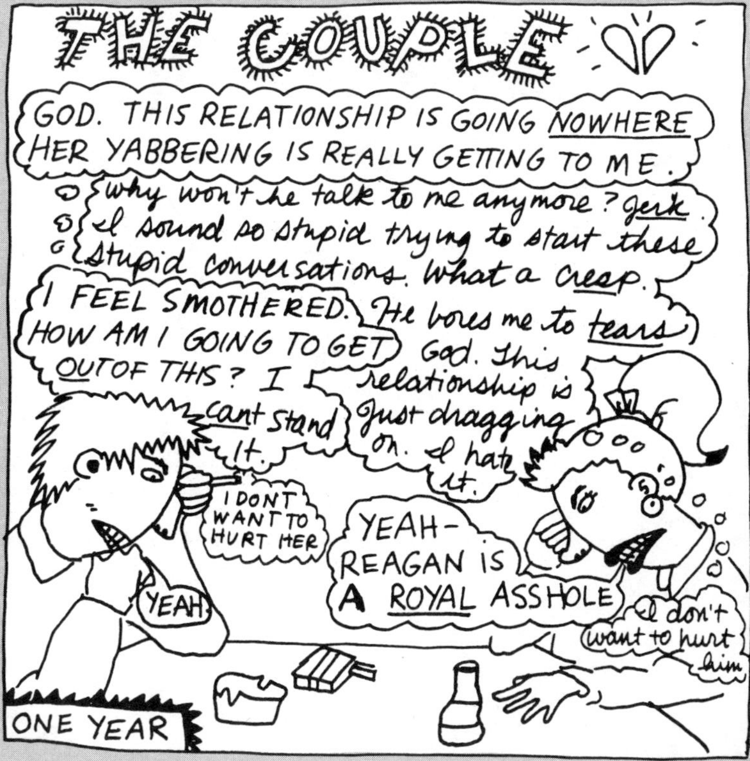
THE COUPLE
GOD. THIS RELATIONSHIP IS GOING NOWHERE HER YABBERING IS REALLY GETTING TO ME.
why won't he talk to me anymore? Jerk. I sound so stupid trying to start these stupid conversations. What a creep.
I FEEL SMOTHERED.
He bores me to tears
HOW AM I GOING TO GET OUT OF THIS? I cant stand it.
God. This relationship is just dragging on. I hate it.
I DONT WANT TO HURT HER
YEAH-REAGAN IS A ROYAL ASSHOLE
YEAH
I don't want to hurt him
ONE YEAR

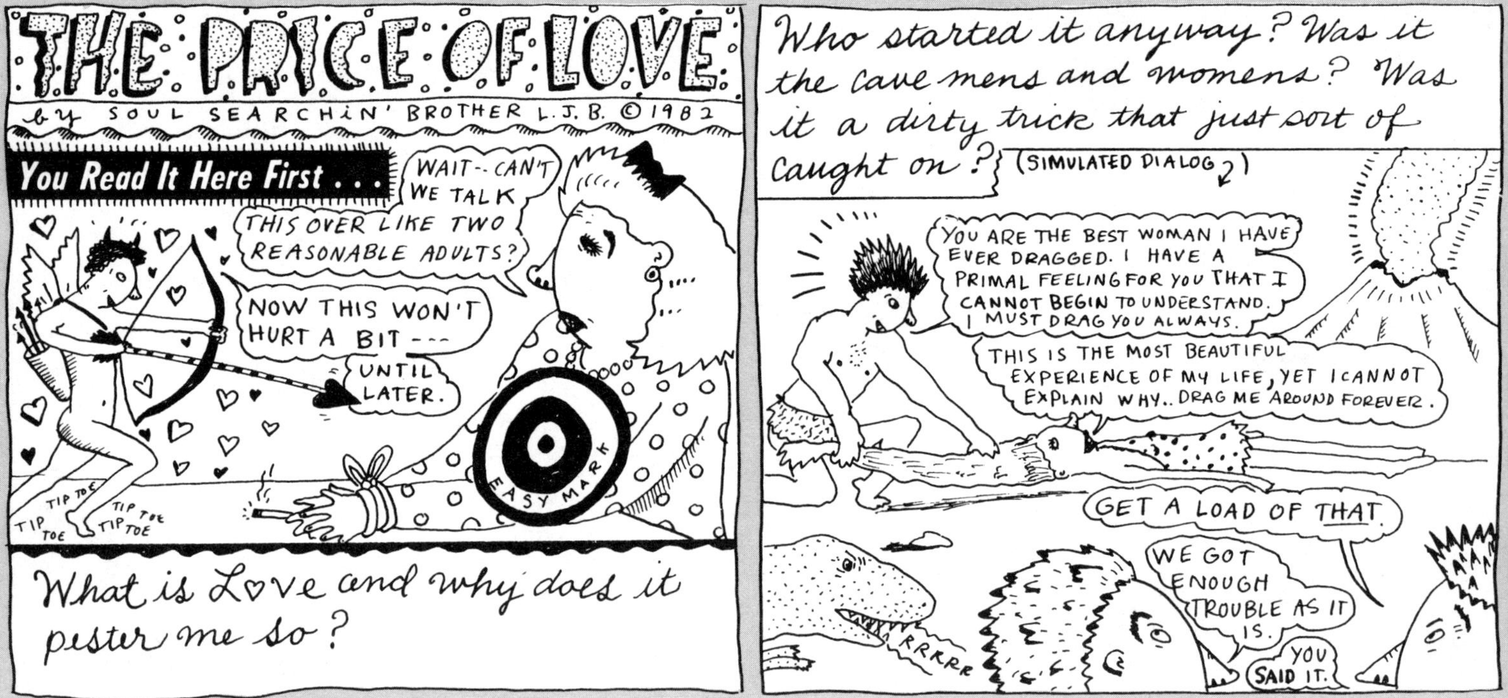

THE PRICE OF LOVE
by SOUL SEARCHIN' BROTHER L.J.B. ©1982
You Read It Here First . . .
WAIT-- CAN'T WE TALK THIS OVER LIKE TWO REASONABLE ADULTS?
NOW THIS WON'T HURT A BIT---
UNTIL LATER.
EASY MARK
TIP TOE TIP TOE TIP TOE TIP TOE
What is Love and why does it pester me so?
Who started it anyway? Was it the cave mens and womens? Was it a dirty trick that just sort of caught on?
(SIMULATED DIALOG)
YOU ARE THE BEST WOMAN I HAVE EVER DRAGGED. I HAVE A PRIMAL FEELING FOR YOU THAT I CANNOT BEGIN TO UNDERSTAND. I MUST DRAG YOU ALWAYS.
THIS IS THE MOST BEAUTIFUL EXPERIENCE OF MY LIFE, YET I CANNOT EXPLAIN WHY.. DRAG ME AROUND FOREVER.
GET A LOAD OF THAT.
WE GOT ENOUGH TROUBLE AS IT IS.
YOU SAID IT.
RRRRRR

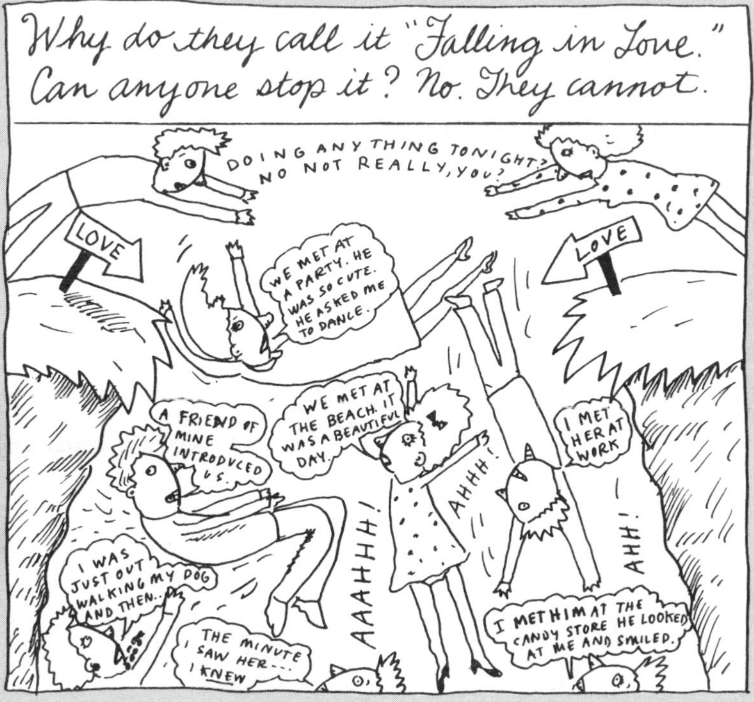
Why do they call it "Falling in Love." Can anyone stop it? No. They cannot.
DOING ANYTHING TONIGHT?
NO NOT REALLY, YOU?
LOVE
LOVE
WE MET AT A PARTY. HE WAS SO CUTE. HE ASKED ME TO DANCE.
A FRIEND OF MINE INTRODUCED US.
WE MET AT THE BEACH. IT WAS A BEAUTIFUL DAY.
AHHH!
I MET HER AT WORK
AAAHHH!
AHH!
I WAS JUST OUT WALKING MY DOG AND THEN...
THE MINUTE I SAW HER--- I KNEW
I MET HIM AT THE CANDY STORE HE LOOKED AT ME AND SMILED.

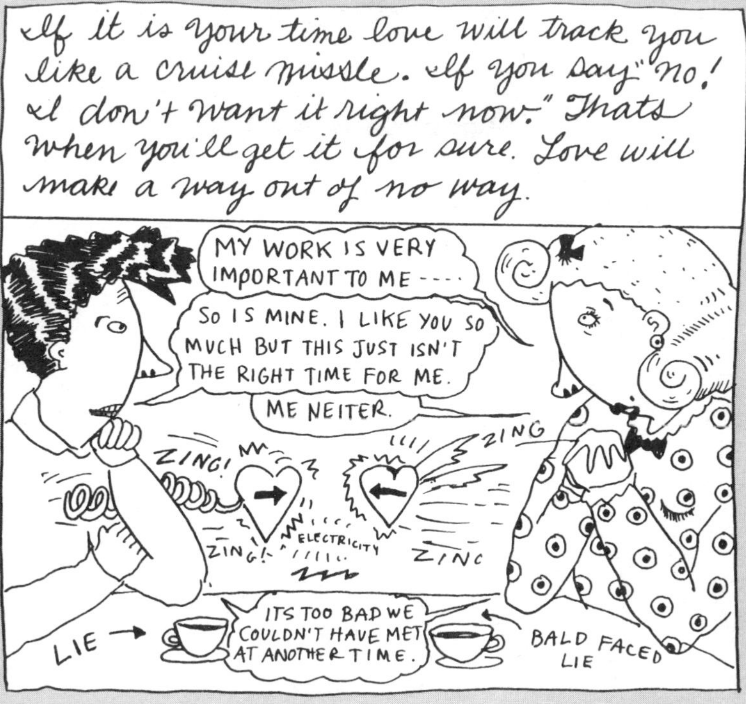
If it is your time love will track you like a cruise missle. If you say "No! I don't want it right now." Thats when you'll get it for sure. Love will make a way out of no way.
MY WORK IS VERY IMPORTANT TO ME ----
SO IS MINE. I LIKE YOU SO MUCH BUT THIS JUST ISN'T THE RIGHT TIME FOR ME.
ME NEITER.
ZING!
ZING
ZING!
ELECTRICITY
ZINC
LIE
ITS TOO BAD WE COULDN'T HAVE MET AT ANOTHER TIME.
BALD FACED LIE

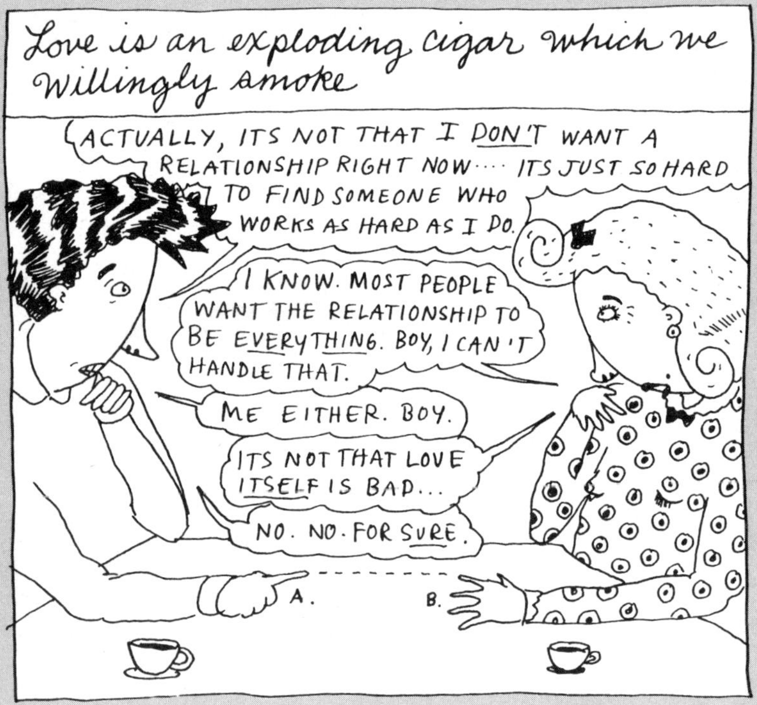
Love is an exploding cigar which we willingly smoke
ACTUALLY, ITS NOT THAT I DON'T WANT A RELATIONSHIP RIGHT NOW.... ITS JUST SO HARD TO FIND SOMEONE WHO WORKS AS HARD AS I DO.
I KNOW. MOST PEOPLE WANT THE RELATIONSHIP TO BE EVERYTHING. BOY, I CAN'T HANDLE THAT.
ME EITHER. BOY.
ITS NOT THAT LOVE ITSELF IS BAD...
NO. NO. FOR SURE.
A.
B.

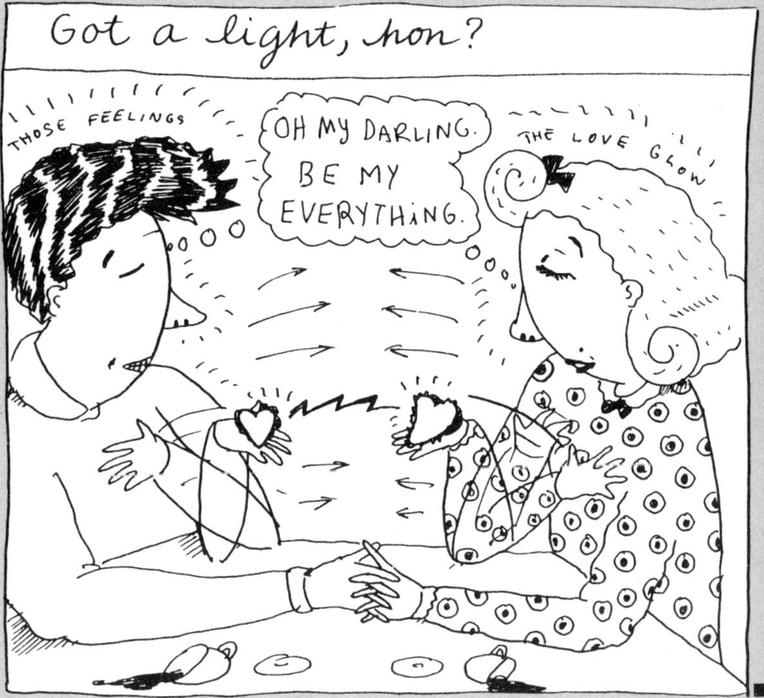
Got a light, hon?
THOSE FEELINGS
OH MY DARLING. BE MY EVERYTHING.
THE LOVE GLOW

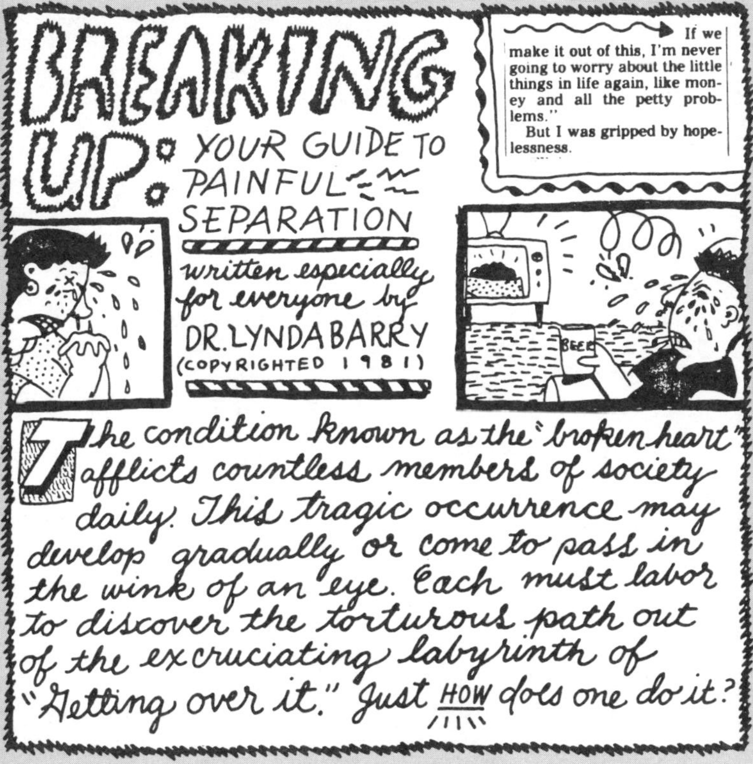
BREAKING UP: YOUR GUIDE TO PAINFUL SEPARATION
If we make it out of this, I'm never going to worry about the little things in life again, like money and all the petty problems."
But I was gripped by hopelessness.
written especially for everyone by DR. LYNDA BARRY
(COPYRIGHTED 1981)
BEER
The condition known as the "broken heart" afflicts countless members of society daily. This tragic occurrence may develop gradually or come to pass in the wink of an eye. Each must labor to discover the torturous path out of the excruciating labyrinth of "Getting over it." Just HOW does one do it?

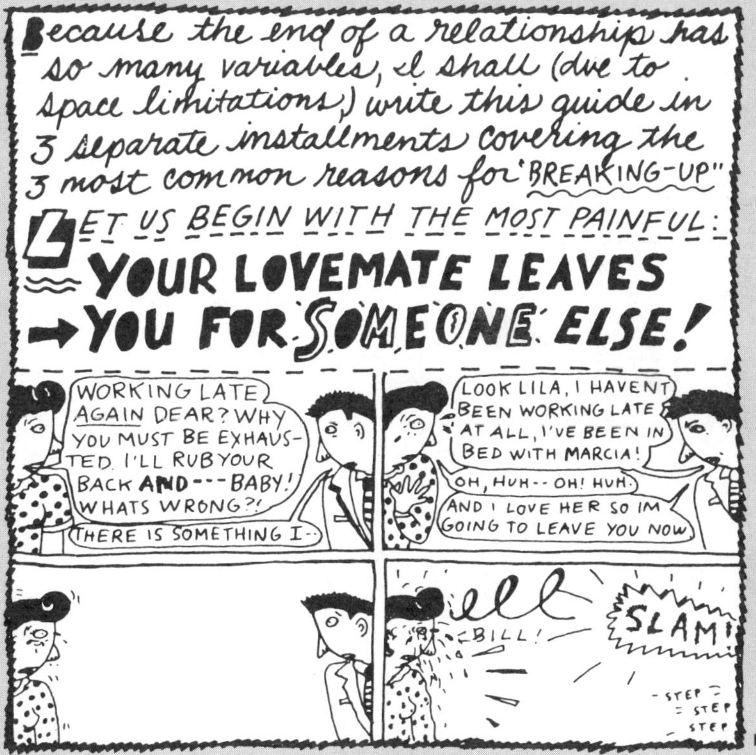
Because the end of a relationship has so many variables, I shall (due to space limitations,) write this guide in 3 separate installments covering the 3 most common reasons for "BREAKING-UP"
LET US BEGIN WITH THE MOST PAINFUL:
YOUR LOVEMATE LEAVES YOU FOR SOMEONE ELSE!
WORKING LATE AGAIN DEAR? WHY YOU MUST BE EXHAUSTED. I'LL RUB YOUR BACK AND--- BABY! WHATS WRONG?!
THERE IS SOMETHING I--
LOOK LILA, I HAVENT BEEN WORKING LATE AT ALL, I'VE BEEN IN BED WITH MARCIA!
OH, HUH--OH! HUH.
AND I LOVE HER SO IM GOING TO LEAVE YOU NOW
BILL!
SLAM!
STEP
STEP
STEP

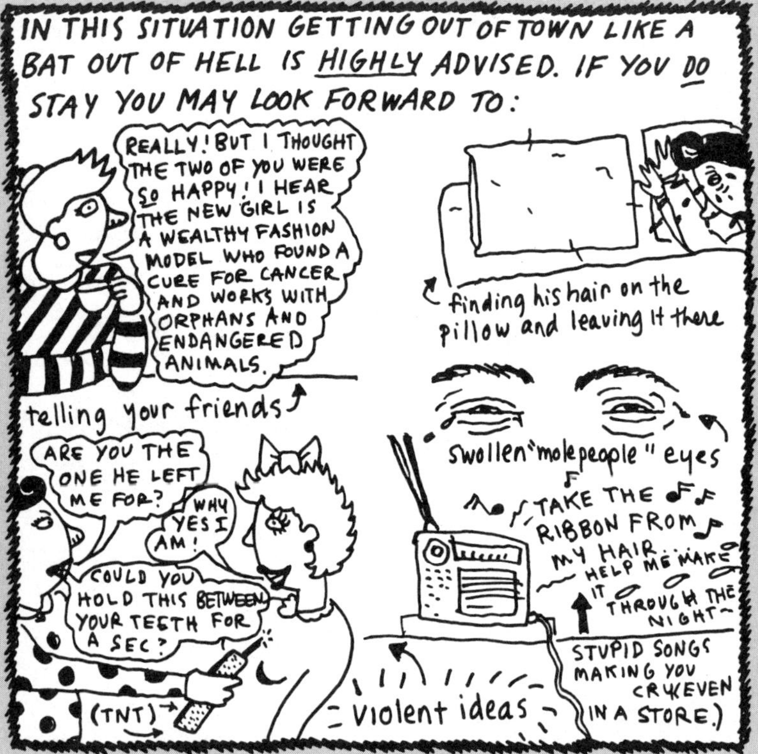
IN THIS SITUATION GETTING OUT OF TOWN LIKE A BAT OUT OF HELL IS HIGHLY ADVISED. IF YOU DO STAY YOU MAY LOOK FORWARD TO:
REALLY! BUT I THOUGHT THE TWO OF YOU WERE SO HAPPY! I HEAR THE NEW GIRL IS A WEALTHY FASHION MODEL WHO FOUND A CURE FOR CANCER AND WORKS WITH ORPHANS AND ENDANGERED ANIMALS.
telling your friends
finding his hair on the pillow and leaving it there
swollen "molepeople" eyes
ARE YOU THE ONE HE LEFT ME FOR?
WHY YES I AM!
COULD YOU HOLD THIS BETWEEN YOUR TEETH FOR A SEC?
(TNT)
violent ideas
TAKE THE RIBBON FROM MY HAIR HELP ME MAKE IT THROUGH THE NIGHT
STUPID SONGS MAKING YOU CRY (EVEN IN A STORE.)

WARNING SIGNS

STOP!

WHEN YOU FIND YOURSELF IN ANY OF THE FOLLOWING SITUATIONS, YOU ARE GETTING IN OVER YOUR HEAD. YOU MUST CALL A FRIEND AND DEMAND THEY CARE FOR YOU FOR A MINIMUM OF 3 HOURS UNTIL YOUR SENSES RETURN. CARRY THIS LIST WITH YOU AT ALL TIMES.

1. You feel a strong urge to go to your ex and his new love and dine with them, and give her gifts and tell him "it all makes sense to you" and "shes a wonderful human being."

2. You jump onto speeding vehicals from the sidewalk.

3. Men you have avoided for months suddenly look good to you.

4. You think it would be a "unique" idea to shave your head and eyebrows

5. You want to find out once and for all if Clorox and drano make a toxic gas.

6. You have a desire to tell everyone you know what you really think of them and tell your parents about your LSD trips at age 12 becarse there should be no more lies in this world

7. You kiss dogs on the lips with your eyes closed.

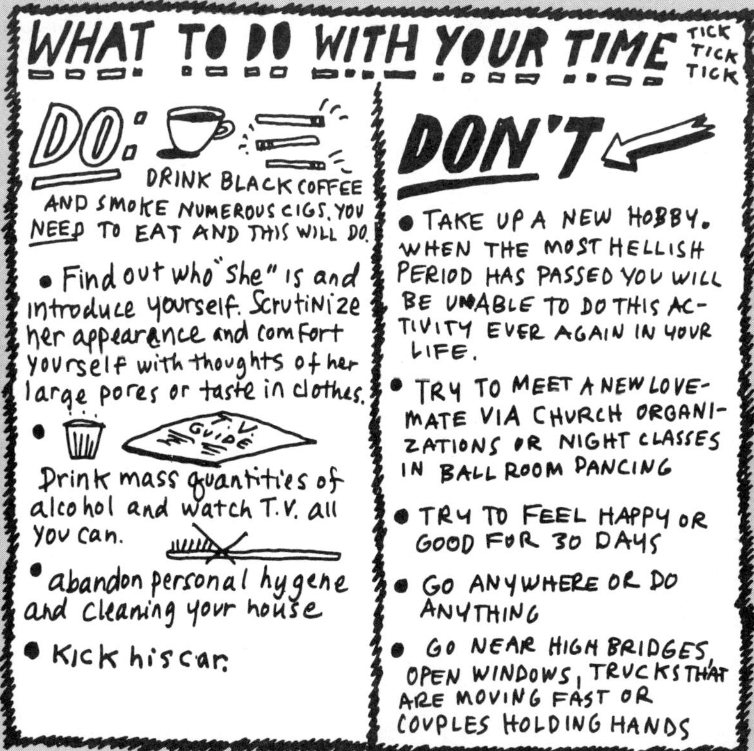
WHAT TO DO WITH YOUR TIME
TICK TICK TICK
DO:
DRINK BLACK COFFEE AND SMOKE NUMEROUS CIGS. YOU NEED TO EAT AND THIS WILL DO.
• Find out who "she" is and introduce yourself. Scrutinize her appearance and comfort yourself with thoughts of her large pores or taste in clothes.
T.V. GUIDE
• Drink mass quantities of alcohol and watch T.V. all you can.
• abandon personal hygene and cleaning your house
• Kick his car.
DON'T
• TAKE UP A NEW HOBBY. WHEN THE MOST HELLISH PERIOD HAS PASSED YOU WILL BE UNABLE TO DO THIS ACTIVITY EVER AGAIN IN YOUR LIFE.
• TRY TO MEET A NEW LOVE-MATE VIA CHURCH ORGANIZATIONS OR NIGHT CLASSES IN BALL ROOM DANCING
• TRY TO FEEL HAPPY OR GOOD FOR 30 DAYS
• GO ANYWHERE OR DO ANYTHING
• GO NEAR HIGH BRIDGES, OPEN WINDOWS, TRUCKS THAT ARE MOVING FAST OR COUPLES HOLDING HANDS

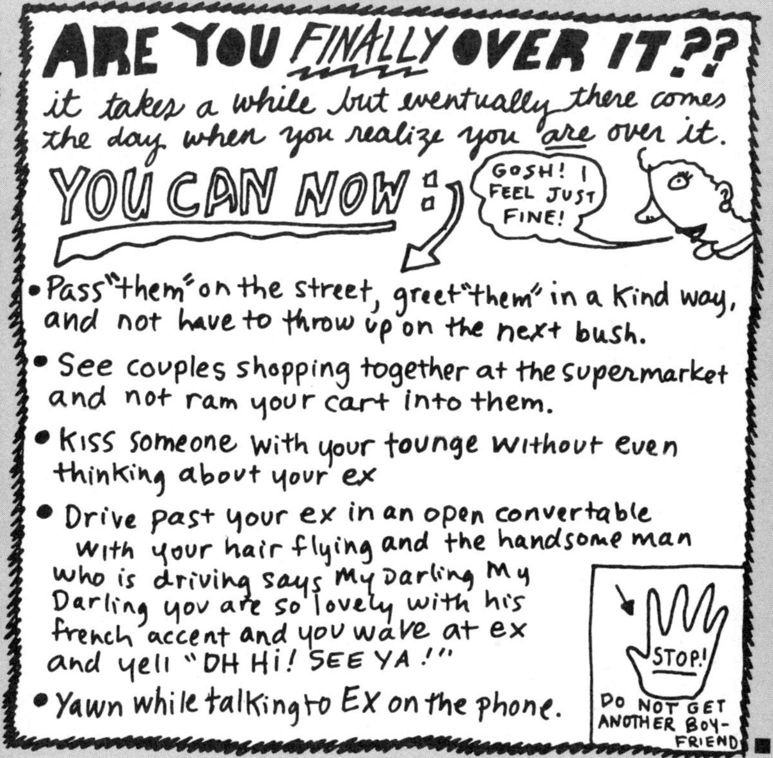
ARE YOU FINALLY OVER IT??
it takes a while but eventually there comes the day when you realize you are over it.
YOU CAN NOW:
GOSH! I FEEL JUST FINE!
• Pass "them" on the street, greet "them" in a kind way, and not have to throw up on the next bush.
• See couples shopping together at the supermarket and not ram your cart into them.
• Kiss someone with your tounge without even thinking about your ex
• Drive past your ex in an open convertable with your hair flying and the handsome man who is driving says My Darling My Darling you are so lovely with his french accent and you wave at ex and yell "OH Hi! SEE YA!"
• Yawn while talking to EX on the phone.
STOP!
DO NOT GET ANOTHER BOY-FRIEND

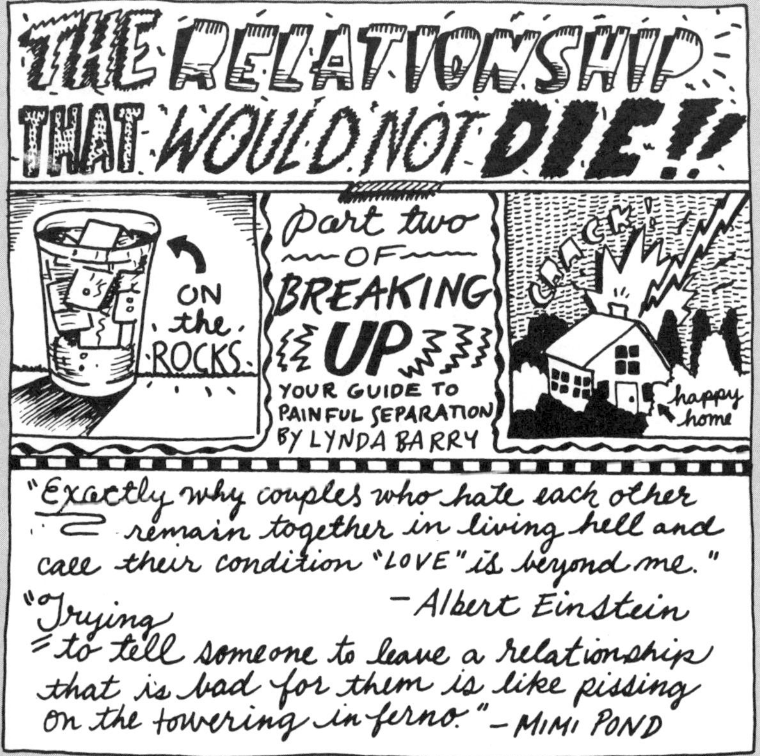

THE RELATIONSHIP THAT WOULD NOT DIE!!
ON the ROCKS
Part two —OF— BREAKING UP
YOUR GUIDE TO PAINFUL SEPARATION BY LYNDA BARRY
CRACK!
happy home
"Exactly why couples who hate each other remain together in living hell and call their condition "LOVE" is beyond me." —Albert Einstein
"Trying to tell someone to leave a relationship that is bad for them is like pissing on the towering inferno." —MIMI POND

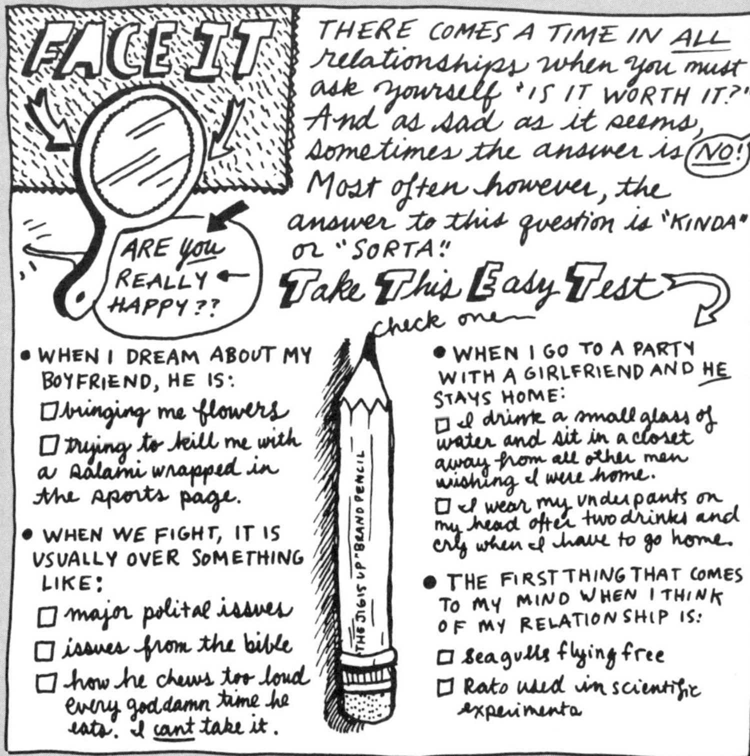

FACE IT
ARE you REALLY HAPPY??
THERE COMES A TIME IN ALL relationships when you must ask yourself "IS IT WORTH IT?" And as sad as it seems, sometimes the answer is NO! Most often however, the answer to this question is "KINDA" or "SORTA!"
Take This Easy Test
check one
• WHEN I DREAM ABOUT MY BOYFRIEND, HE IS:
☐ bringing me flowers
☐ trying to kill me with a salami wrapped in the sports page.
• WHEN WE FIGHT, IT IS USUALLY OVER SOMETHING LIKE:
☐ major polital issues
☐ issues from the bible
☐ how he chews too loud every goddamn time he eats. I cant take it.
THE "JIG IS UP" BRAND PENCIL
• WHEN I GO TO A PARTY WITH A GIRLFRIEND AND HE STAYS HOME:
☐ I drink a small glass of water and sit in a closet away from all other men wishing I were home.
☐ I wear my underpants on my head after two drinks and cry when I have to go home.
• THE FIRST THING THAT COMES TO MY MIND WHEN I THINK OF MY RELATIONSHIP IS:
☐ Seagulls flying free
☐ Rats used in scientific experiments

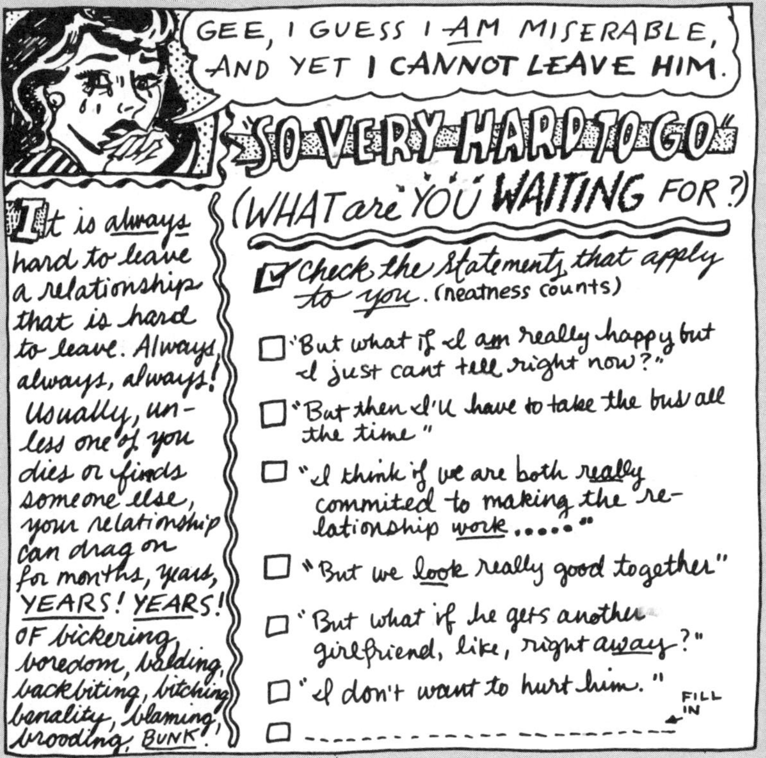
GEE, I GUESS I AM MISERABLE, AND YET I CANNOT LEAVE HIM.
"SO VERY HARD TO GO"
(WHAT are YOU WAITING FOR?)
It is always hard to leave a relationship that is hard to leave. Always, always, always! Usually, unless one of you dies or finds someone else, your relationship can drag on for months, years, YEARS! YEARS! OF bickering, boredom, balding, backbiting, bitching, banality, blaming, brooding, BUNK!
Check the statements that apply to you. (neatness counts)
"But what if I am really happy but I just cant tell right now?"
"But then I'll have to take the bus all the time"
"I think if we are both really commited to making the relationship work....."
"But we look really good together"
"But what if he gets another girlfriend, like, right away?"
"I don't want to hurt him."
FILL IN

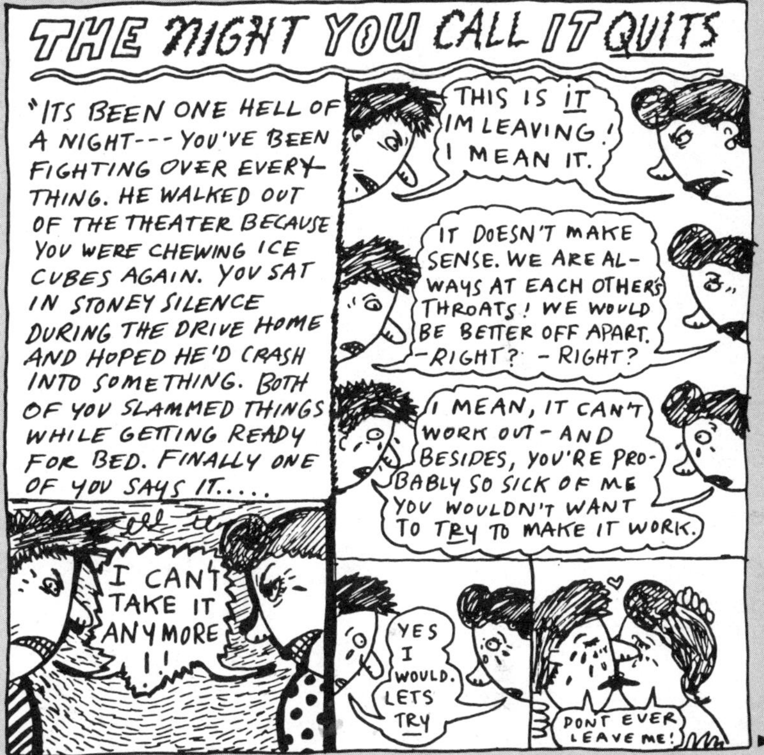
THE NIGHT YOU CALL IT QUITS
"ITS BEEN ONE HELL OF A NIGHT--- YOU'VE BEEN FIGHTING OVER EVERYTHING. HE WALKED OUT OF THE THEATER BECAUSE YOU WERE CHEWING ICE CUBES AGAIN. YOU SAT IN STONEY SILENCE DURING THE DRIVE HOME AND HOPED HE'D CRASH INTO SOMETHING. BOTH OF YOU SLAMMED THINGS WHILE GETTING READY FOR BED. FINALLY ONE OF YOU SAYS IT....
I CAN'T TAKE IT ANYMORE!!
THIS IS IT IM LEAVING! I MEAN IT.
IT DOESN'T MAKE SENSE. WE ARE ALWAYS AT EACH OTHER'S THROATS! WE WOULD BE BETTER OFF APART. -RIGHT? -RIGHT?
I MEAN, IT CAN'T WORK OUT - AND BESIDES, YOU'RE PROBABLY SO SICK OF ME YOU WOULDN'T WANT TO TRY TO MAKE IT WORK.
YES I WOULD. LETS TRY
DONT EVER LEAVE ME!

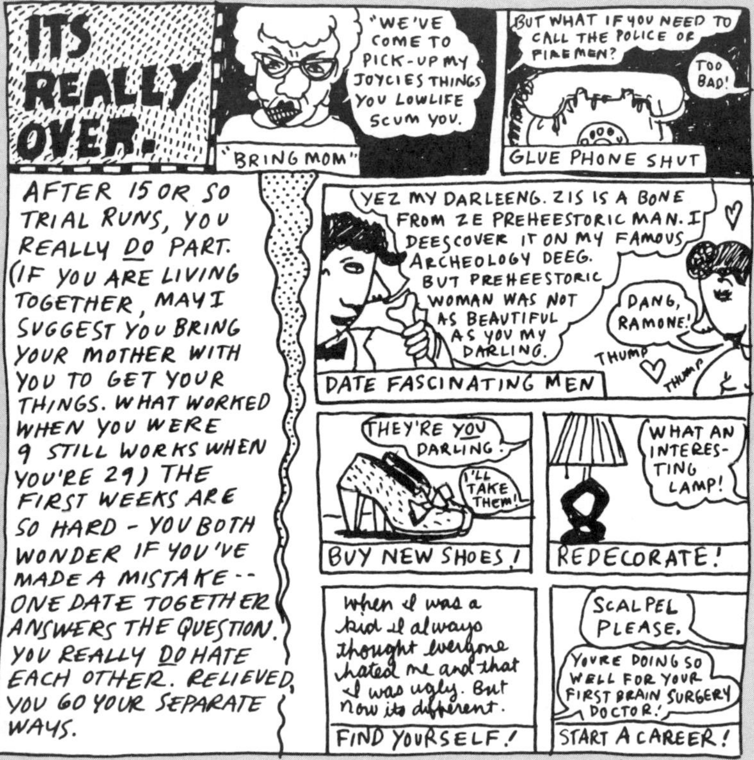
ITS REALLY OVER.
"WE'VE COME TO PICK-UP MY JOYCIES THINGS YOU LOWLIFE SCUM YOU.
"BRING MOM"
BUT WHAT IF YOU NEED TO CALL THE POLICE OR FIREMEN?
TOO BAD!
GLUE PHONE SHUT
AFTER 15 OR SO TRIAL RUNS, YOU REALLY DO PART. (IF YOU ARE LIVING TOGETHER, MAY I SUGGEST YOU BRING YOUR MOTHER WITH YOU TO GET YOUR THINGS. WHAT WORKED WHEN YOU WERE 9 STILL WORKS WHEN YOU'RE 29) THE FIRST WEEKS ARE SO HARD - YOU BOTH WONDER IF YOU'VE MADE A MISTAKE -- ONE DATE TOGETHER ANSWERS THE QUESTION. YOU REALLY DO HATE EACH OTHER. RELIEVED, YOU GO YOUR SEPARATE WAYS.
YEZ MY DARLEENG. ZIS IS A BONE FROM ZE PREHEESTORIC MAN. I DEESCOVER IT ON MY FAMOUS ARCHEOLOGY DEEG. BUT PREHEESTORIC WOMAN WAS NOT AS BEAUTIFUL AS YOU MY DARLING.
DANG, RAMONE!
THUMP
THUMP
DATE FASCINATING MEN
THEY'RE YOU DARLING.
I'LL TAKE THEM!
BUY NEW SHOES!
WHAT AN INTERESTING LAMP!
REDECORATE!
When I was a kid I always thought everyone hated me and that I was ugly. But now its different.
FIND YOURSELF!
SCALPEL PLEASE.
YOU'RE DOING SO WELL FOR YOUR FIRST BRAIN SURGERY DOCTOR!
START A CAREER!

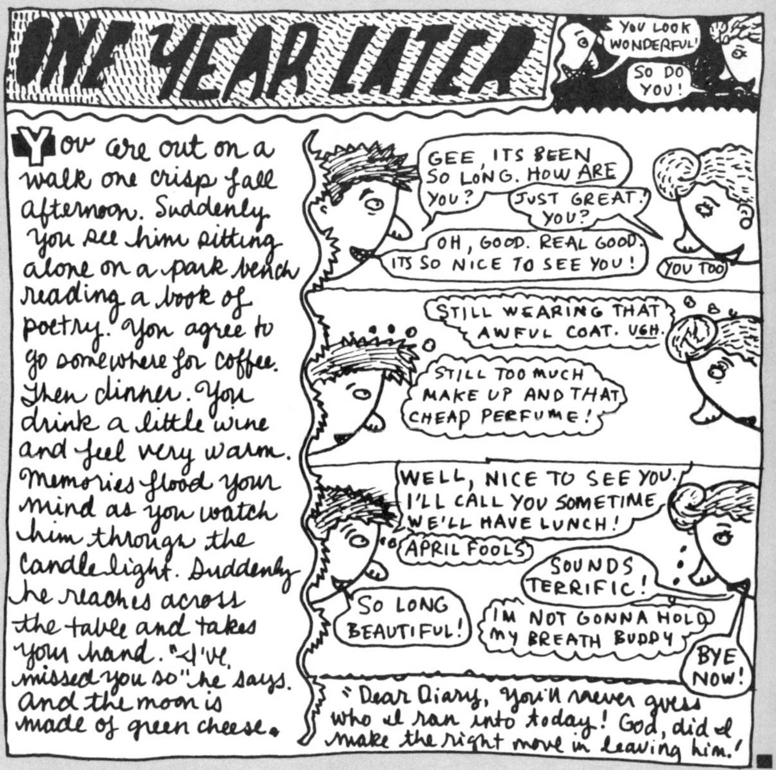
ONE YEAR LATER
YOU LOOK WONDERFUL!
SO DO YOU!
You are out on a walk one crisp fall afternoon. Suddenly you see him sitting alone on a park bench reading a book of poetry. You agree to go somewhere for coffee. Then dinner. You drink a little wine and feel very warm. Memories flood your mind as you watch him through the candle light. Suddenly he reaches across the table and takes your hand. "I've missed you so" he says. And the moon is made of green cheese.
GEE, ITS BEEN SO LONG. HOW ARE YOU?
JUST GREAT. YOU?
OH, GOOD. REAL GOOD. ITS SO NICE TO SEE YOU!
YOU TOO
STILL WEARING THAT AWFUL COAT. UGH.
STILL TOO MUCH MAKE UP AND THAT CHEAP PERFUME!
WELL, NICE TO SEE YOU. I'LL CALL YOU SOMETIME WE'LL HAVE LUNCH!
APRIL FOOLS
SOUNDS TERRIFIC!
SO LONG BEAUTIFUL!
I'M NOT GONNA HOLD MY BREATH BUDDY
BYE NOW!
"Dear Diary, You'll never guess who I ran into today! God, did I make the right move in leaving him!

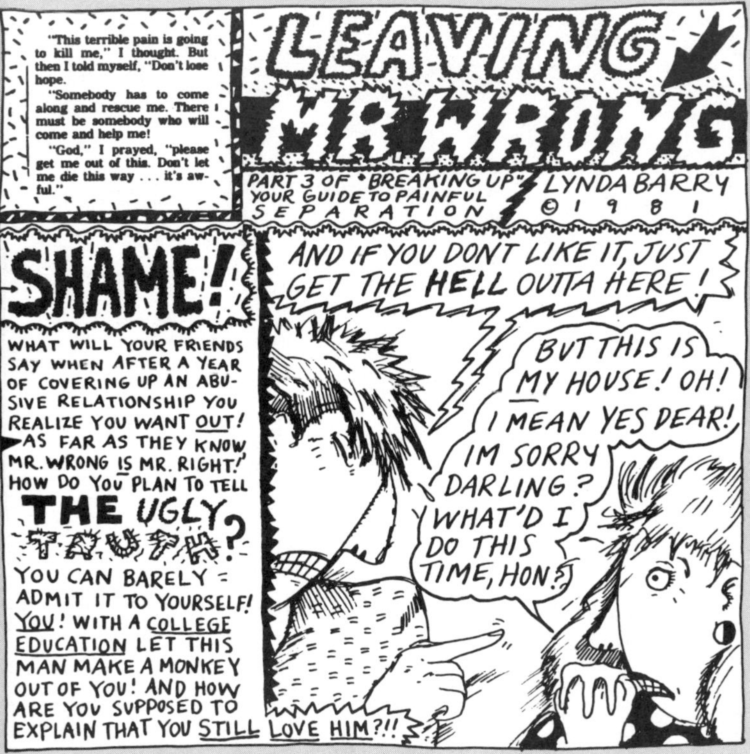
"This terrible pain is going to kill me," I thought. But then I told myself, "Don't lose hope.
"Somebody has to come along and rescue me. There must be somebody who will come and help me!
"God," I prayed, "please get me out of this. Don't let me die this way . . . it's awful."
LEAVING MR WRONG
PART 3 OF "BREAKING UP" YOUR GUIDE TO PAINFUL SEPARATION
LYNDA BARRY ©1981
SHAME!
WHAT WILL YOUR FRIENDS SAY WHEN AFTER A YEAR OF COVERING UP AN ABUSIVE RELATIONSHIP YOU REALIZE YOU WANT OUT! AS FAR AS THEY KNOW MR. WRONG IS MR. RIGHT! HOW DO YOU PLAN TO TELL THE UGLY TRUTH? YOU CAN BARELY ADMIT IT TO YOURSELF! YOU! WITH A COLLEGE EDUCATION LET THIS MAN MAKE A MONKEY OUT OF YOU! AND HOW ARE YOU SUPPOSED TO EXPLAIN THAT YOU STILL LOVE HIM?!!
AND IF YOU DONT LIKE IT, JUST GET THE HELL OUTTA HERE!
BUT THIS IS MY HOUSE! OH! I MEAN YES DEAR!
IM SORRY DARLING? WHAT'D I DO THIS TIME, HON?

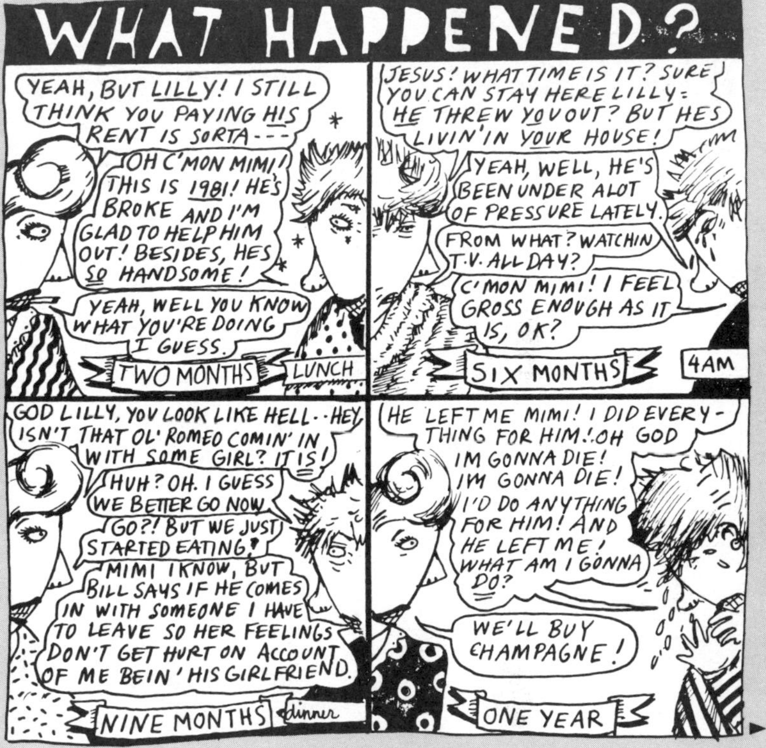
WHAT HAPPENED?
YEAH, BUT LILLY! I STILL THINK YOU PAYING HIS RENT IS SORTA---
OH C'MON MIMI! THIS IS 1981! HE'S BROKE AND I'M GLAD TO HELP HIM OUT! BESIDES, HES SO HANDSOME!
YEAH, WELL YOU KNOW WHAT YOU'RE DOING I GUESS.
TWO MONTHS
LUNCH
JESUS! WHAT TIME IS IT? SURE YOU CAN STAY HERE LILLY- HE THREW YOU OUT? BUT HES LIVIN' IN YOUR HOUSE!
YEAH, WELL, HE'S BEEN UNDER ALOT OF PRESSURE LATELY.
FROM WHAT? WATCHIN T.V. ALL DAY?
C'MON MIMI! I FEEL GROSS ENOUGH AS IT IS, OK?
SIX MONTHS
4AM
GOD LILLY, YOU LOOK LIKE HELL--HEY, ISN'T THAT OL' ROMEO COMIN' IN WITH SOME GIRL? IT IS!
HUH? OH. I GUESS WE BETTER GO NOW.
GO?! BUT WE JUST STARTED EATING!
MIMI I KNOW, BUT BILL SAYS IF HE COMES IN WITH SOMEONE I HAVE TO LEAVE SO HER FEELINGS DON'T GET HURT ON ACCOUNT OF ME BEIN' HIS GIRLFRIEND.
NINE MONTHS
dinner
HE LEFT ME MIMI! I DID EVERYTHING FOR HIM! OH GOD IM GONNA DIE! IM GONNA DIE! I'D DO ANYTHING FOR HIM! AND HE LEFT ME! WHAT AM I GONNA DO?
WE'LL BUY CHAMPAGNE!
ONE YEAR

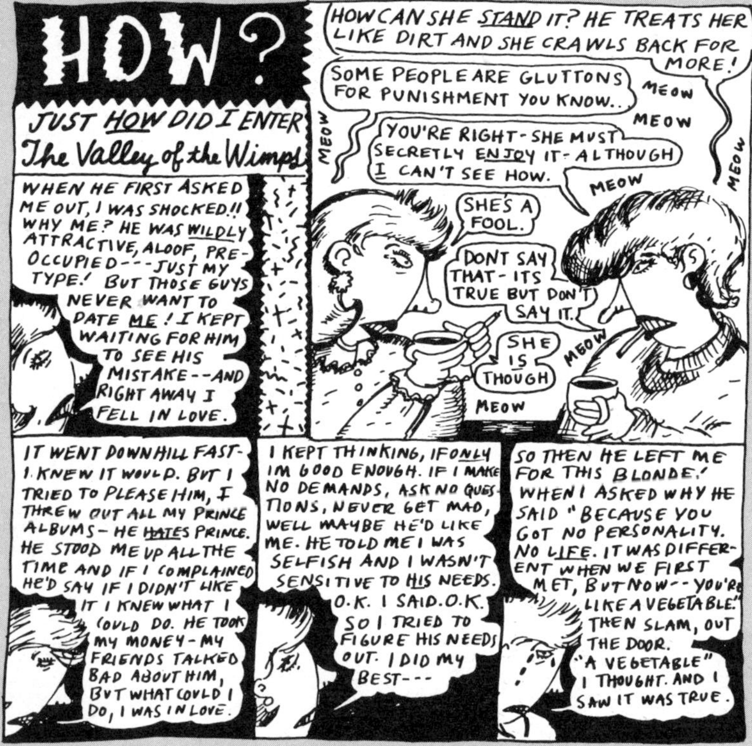
HOW?
JUST HOW DID I ENTER The Valley of the Wimps!
WHEN HE FIRST ASKED ME OUT, I WAS SHOCKED!! WHY ME? HE WAS WILDLY ATTRACTIVE, ALOOF, PRE-OCCUPIED---JUST MY TYPE! BUT THOSE GUYS NEVER WANT TO DATE ME! I KEPT WAITING FOR HIM TO SEE HIS MISTAKE--AND RIGHT AWAY I FELL IN LOVE.
HOW CAN SHE STAND IT? HE TREATS HER LIKE DIRT AND SHE CRAWLS BACK FOR MORE!
SOME PEOPLE ARE GLUTTONS FOR PUNISHMENT YOU KNOW..
MEOW
MEOW
MEOW
YOU'RE RIGHT- SHE MUST SECRETLY ENJOY IT- ALTHOUGH I CAN'T SEE HOW.
MEOW
MEOW
SHE'S A FOOL.
DONT SAY THAT- ITS TRUE BUT DON'T SAY IT.
SHE IS THOUGH
MEOW
MEOW
IT WENT DOWNHILL FAST- I KNEW IT WOULD. BUT I TRIED TO PLEASE HIM, I THREW OUT ALL MY PRINCE ALBUMS- HE HATES PRINCE. HE STOOD ME UP ALL THE TIME AND IF I COMPLAINED HE'D SAY IF I DIDN'T LIKE IT I KNEW WHAT I COULD DO. HE TOOK MY MONEY- MY FRIENDS TALKED BAD ABOUT HIM, BUT WHAT COULD I DO, I WAS IN LOVE.
I KEPT THINKING, IF ONLY IM GOOD ENOUGH. IF I MAKE NO DEMANDS, ASK NO QUESTIONS, NEVER GET MAD, WELL MAYBE HE'D LIKE ME. HE TOLD ME I WAS SELFISH AND I WASN'T SENSITIVE TO HIS NEEDS.
O.K. I SAID. O.K. SO I TRIED TO FIGURE HIS NEEDS OUT. I DID MY BEST---
SO THEN HE LEFT ME FOR THIS BLONDE! WHEN I ASKED WHY HE SAID "BECAUSE YOU GOT NO PERSONALITY. NO LIFE. IT WAS DIFFERENT WHEN WE FIRST MET, BUT NOW-- YOU'RE LIKE A VEGETABLE." THEN SLAM, OUT THE DOOR. "A VEGETABLE" I THOUGHT. AND I SAW IT WAS TRUE.

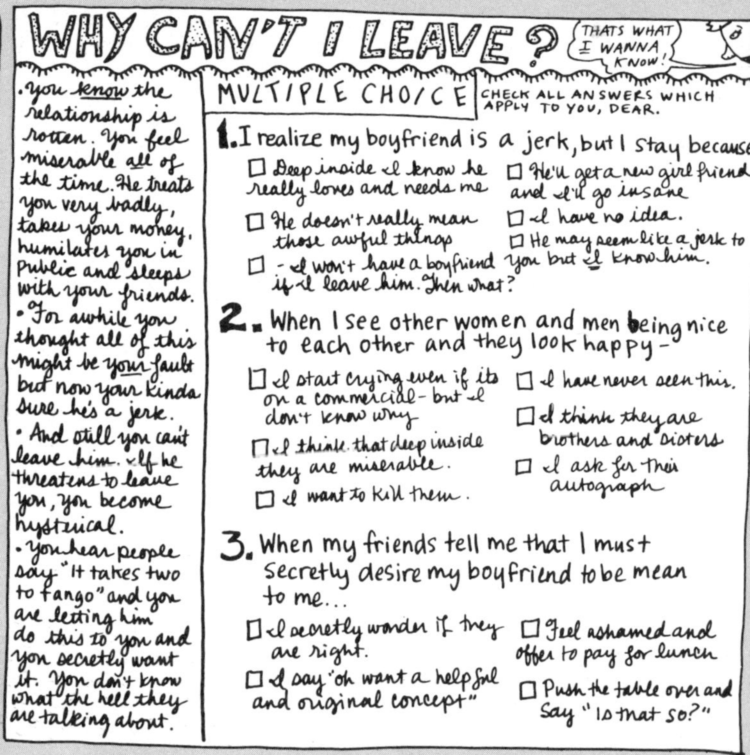
WHY CAN'T I LEAVE?
THATS WHAT I WANNA KNOW!
• you know the relationship is rotten. You feel miserable all of the time. He treats you very badly, takes your money, humilates you in public and sleeps with your friends.
• For awhile you thought all of this might be your fault but now your kinda sure he's a jerk.
• And still you can't leave him. If he threatens to leave you, you become hysterical.
• You hear people say "It takes two to tango" and you are letting him do this to you and you secretly want it. You don't know what the hell they are talking about.
MULTIPLE CHOICE
CHECK ALL ANSWERS WHICH APPLY TO YOU, DEAR.
1. I realize my boyfriend is a jerk, but I stay because
☐ Deep inside I know he really loves and needs me
☐ He doesn't really mean those awful things
☐ - I won't have a boyfriend if I leave him. Then what?
☐ He'll get a new girl friend and I'll go insane
☐ I have no idea.
☐ He may seem like a jerk to you but I know him.
2. When I see other women and men being nice to each other and they look happy-
☐ I start crying even if its on a commercial- but I don't know why
☐ I think that deep inside they are miserable.
☐ I want to kill them.
☐ I have never seen this.
☐ I think they are brothers and sisters
☐ I ask for their autograph
3. When my friends tell me that I must secretly desire my boyfriend to be mean to me...
☐ I secretly wonder if they are right.
☐ I say "oh want a helpful and original concept"
☐ Feel ashamed and offer to pay for lunch
☐ Push the table over and Say "Is that So?"

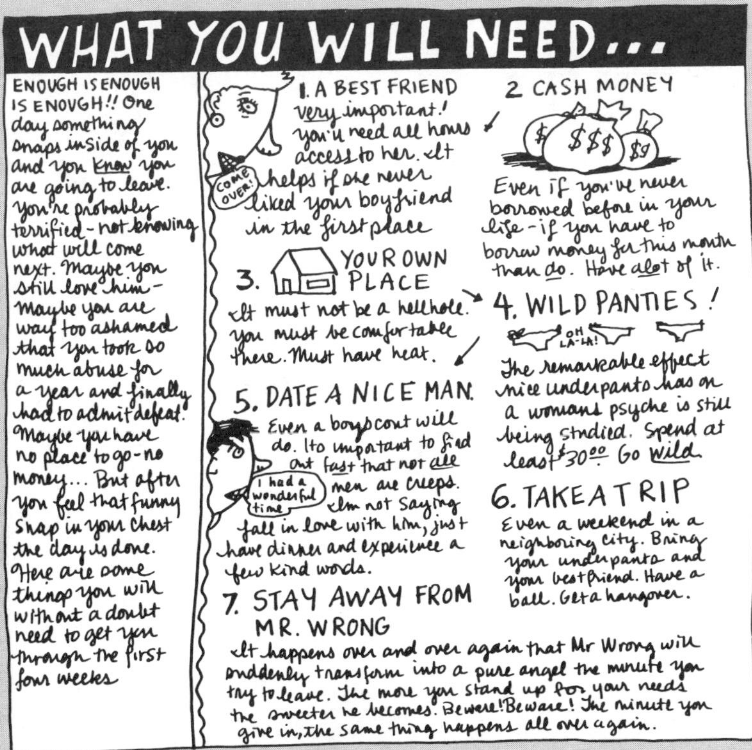
WHAT YOU WILL NEED...
ENOUGH IS ENOUGH IS ENOUGH!! One day something snaps inside of you and you know you are going to leave. You're probably terrified - not knowing what will come next. Maybe you still love him - Maybe you are way too ashamed that you took so much abuse for a year and finally had to admit defeat. Maybe you have no place to go - no money... But after you feel that funny snap in your chest the day is done. Here are some things you will without a doubt need to get you through the first four weeks
1. A BEST FRIEND very important! you'll need all hours access to her. It helps if she never liked your boyfriend in the first place
COME OVER!
2 CASH MONEY
$
$$$
$$
Even if you've never borrowed before in your life - if you have to borrow money for this month than do. Have alot of it.
3. YOUR OWN PLACE
It must not be a hellhole. You must be comfortable there. Must have heat.
4. WILD PANTIES!
OH LA-LA!
The remarkable effect nice underpants has on a womans psyche is still being studied. Spend at least $30.00 Go wild.
5. DATE A NICE MAN. Even a boy scout will do. Its important to find out fast that not all men are creeps. I'm not saying fall in love with him, just have dinner and experience a few kind words.
I had a wonderful time
6. TAKE A TRIP
Even a weekend in a neighboring city. Bring your underpants and your best friend. Have a ball. Get a hangover.
7. STAY AWAY FROM MR. WRONG
It happens over and over again that Mr Wrong will suddenly transform into a pure angel the minute you try to leave. The more you stand up for your needs the sweeter he becomes. Beware! Beware! The minute you give in, the same thing happens all over again.

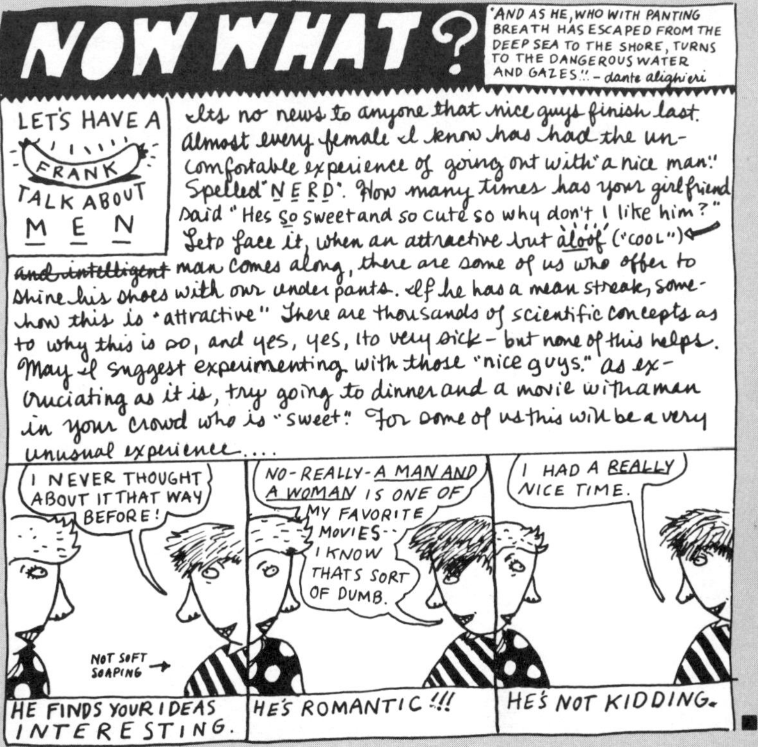
NOW WHAT?
"AND AS HE, WHO WITH PANTING BREATH HAS ESCAPED FROM THE DEEP SEA TO THE SHORE, TURNS TO THE DANGEROUS WATER AND GAZES!!. - dante alighieri
LET'S HAVE A FRANK TALK ABOUT MEN
Its no news to anyone that nice guys finish last. Almost every female I know has had the uncomfortable experience of going out with "a nice man." Spelled "N E R D". How many times has your girlfriend said "Hes so sweet and so cute so why don't I like him?" Lets face it, when an attractive but aloof ("COOL") ~~and intelligent~~ man comes along, there are some of us who offer to shine his shoes with our underpants. If he has a mean streak, somehow this is "attractive" There are thousands of scientific concepts as to why this is so, and yes, yes, its very sick - but none of this helps. May I suggest experimenting with those "nice guys." as excruciating as it is, try going to dinner and a movie with a man in your crowd who is "sweet." For some of us this will be a very unusual experience....
I NEVER THOUGHT ABOUT IT THAT WAY BEFORE!
NOT SOFT SOAPING
HE FINDS YOUR IDEAS INTERESTING.
NO - REALLY - A MAN AND A WOMAN IS ONE OF MY FAVORITE MOVIES - I KNOW THATS SORT OF DUMB.
HE'S ROMANTIC!!!
I HAD A REALLY NICE TIME.
HE'S NOT KIDDING.

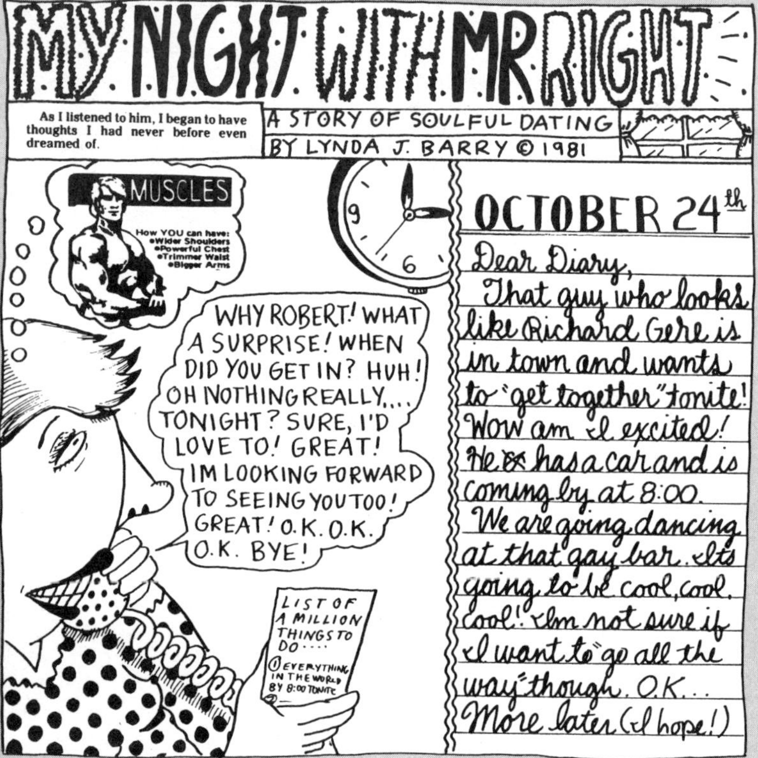

MY NIGHT WITH MR RIGHT
As I listened to him, I began to have thoughts I had never before even dreamed of.
A STORY OF SOULFUL DATING
BY LYNDA J. BARRY © 1981
MUSCLES
How YOU can have:
•Wider Shoulders
•Powerful Chest
•Trimmer Waist
•Bigger Arms
WHY ROBERT! WHAT A SURPRISE! WHEN DID YOU GET IN? HUH! OH NOTHING REALLY,... TONIGHT? SURE, I'D LOVE TO! GREAT! IM LOOKING FORWARD TO SEEING YOU TOO! GREAT! O.K. O.K. O.K. BYE!
LIST OF A MILLION THINGS TO DO....
① EVERYTHING IN THE WORLD BY 8:00 TONITE
OCTOBER 24th
Dear Diary,
That guy who looks like Richard Gere is in town and wants to "get together" tonite! Wow am I excited! He has a car and is coming by at 8:00. We are going dancing at that gay bar. Its going to be cool, cool, cool! I'm not sure if I want to go all the way though. O.K... More later (I hope!)

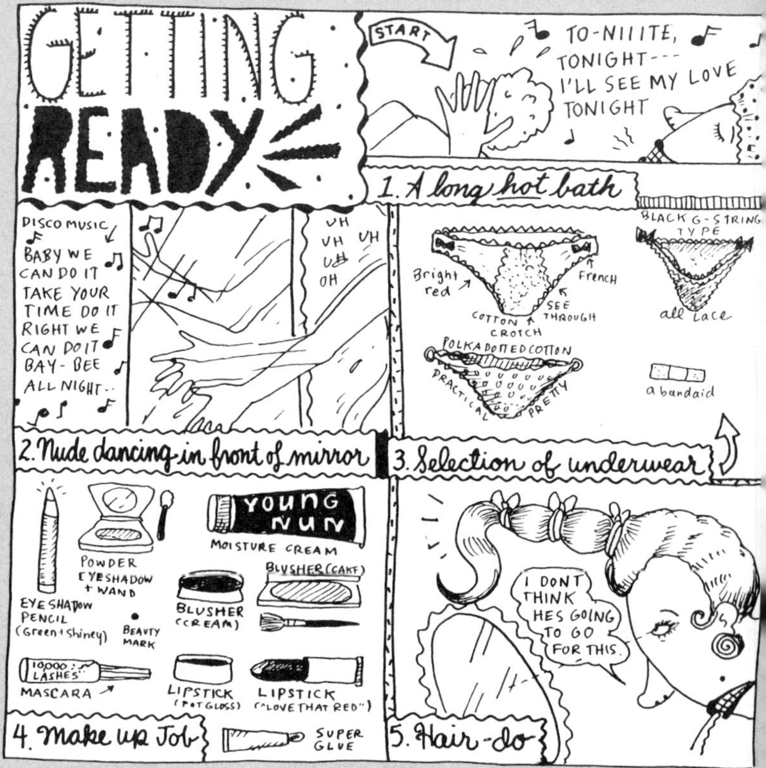

GETTING READY
START
TO-NIIITE, TONIGHT--- I'LL SEE MY LOVE TONIGHT
1. A long hot bath
DISCO MUSIC
BABY WE CAN DO IT TAKE YOUR TIME DO IT RIGHT WE CAN DO IT BAY-BEE ALL NIGHT..
UH UH UH UH OH
2. Nude dancing in front of mirror
Bright red
French
SEE THROUGH
COTTON CROTCH
BLACK G-STRING TYPE
all Lace
POLKA DOTTED COTTON
PRACTICAL
PRETTY
a bandaid
3. Selection of underwear
EYE SHADOW PENCIL (Green + Shiney)
POWDER EYESHADOW + WAND
BEAUTY MARK
YOUNG NUN
MOISTURE CREAM
BLUSHER (CAKE)
BLUSHER (CREAM)
10,000 LASHES
MASCARA
LIPSTICK (POT GLOSS)
LIPSTICK ("LOVE THAT RED")
4. Make up Job
SUPER GLUE
I DONT THINK HES GOING TO GO FOR THIS.
5. Hair-do

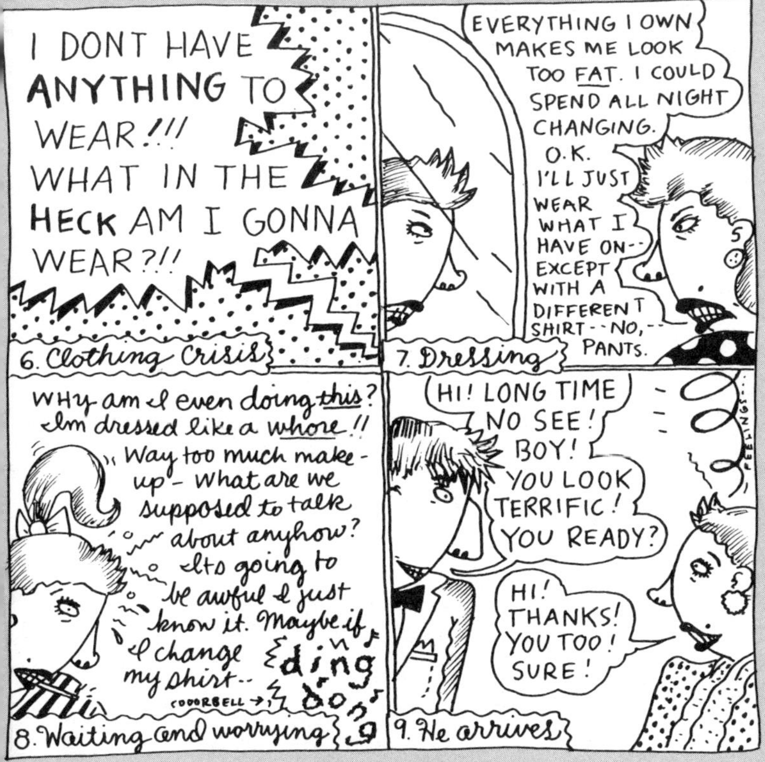
I DONT HAVE ANYTHING TO WEAR!!! WHAT IN THE HECK AM I GONNA WEAR?!!
6. Clothing Crisis
EVERYTHING I OWN MAKES ME LOOK TOO FAT. I COULD SPEND ALL NIGHT CHANGING.
O.K. I'LL JUST WEAR WHAT I HAVE ON-- EXCEPT WITH A DIFFERENT SHIRT--NO,--PANTS.
7. Dressing
WHY am I even doing this? I'm dressed like a whore!! Way too much make-up- What are we supposed to talk about anyhow? It's going to be awful I just know it. Maybe if I change my shirt--
ding dong
DOORBELL
8. Waiting and worrying
HI! LONG TIME NO SEE! BOY! YOU LOOK TERRIFIC! YOU READY?
HI! THANKS! YOU TOO! SURE!
FEELINGS
9. He arrives

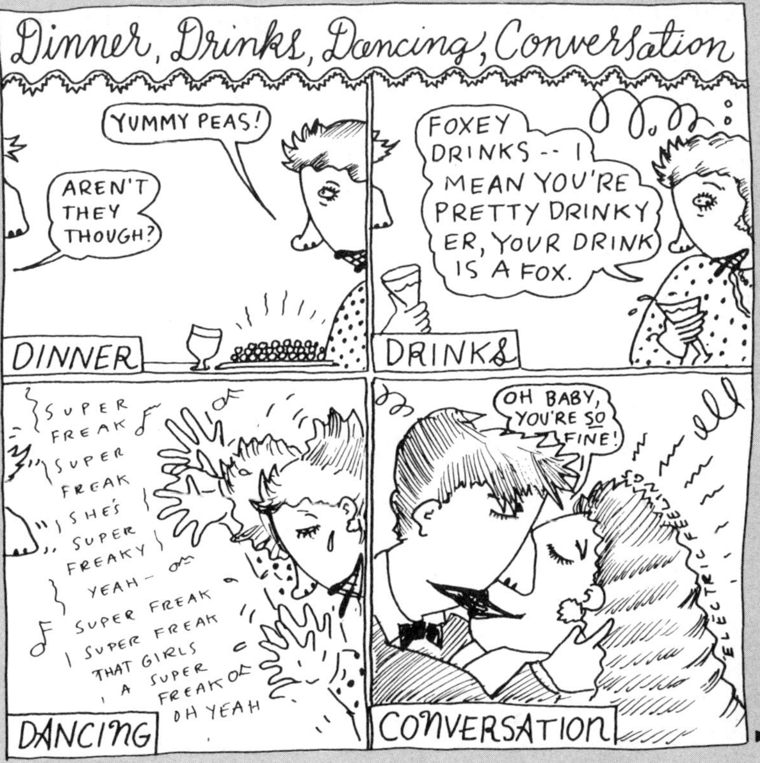
Dinner, Drinks, Dancing, Conversation
YUMMY PEAS!
AREN'T THEY THOUGH?
DINNER
FOXEY DRINKS -- I MEAN YOU'RE PRETTY DRINKY ER, YOUR DRINK IS A FOX.
DRINKS
SUPER FREAK SUPER FREAK SHE'S SUPER FREAKY YEAH- SUPER FREAK SUPER FREAK THAT GIRLS A SUPER FREAK OH YEAH
DANCING
OH BABY, YOU'RE SO FINE!
CONVERSATION

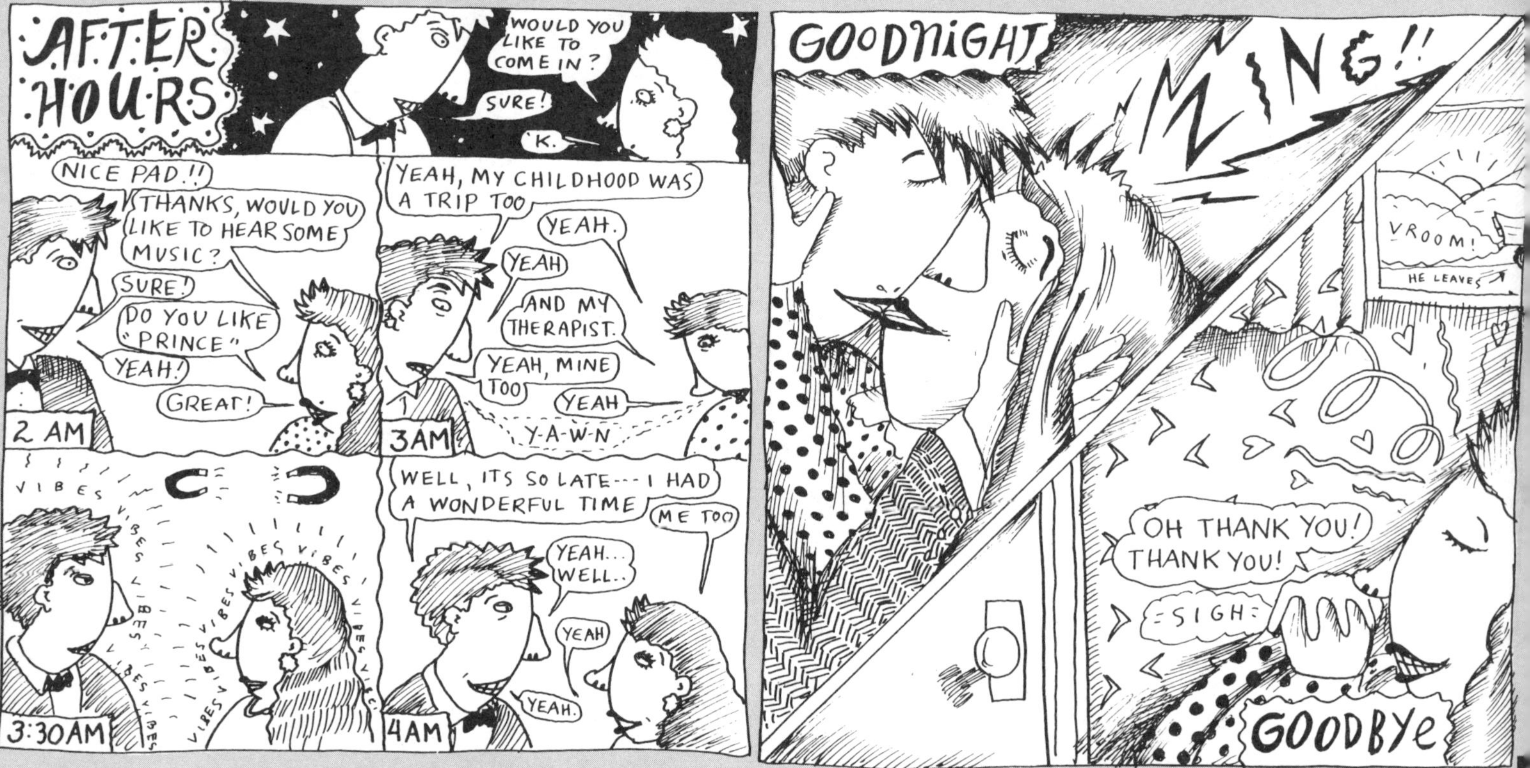
AFTER HOURS
WOULD YOU LIKE TO COME IN?
SURE!
'K.
NICE PAD!!
THANKS, WOULD YOU LIKE TO HEAR SOME MUSIC?
SURE!
DO YOU LIKE "PRINCE"
YEAH!
GREAT!
2 AM
YEAH, MY CHILDHOOD WAS A TRIP TOO
YEAH.
YEAH
AND MY THERAPIST.
YEAH, MINE TOO
YEAH
Y-A-W-N
3AM
VIBES
VIBES VIBES VIBES
3:30AM
WELL, ITS SO LATE--- I HAD A WONDERFUL TIME
ME TOO
YEAH... WELL..
YEAH
YEAH.
4AM
GOODNIGHT
ZING!!
VROOM!
HE LEAVES
OH THANK YOU! THANK YOU!
SIGH
GOODBYE

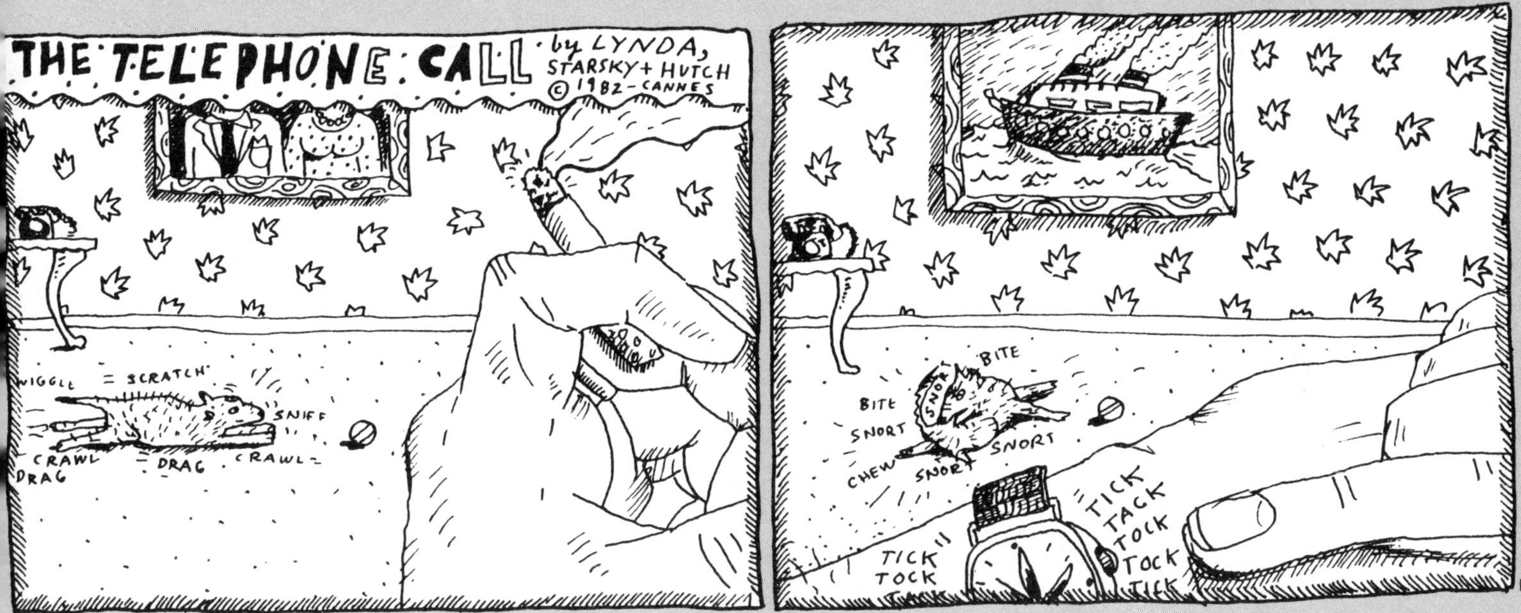
THE TELEPHONE CALL
by LYNDA, STARSKY + HUTCH © 1982 - CANNES
WIGGLE = SCRATCH
SNIFF
CRAWL
DRAG
= DRAG
CRAWL
BITE
BITE
SNORT
SNORT
CHEW
SNORT
TICK
TOCK
TICK
TACK
TOCK
TOCK
TICK

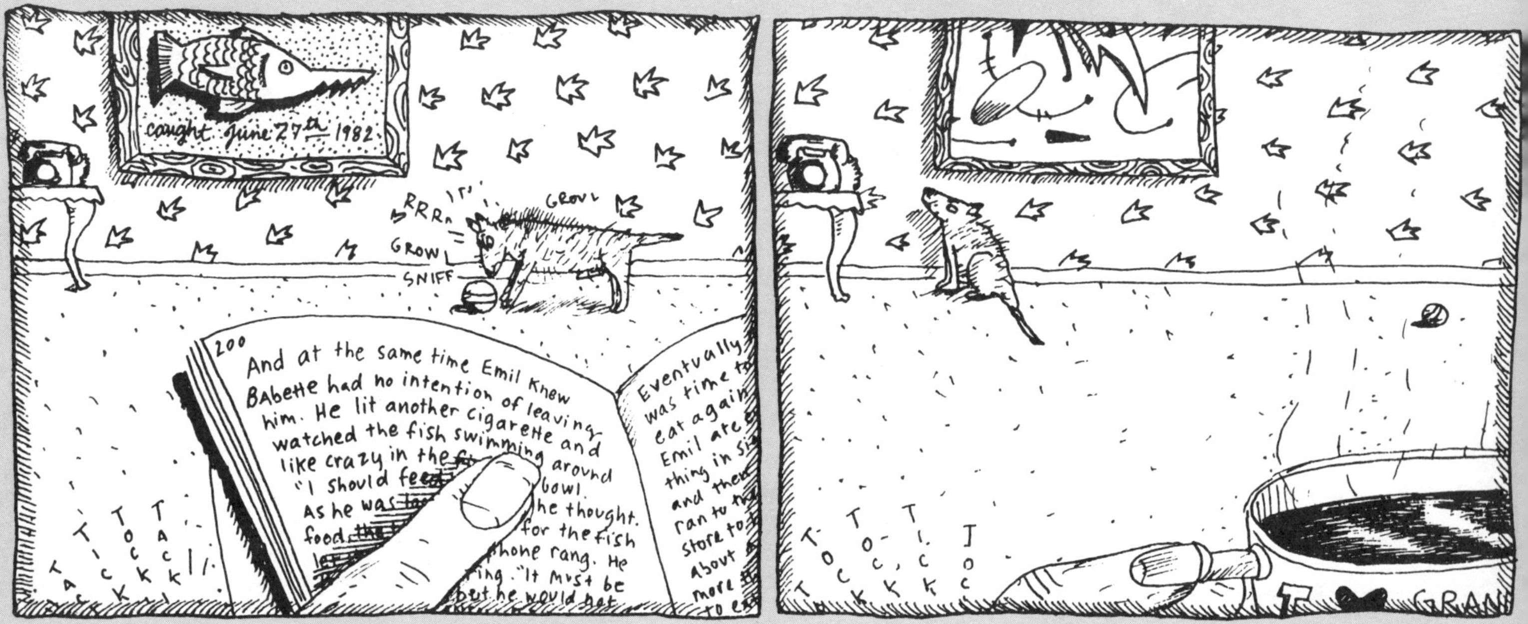

caught June 27th 1982
RRRr
GROWL
GROWL
SNIFF
200
And at the same time Emil knew
Babette had no intention of leaving
him. He lit another cigarette and
watched the fish swimming around
like crazy in the
bowl.
"I should
he thought.
As he
for the fish
food
phone rang. He
"It must be
Eventually
was time
eat again
Emil ate
thing in
and then
ran to
store to
about
more
TICK TOCK
TACK
TICK TOCK

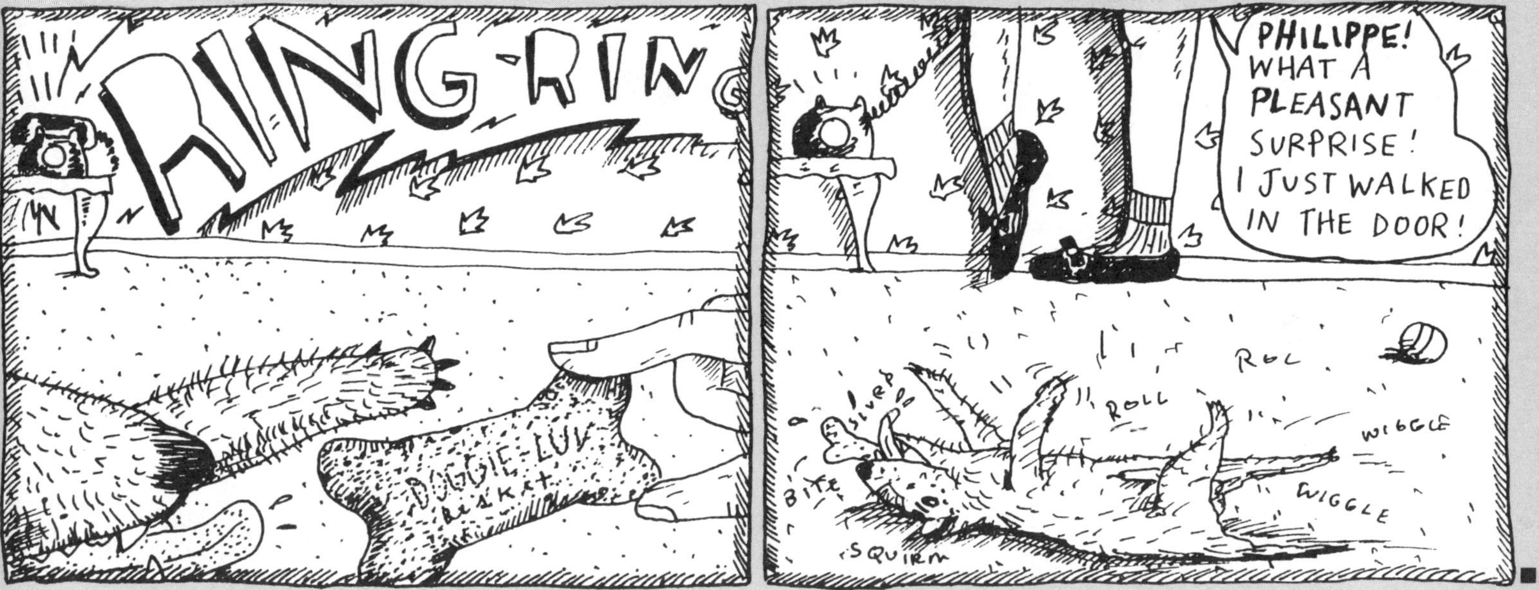
RING-RING
DOGGIE-LUV
PHILIPPE! WHAT A PLEASANT SURPRISE! I JUST WALKED IN THE DOOR!
SLURP
BITE
SQUIRM
ROL
ROLL
WIGGLE
WIGGLE

Nutrition

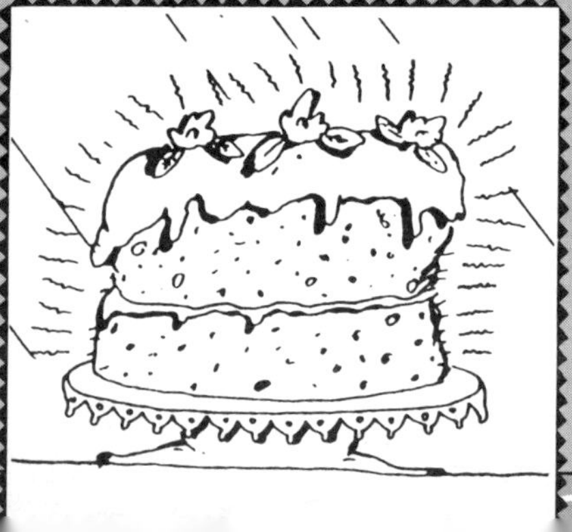

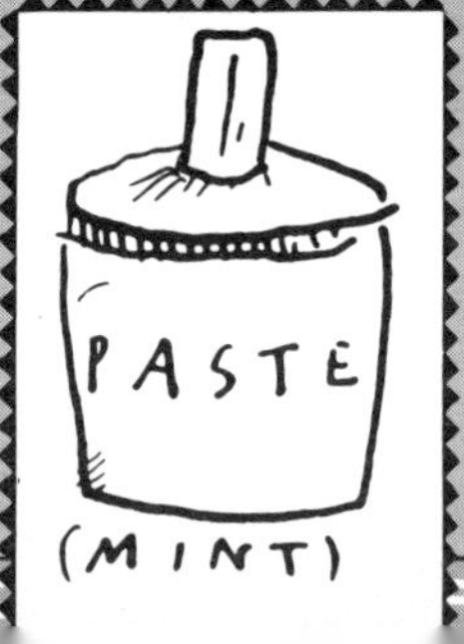
PASTE
(MINT)

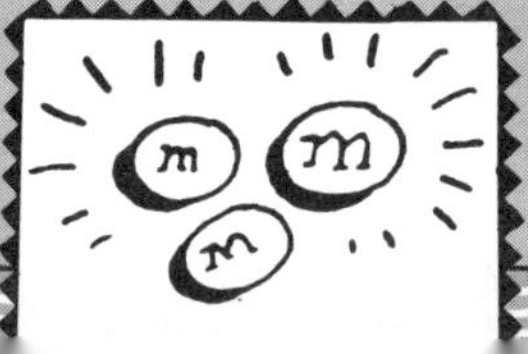
m
m
m

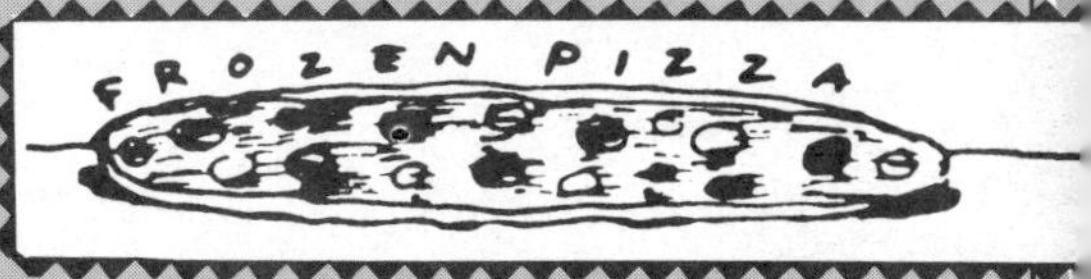
FROZEN PIZZA

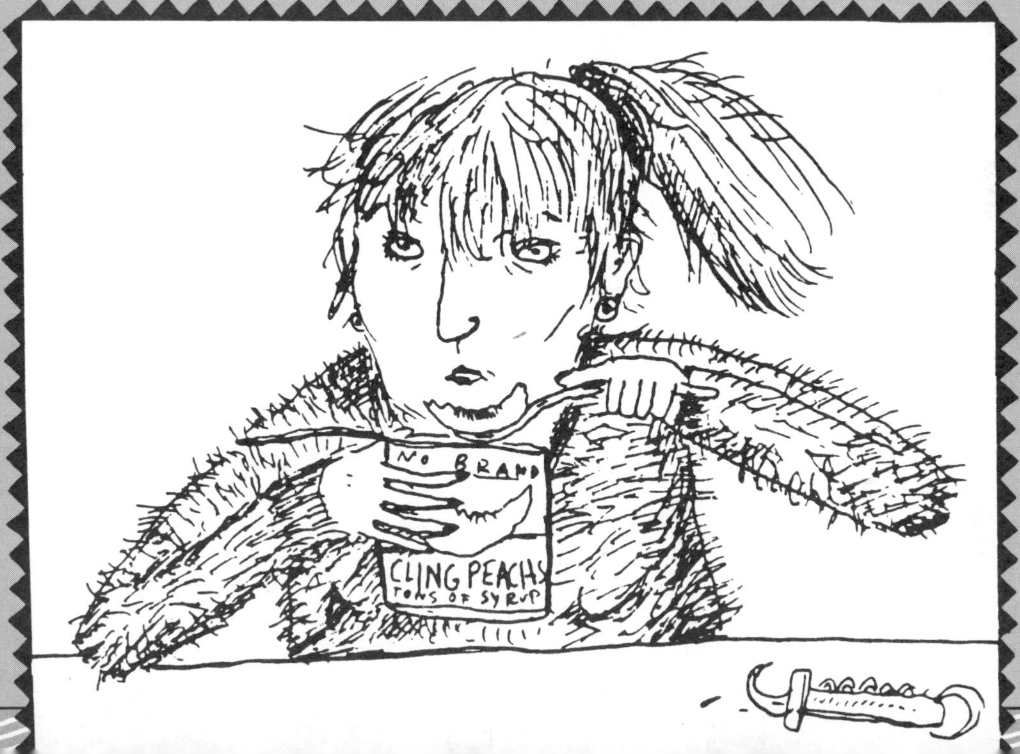
NO BRAND
CLING PEACHS
TONS OF SYRUP

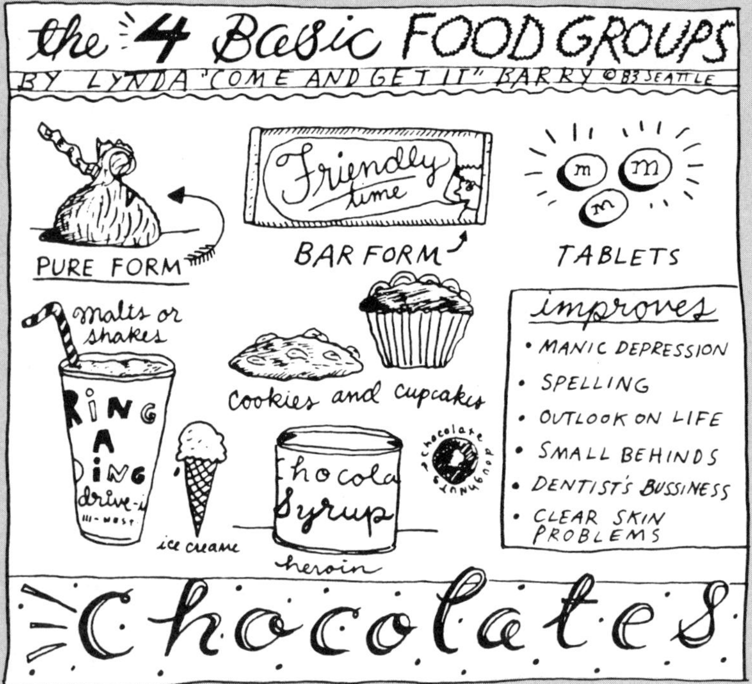
the 4 Basic FOOD GROUPS
BY LYNDA "COME AND GET IT" BARRY ©83 SEATTLE
PURE FORM
Friendly time
BAR FORM
m m m
TABLETS
malts or shakes
RING A DING drive-in
cookies and cupcakes
ice cream
Chocolate Syrup
heroin
chocolate doughnuts
improves
• MANIC DEPRESSION
• SPELLING
• OUTLOOK ON LIFE
• SMALL BEHINDS
• DENTIST'S BUSSINESS
• CLEAR SKIN PROBLEMS
Chocolates

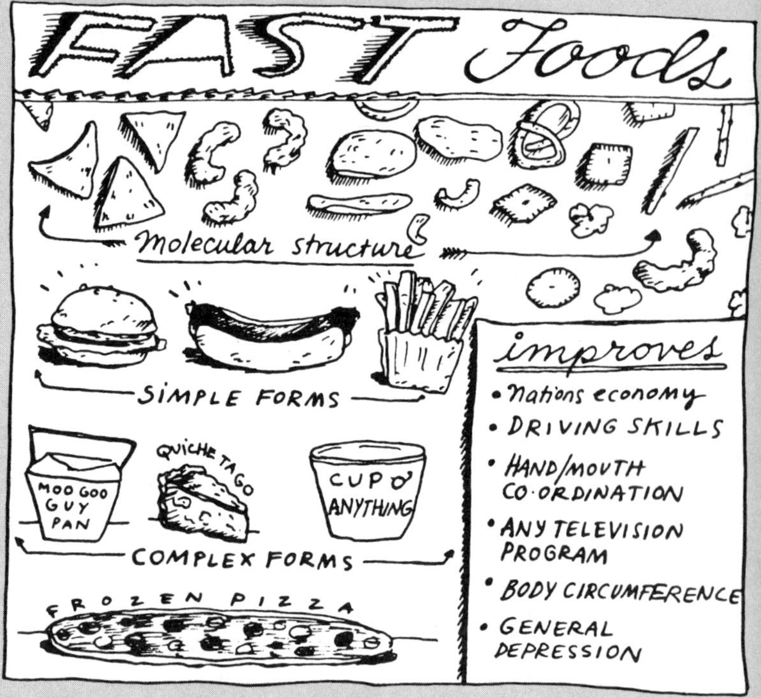
FAST Foods
molecular structure
SIMPLE FORMS
MOO GOO GUY PAN
QUICHE TAGO
CUP O' ANYTHING
COMPLEX FORMS
FROZEN PIZZA
improves
• nations economy
• DRIVING SKILLS
• HAND/MOUTH CO-ORDINATION
• ANY TELEVISION PROGRAM
• BODY CIRCUMFERENCE
• GENERAL DEPRESSION

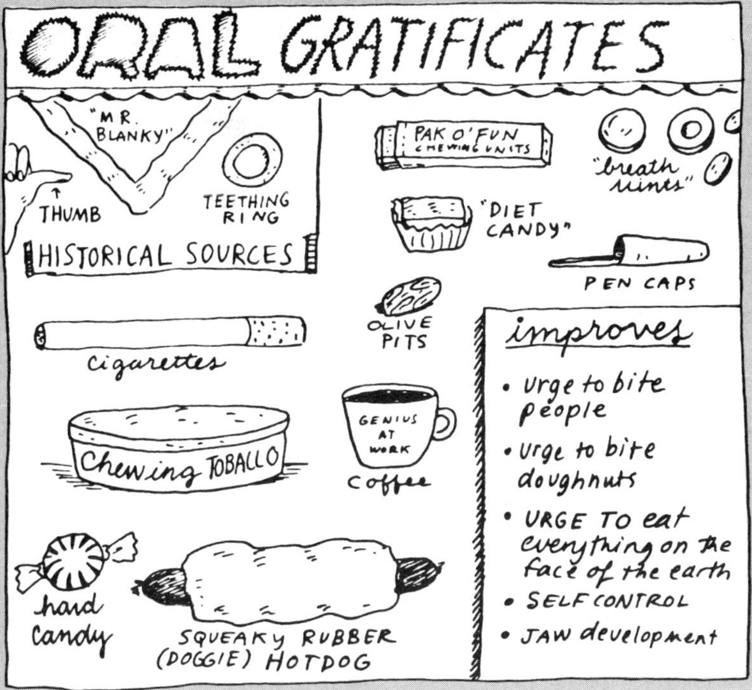
ORAL GRATIFICATES
"MR. BLANKY"
THUMB
TEETHING RING
HISTORICAL SOURCES
PAK O' FUN CHEWING UNITS
"breath mints"
"DIET CANDY"
PEN CAPS
OLIVE PITS
cigarettes
Chewing TOBALLO
GENIUS AT WORK
coffee
hard candy
SQUEAKY RUBBER (DOGGIE) HOTDOG
improves
• urge to bite people
• urge to bite doughnuts
• URGE TO eat everything on the face of the earth
• SELF CONTROL
• JAW development

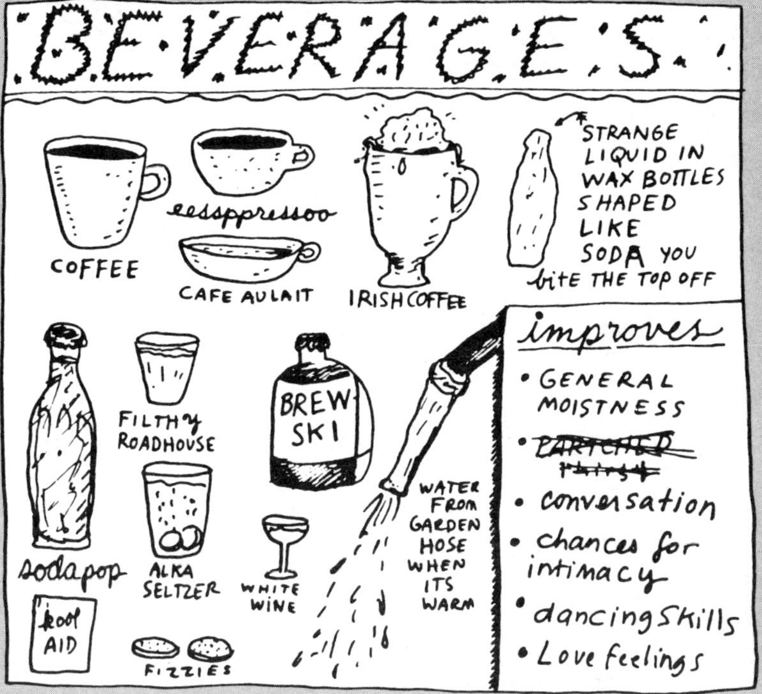
BEVERAGES
COFFEE
eessppressoo
CAFE AULAIT
IRISH COFFEE
STRANGE LIQUID IN WAX BOTTLES SHAPED LIKE SODA YOU bite THE TOP OFF
sodapop
FILTHY ROADHOUSE
BREW SKI
ALKA SELTZER
WHITE WINE
WATER FROM GARDEN HOSE WHEN ITS WARM
kool AID
FIZZIES
improves
• GENERAL MOISTNESS
• conversation
• chances for intimacy
• dancing Skills
• Love feelings

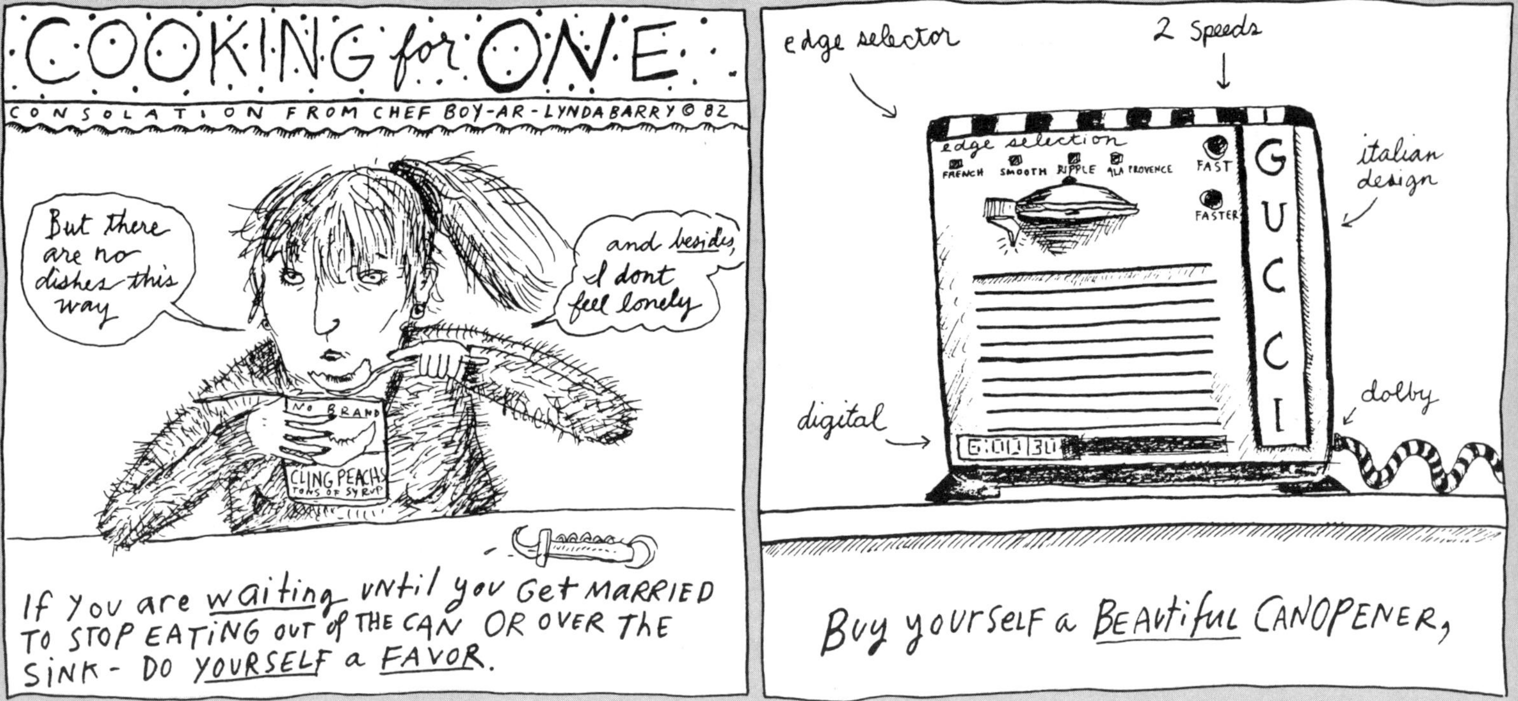

COOKING for ONE
CONSOLATION FROM CHEF BOY-AR-LYNDABARRY © 82
But there are no dishes this way
and besides, I dont feel lonely
NO BRAND
CLING PEACHS
TONS OF SYRUP
IF YOU ARE WAITING UNTIL YOU GET MARRIED TO STOP EATING OUT OF THE CAN OR OVER THE SINK - DO YOURSELF A FAVOR.
edge selector
2 Speeds
edge selection
FRENCH
SMOOTH
RIPPLE
A LA PROVENCE
FAST
FASTER
GUCCI
italian design
digital
dolby
Buy yourself a BEAUTIFUL CANOPENER,

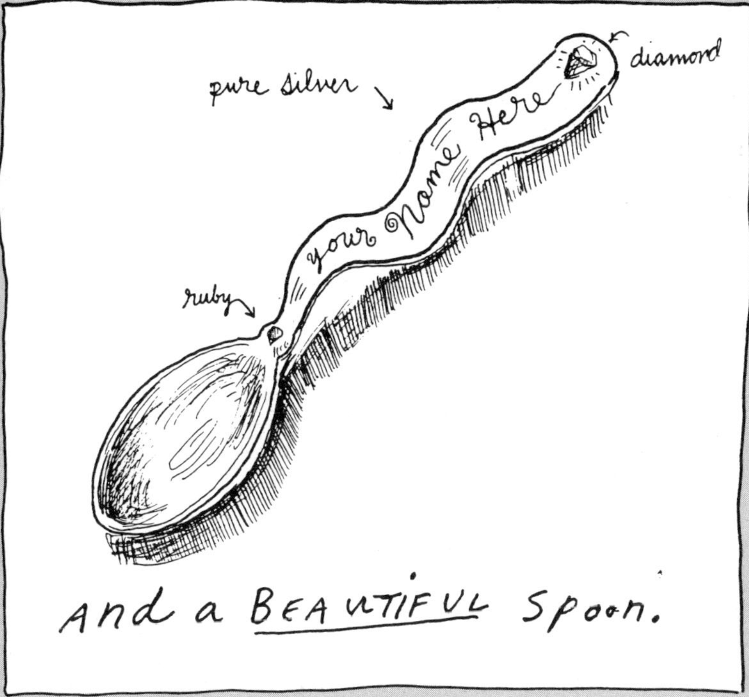
pure silver
diamond
your name Here
ruby
And a BEAUTIFUL Spoon.

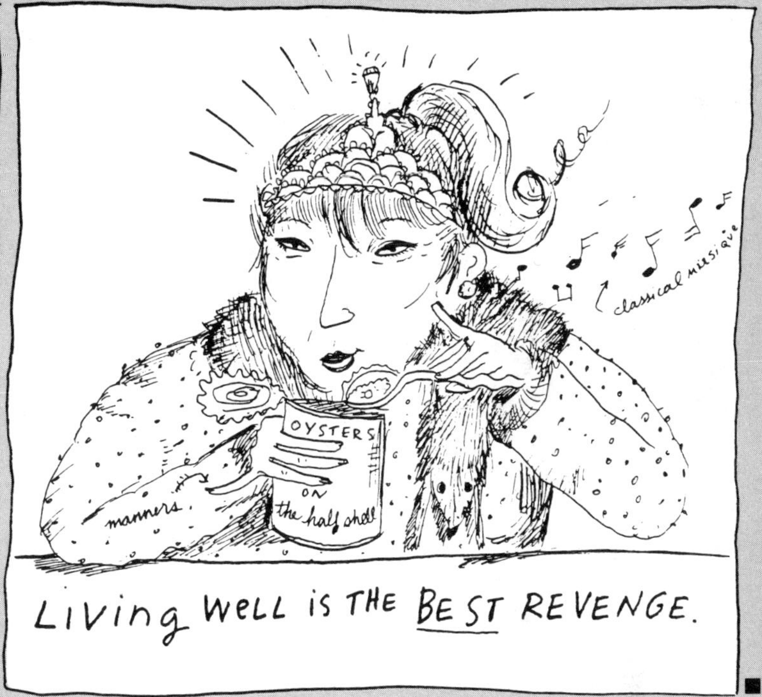
OYSTERS ON the half shell
manners
classical MUSIQUE
LIVING WELL IS THE BEST REVENGE.

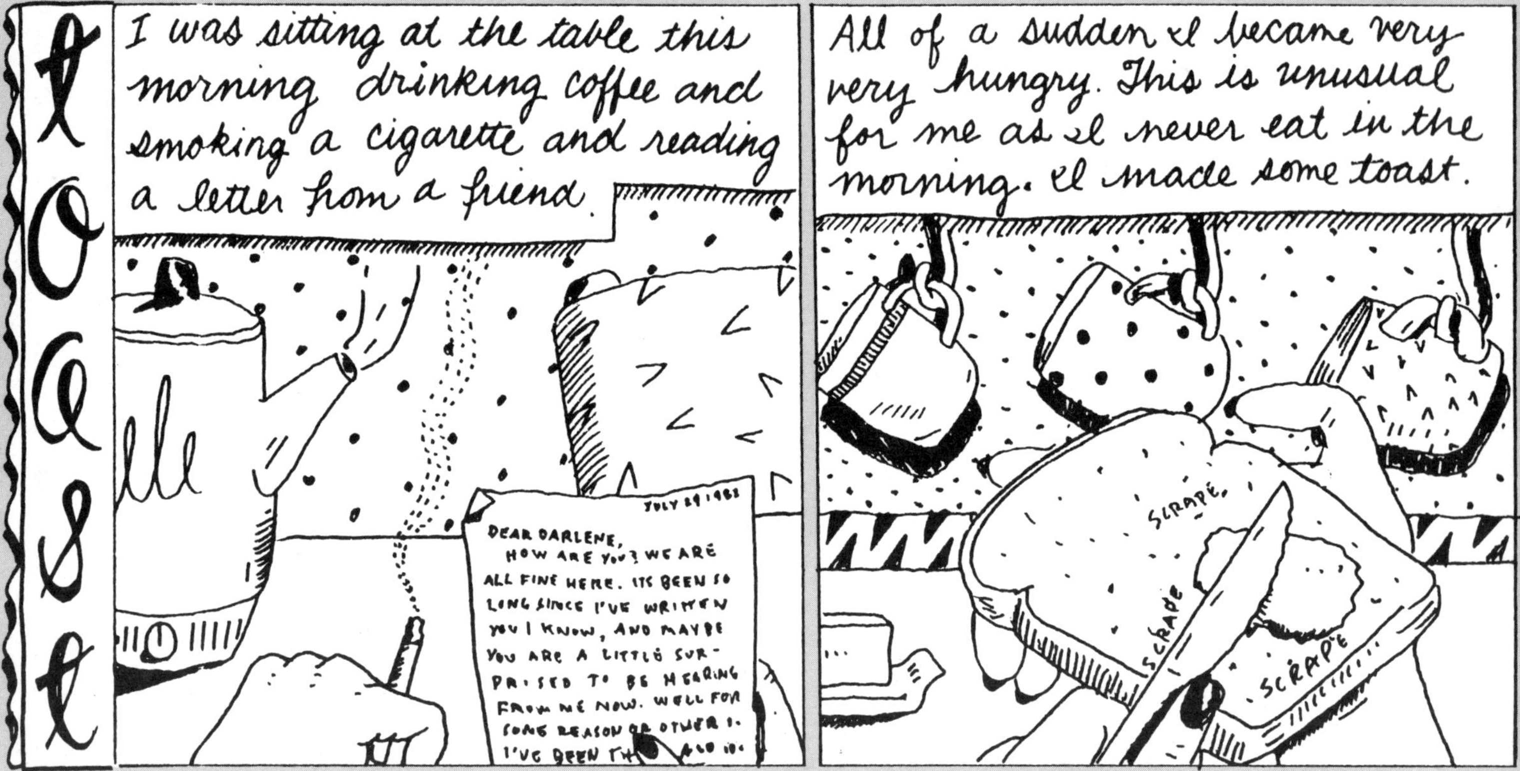
Toast
I was sitting at the table this morning drinking coffee and smoking a cigarette and reading a letter from a friend.
DEAR DARLENE,
HOW ARE YOU? WE ARE ALL FINE HERE. ITS BEEN SO LONG SINCE I'VE WRITTEN YOU I KNOW, AND MAYBE YOU ARE A LITTLE SUR-PRISED TO BE HEARING FROM ME NOW. WELL FOR SOME REASON OR OTHER I.
All of a sudden I became very very hungry. This is unusual for me as I never eat in the morning. I made some toast.
SCRAPE
SCRAPE
SCRAPE

After eating this toast I wanted more toast. You know what they say about toast. I made 4 more slices as my toaster can make this many at any moment. But this is not the reason I bought my toaster.

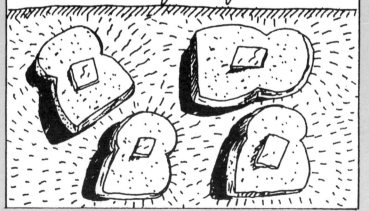

In fact I didn't buy this toaster. It was a gift to me from the person who had written me the letter, Heather is her name. And in fact this toaster is capable of making eight slices of toast should you ever want that many.

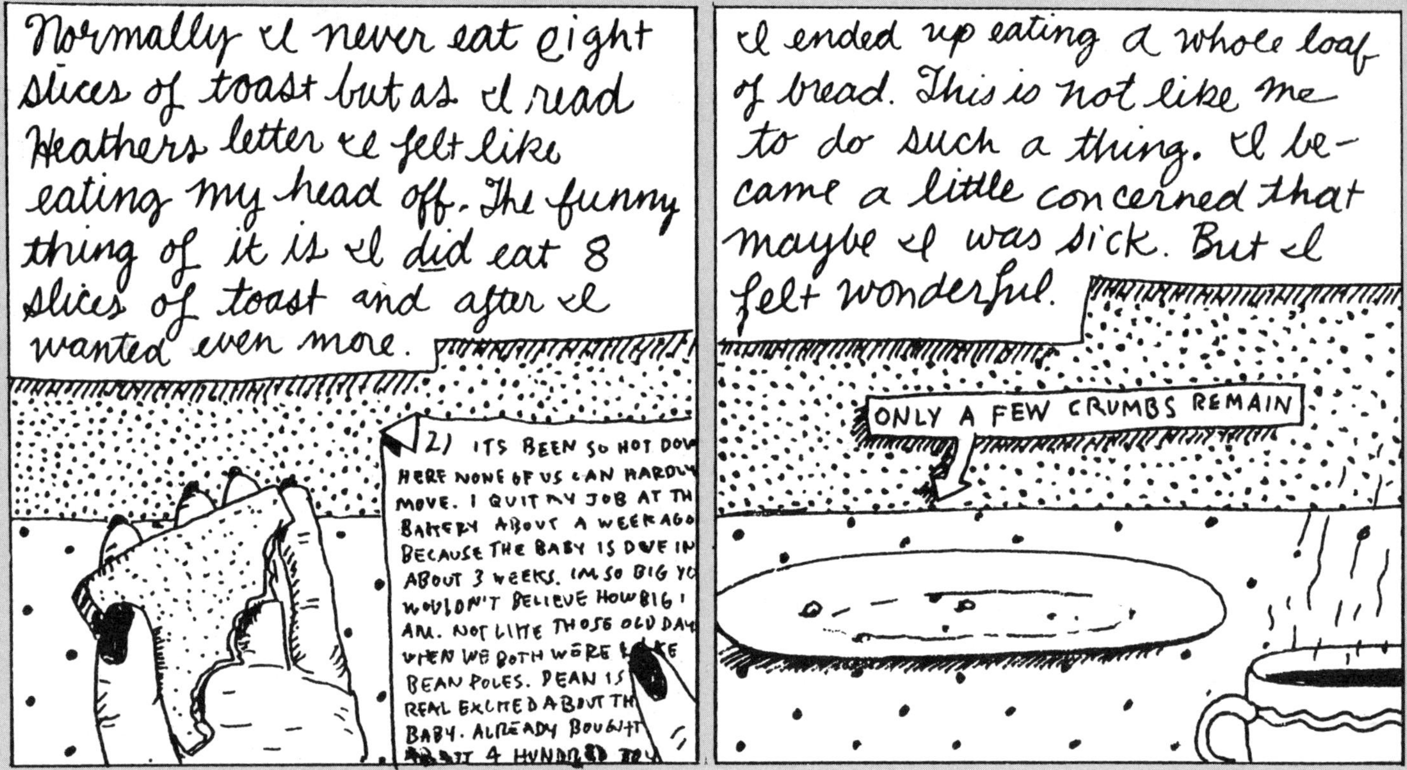
Normally I never eat eight slices of toast but as I read Heathers letter I felt like eating my head off. The funny thing of it is I did eat 8 slices of toast and after I wanted even more.
2) ITS BEEN SO HOT DOW
HERE NONE OF US CAN HARDLY
MOVE. I QUIT MY JOB AT TH
BAKERY ABOUT A WEEK AGO
BECAUSE THE BABY IS DUE IN
ABOUT 3 WEEKS. IM SO BIG YO
WOULDN'T BELIEVE HOW BIG I
AM. NOT LIKE THOSE OLD DAY
WHEN WE BOTH WERE LIKE
BEAN POLES. DEAN IS
REAL EXCITED ABOUT TH
BABY. ALREADY BOUGHT
4 HUNDRED
I ended up eating a whole loaf of bread. This is not like me to do such a thing. I became a little concerned that maybe I was sick. But I felt wonderful.
ONLY A FEW CRUMBS REMAIN

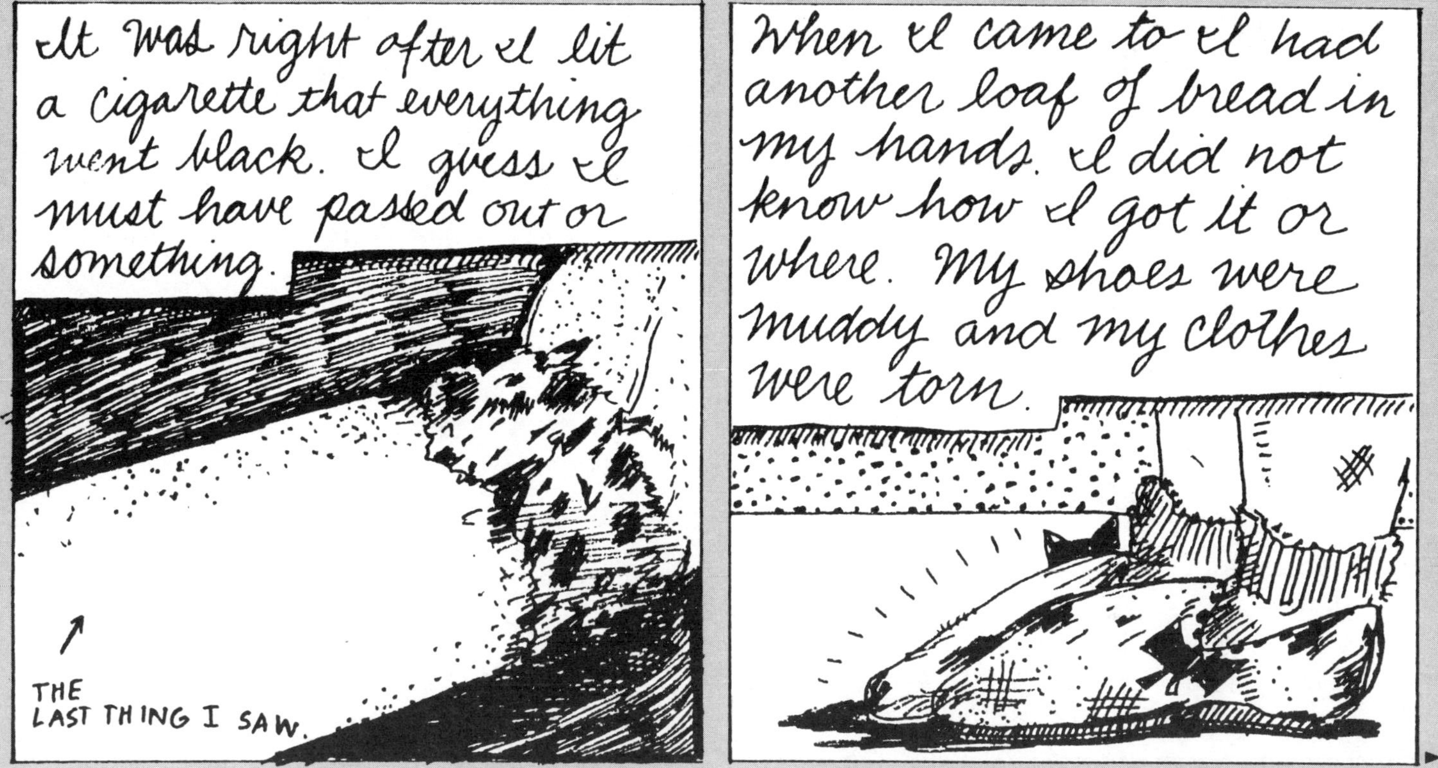
It was right after I lit a cigarette that everything went black. I guess I must have passed out or something.
THE LAST THING I SAW.
When I came to I had another loaf of bread in my hands. I did not know how I got it or where. My shoes were muddy and my clothes were torn.

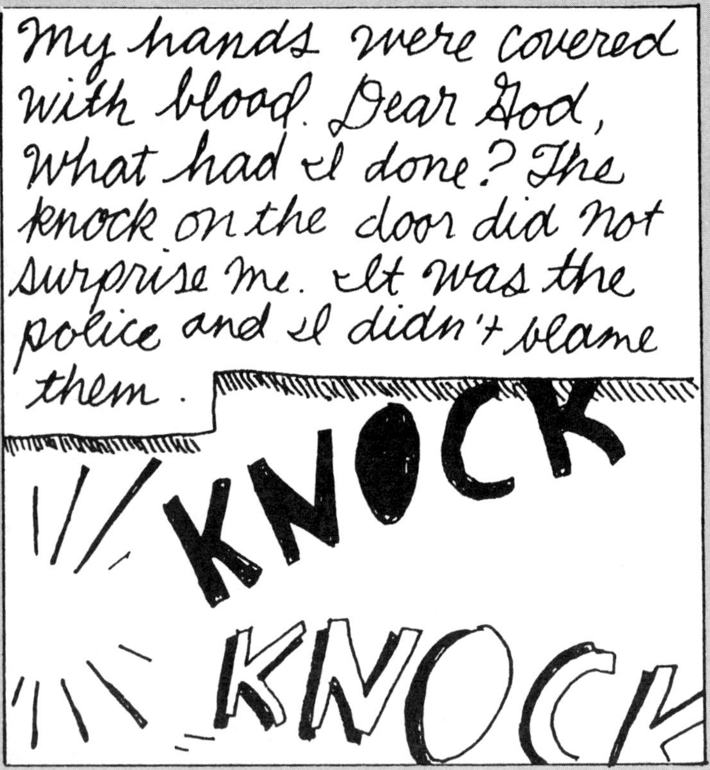
My hands were covered with blood. Dear God, What had I done? The knock on the door did not surprise me. It was the police and I didn't blame them.
KNOCK
KNOCK

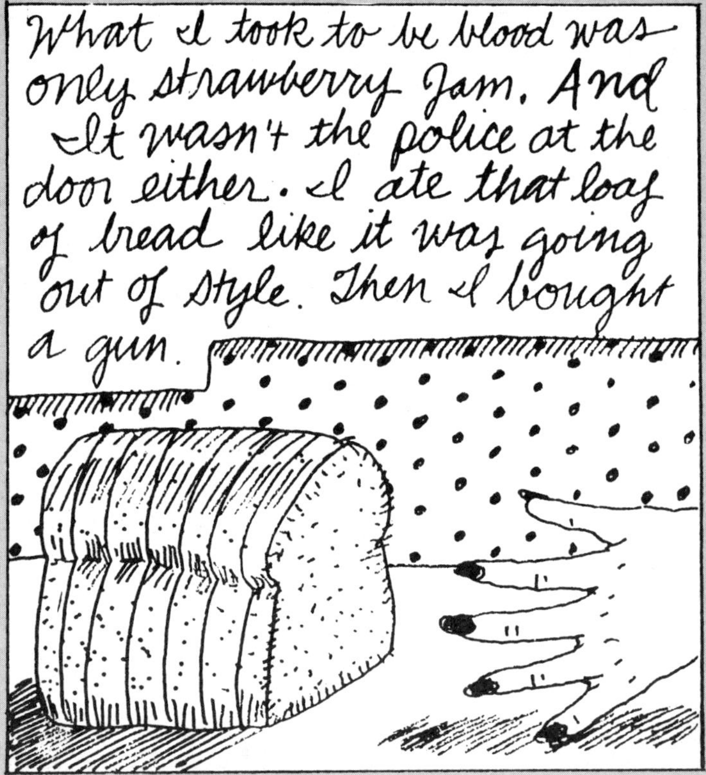
What I took to be blood was only strawberry Jam. And It wasn't the police at the door either. I ate that loaf of bread like it was going out of style. Then I bought a gun.

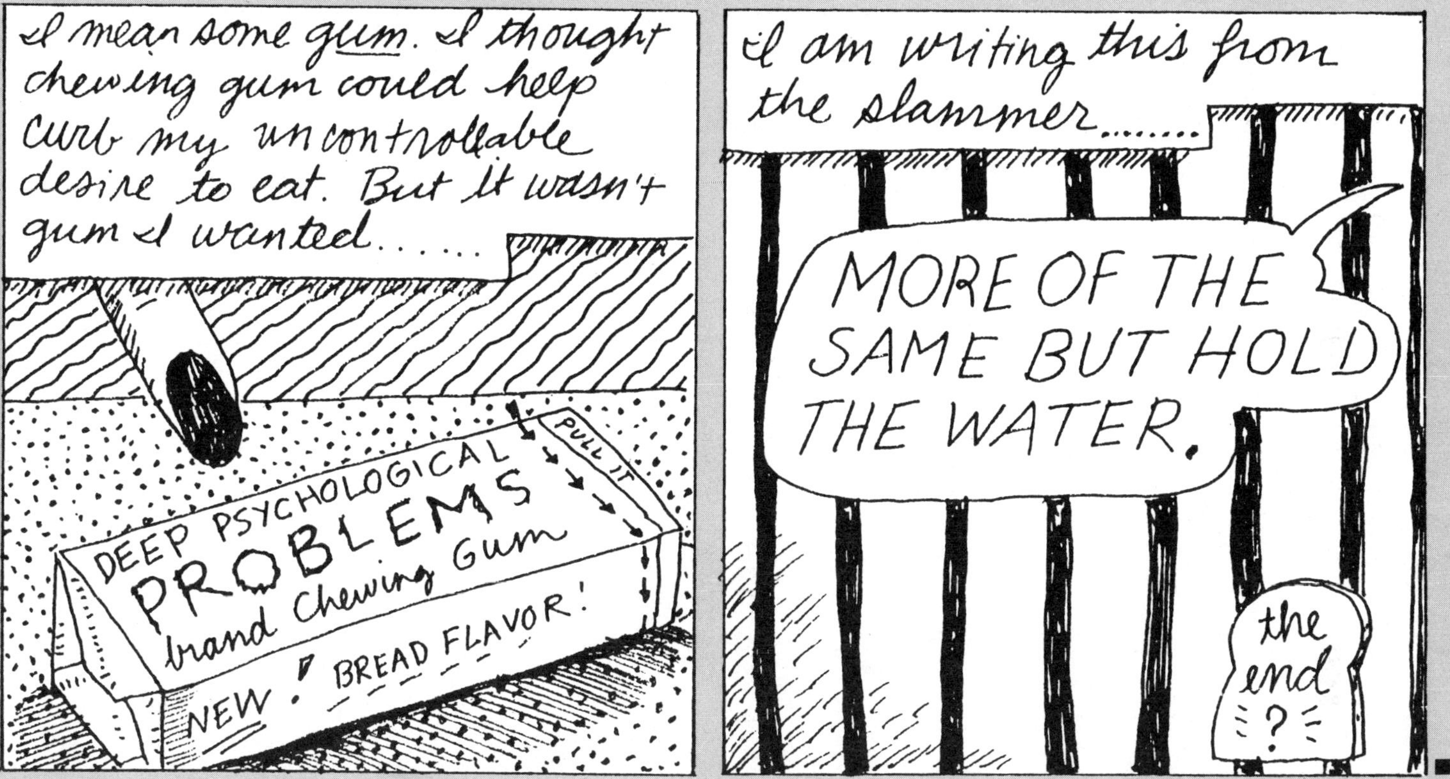

I mean some gum. I thought chewing gum could help curb my uncontrollable desire to eat. But it wasn't gum I wanted......
PULL IT
DEEP PSYCHOLOGICAL PROBLEMS brand Chewing Gum
NEW! BREAD FLAVOR!
I am writing this from the slammer.......
MORE OF THE SAME BUT HOLD THE WATER.
the end ?

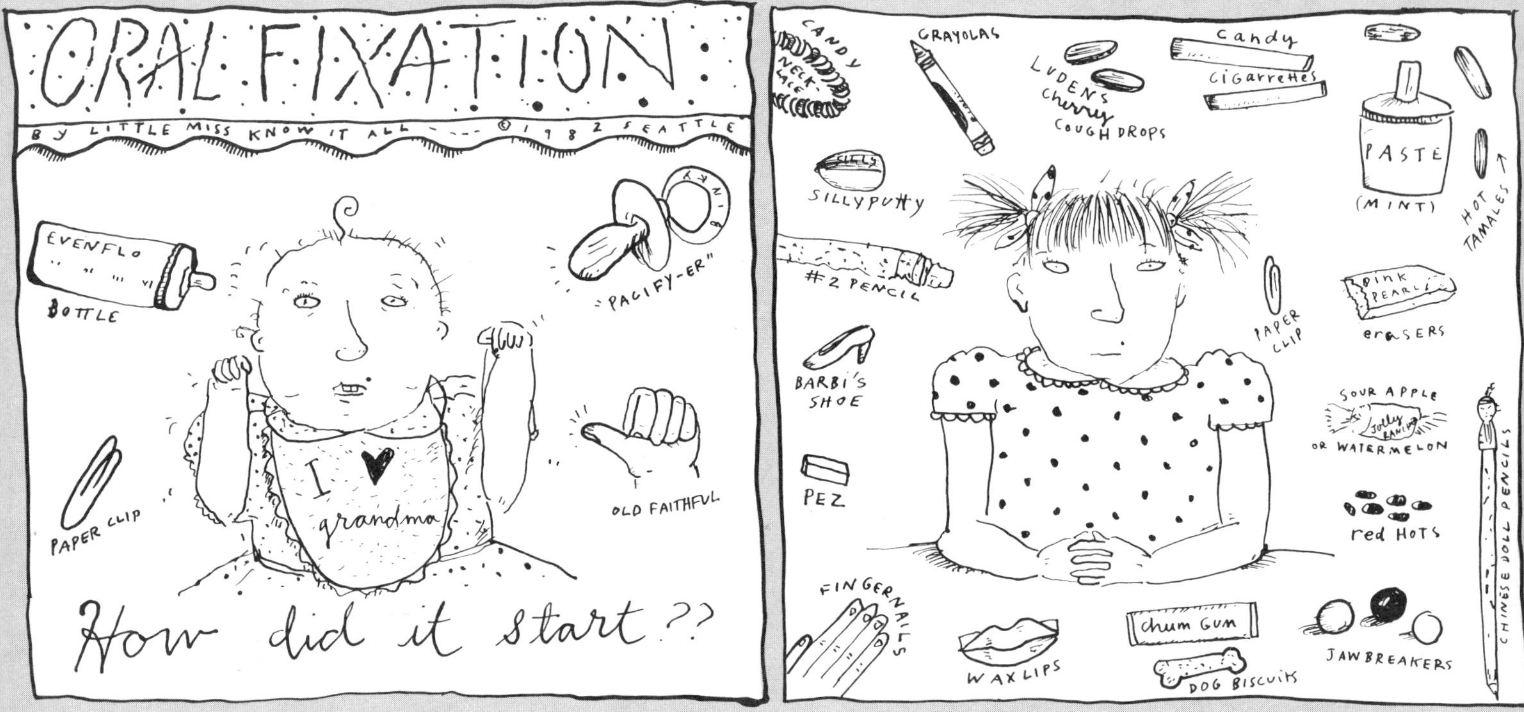
ORAL FIXATION
BY LITTLE MISS KNOW IT ALL — ©1982 SEATTLE
EVENFLO
BOTTLE
BINKY
"PACIFY-ER"
PAPER CLIP
I ♥ grandma
OLD FAITHFUL
How did it start??
CANDY NECK-LACE
CRAYOLAS
LUDENS Cherry COUGH DROPS
candy cigarrettes
PASTE
(MINT)
HOT TAMALES
Sillyputty
#2 PENCIL
PAPER CLIP
pink PEARL
erasers
BARBI'S SHOE
SOUR APPLE
Jolly
OR WATERMELON
PEZ
red HOTS
CHINESE DOLL PENCILS
FINGERNAILS
WAX LIPS
chum Gum
DOG BISCUITS
JAWBREAKERS

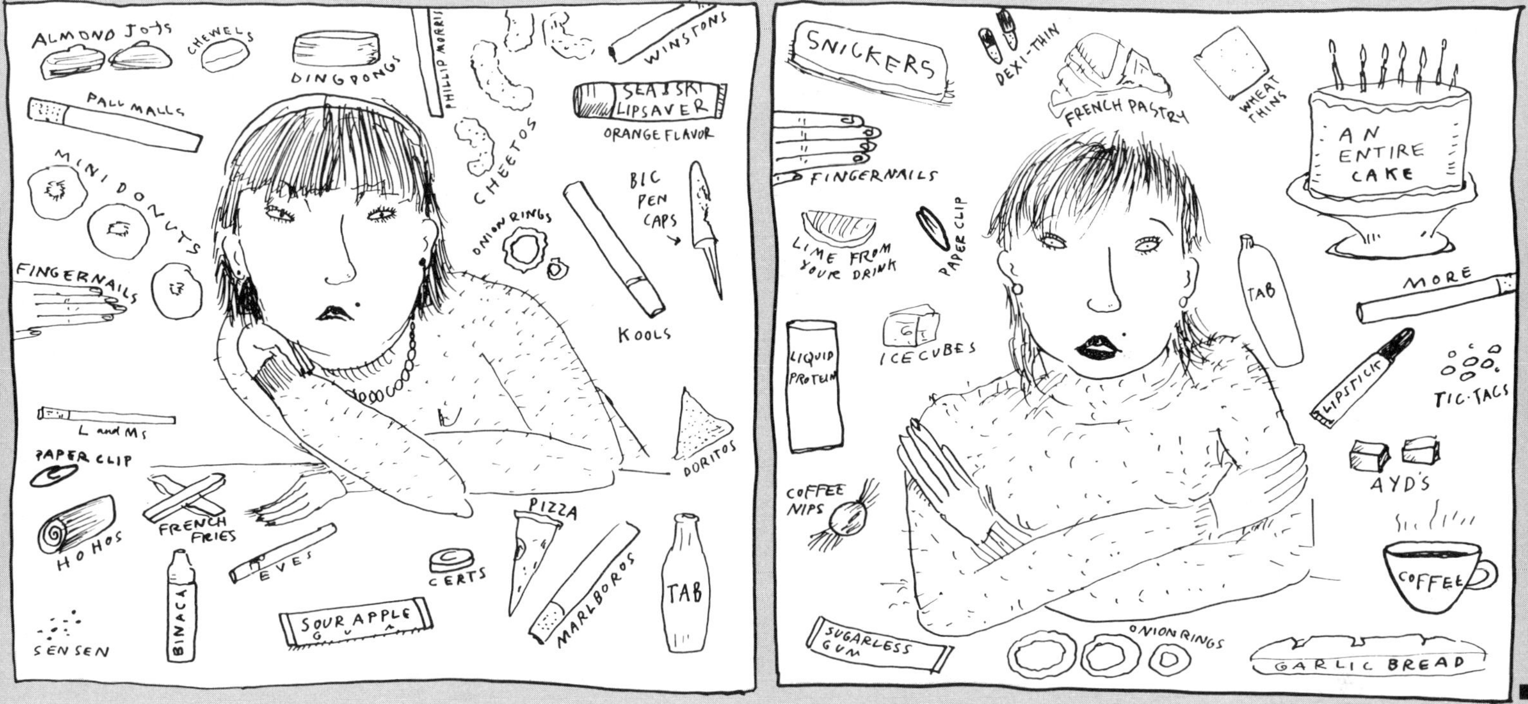
ALMOND JOYS
CHEWELS
DINGDONGS
PHILLIP MORRIS
WINSTONS
PALL MALLS
SEA & SKI LIPSAVER
ORANGE FLAVOR
CHEETOS
MINI DONUTS
FINGERNAILS
ONION RINGS
BIC PEN CAPS
KOOLS
L and Ms
PAPER CLIP
DORITOS
PIZZA
FRENCH FRIES
HO HOS
EVES
CERTS
MARLBOROS
TAB
SOUR APPLE GUM
BINACA
SEN SEN
SNICKERS
DEXI-THIN
FRENCH PASTRY
WHEAT THINS
AN ENTIRE CAKE
FINGERNAILS
LIME FROM YOUR DRINK
PAPER CLIP
TAB
MORE
LIQUID PROTEIN
ICE CUBES
LIPSTICK
TIC-TACS
AYD'S
COFFEE NIPS
COFFEE
SUGARLESS GUM
ONION RINGS
GARLIC BREAD

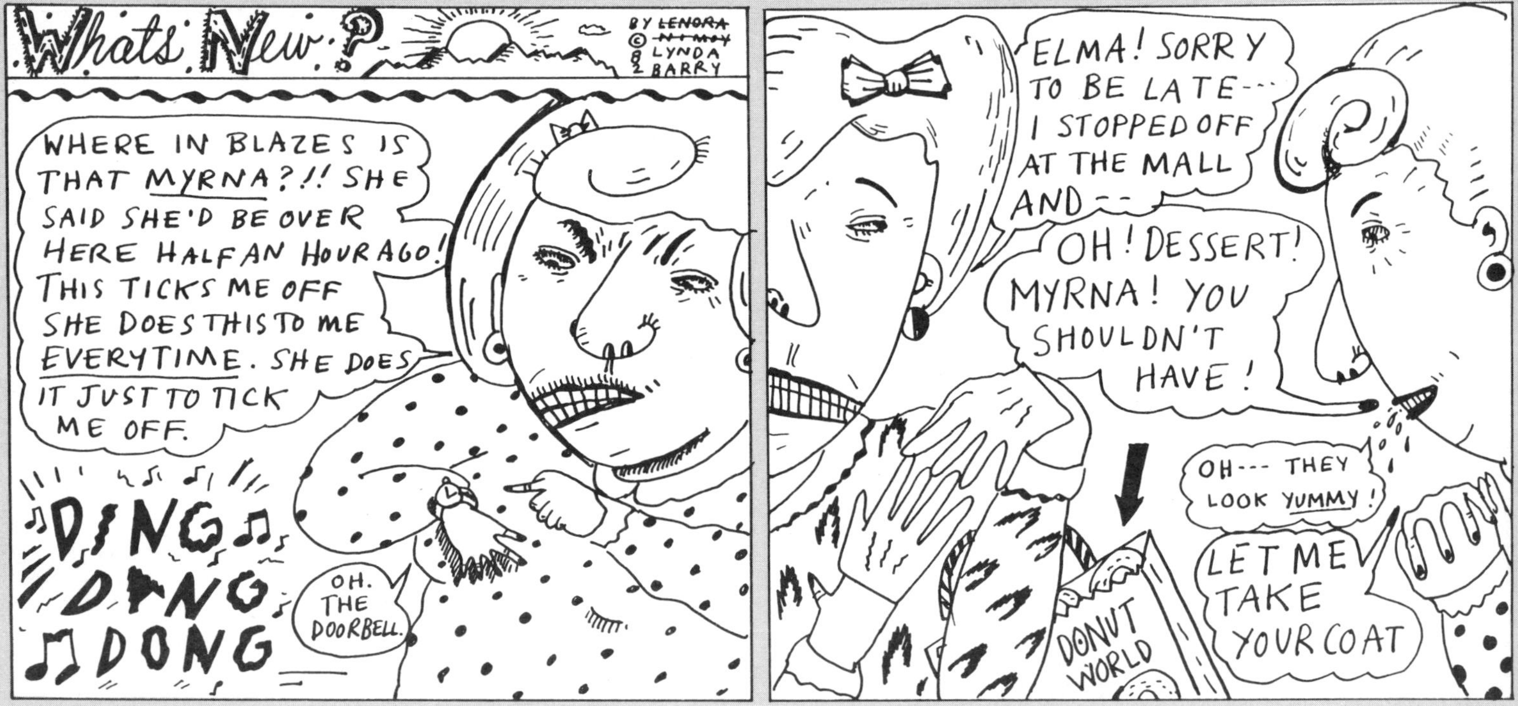
What's New?
BY ~~LENORA NIMOY~~ © 82 LYNDA BARRY
WHERE IN BLAZES IS THAT MYRNA?!! SHE SAID SHE'D BE OVER HERE HALF AN HOUR AGO! THIS TICKS ME OFF SHE DOES THIS TO ME EVERYTIME. SHE DOES IT JUST TO TICK ME OFF.
DING DONG DONG
OH. THE DOORBELL.
ELMA! SORRY TO BE LATE--- I STOPPED OFF AT THE MALL AND---
OH! DESSERT! MYRNA! YOU SHOULDN'T HAVE!
DONUT WORLD
OH--- THEY LOOK YUMMY!
LET ME TAKE YOUR COAT

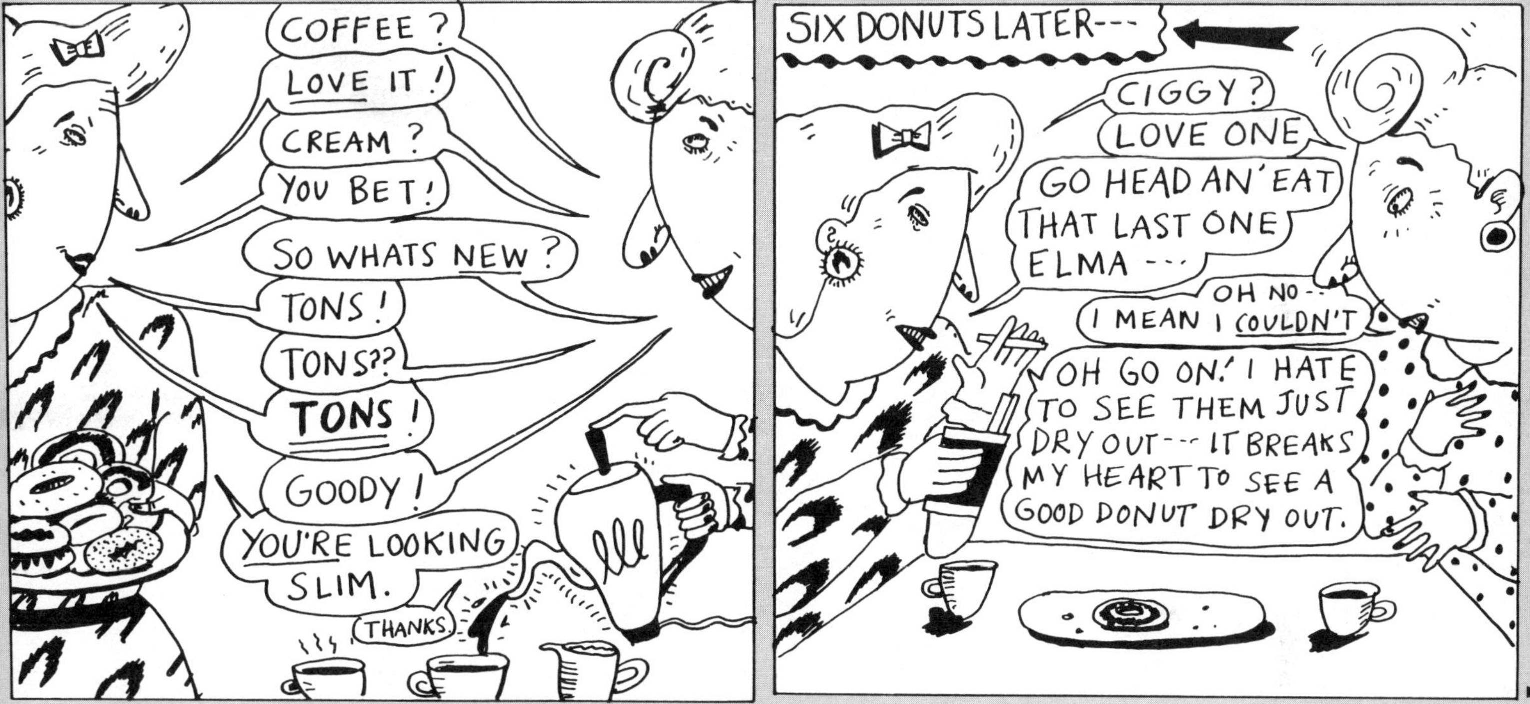
COFFEE?
LOVE IT!
CREAM?
YOU BET!
SO WHATS NEW?
TONS!
TONS??
TONS!
GOODY!
YOU'RE LOOKING SLIM.
THANKS.
SIX DONUTS LATER---
CIGGY?
LOVE ONE
GO HEAD AN' EAT THAT LAST ONE ELMA ---
OH NO-- I MEAN I COULDN'T
OH GO ON! I HATE TO SEE THEM JUST DRY OUT--- IT BREAKS MY HEART TO SEE A GOOD DONUT DRY OUT.

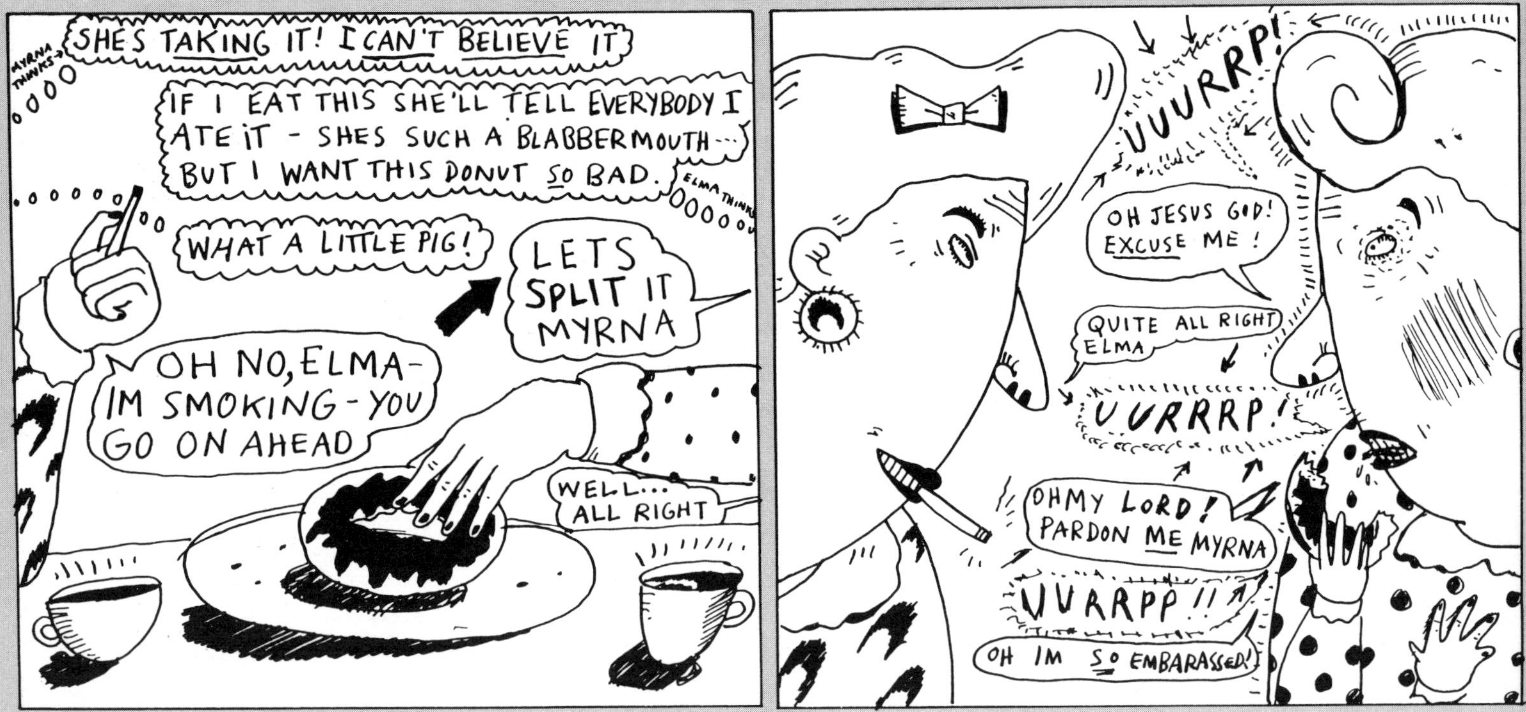
MYRNA THINKS
SHE'S TAKING IT! I CAN'T BELIEVE IT
IF I EAT THIS SHE'LL TELL EVERYBODY I ATE IT - SHES SUCH A BLABBERMOUTH... BUT I WANT THIS DONUT SO BAD.
ELMA THINKS
WHAT A LITTLE PIG!
LETS SPLIT IT MYRNA
OH NO, ELMA - IM SMOKING - YOU GO ON AHEAD
WELL... ALL RIGHT
UUURRP!
OH JESUS GOD! EXCUSE ME!
QUITE ALL RIGHT ELMA
UURRRP!
OHMY LORD! PARDON ME MYRNA
UURRPP!!
OH IM SO EMBARASSED!

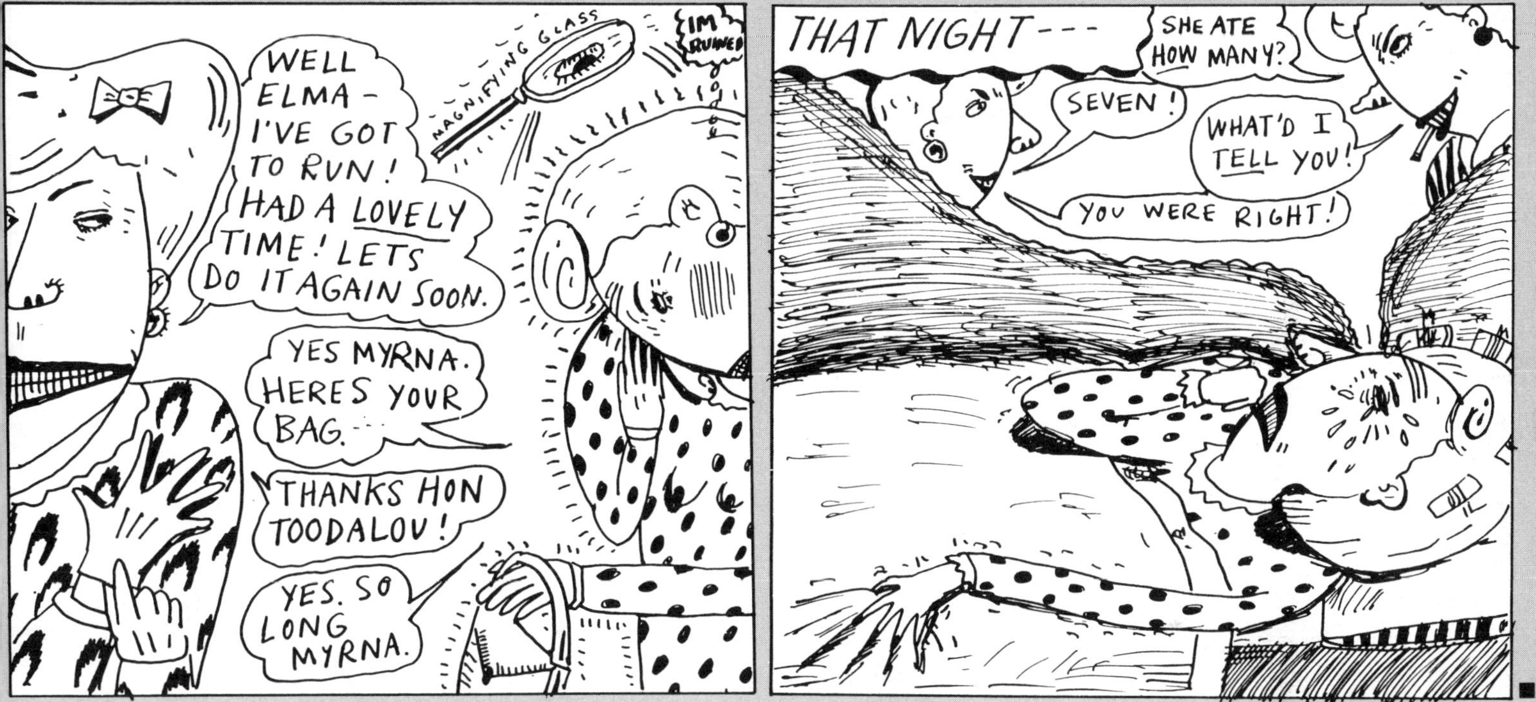
WELL ELMA - I'VE GOT TO RUN! HAD A LOVELY TIME! LETS DO IT AGAIN SOON.
MAGNIFYING GLASS
IM RUINED
YES MYRNA. HERES YOUR BAG.
THANKS HON TOODALOU!
YES. SO LONG MYRNA.
THAT NIGHT---
SHE ATE HOW MANY?
SEVEN!
WHAT'D I TELL YOU!
YOU WERE RIGHT!

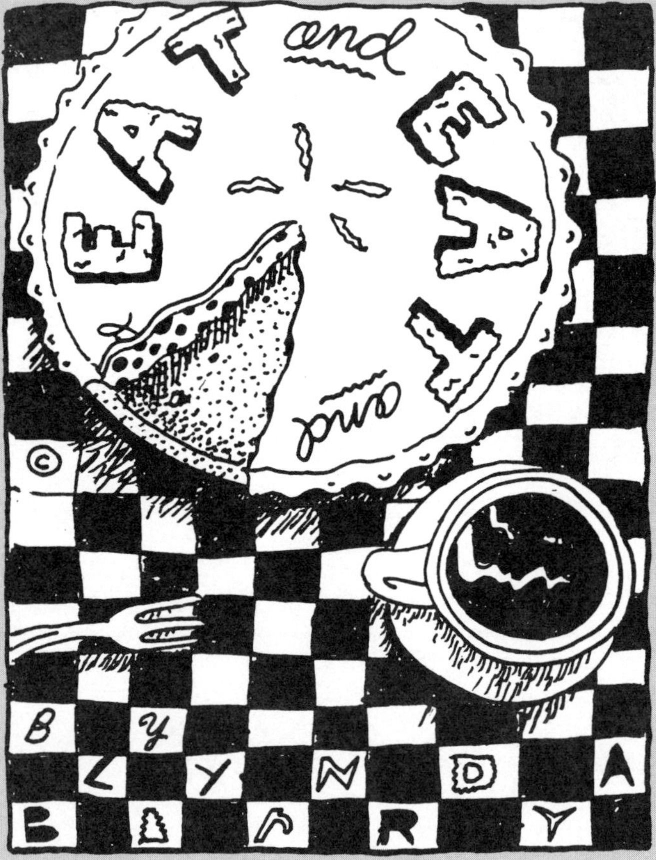
EAT and EAT and
©
By Lynda Barry

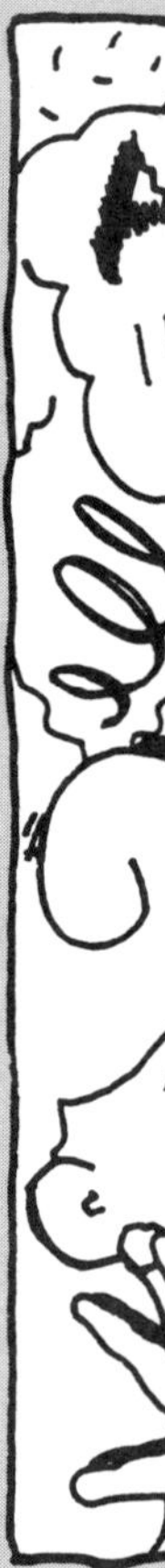
AUGGH!
IM SO FAT!! I LOOK LIKE I HAVE THE MUMPS! MY PANTS ARE TOO TIGHT! PIG!! ITS SO GROSS!
GOOD YEAR
RIN RING

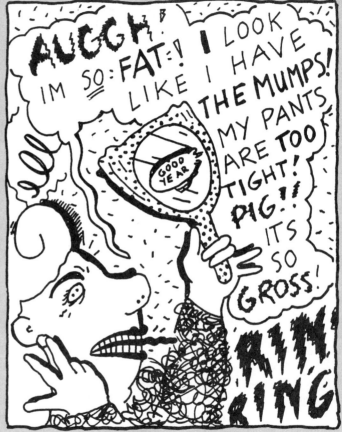

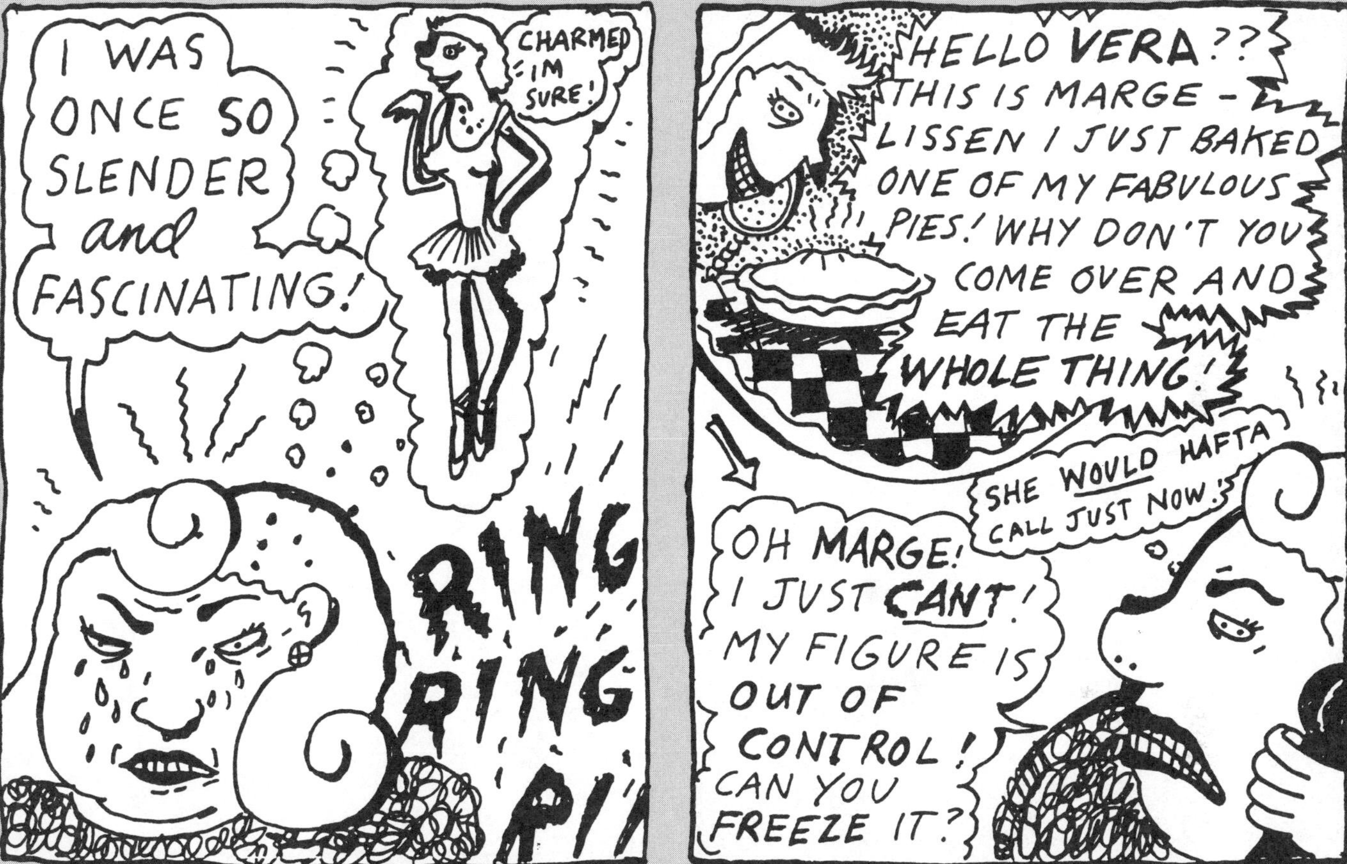
I WAS ONCE SO SLENDER and FASCINATING!
CHARMED I'M SURE!
RING RING
HELLO VERA?? THIS IS MARGE - LISSEN I JUST BAKED ONE OF MY FABULOUS PIES! WHY DON'T YOU COME OVER AND EAT THE WHOLE THING!
SHE WOULD HAFTA CALL JUST NOW!
OH MARGE! I JUST CANT! MY FIGURE IS OUT OF CONTROL! CAN YOU FREEZE IT?

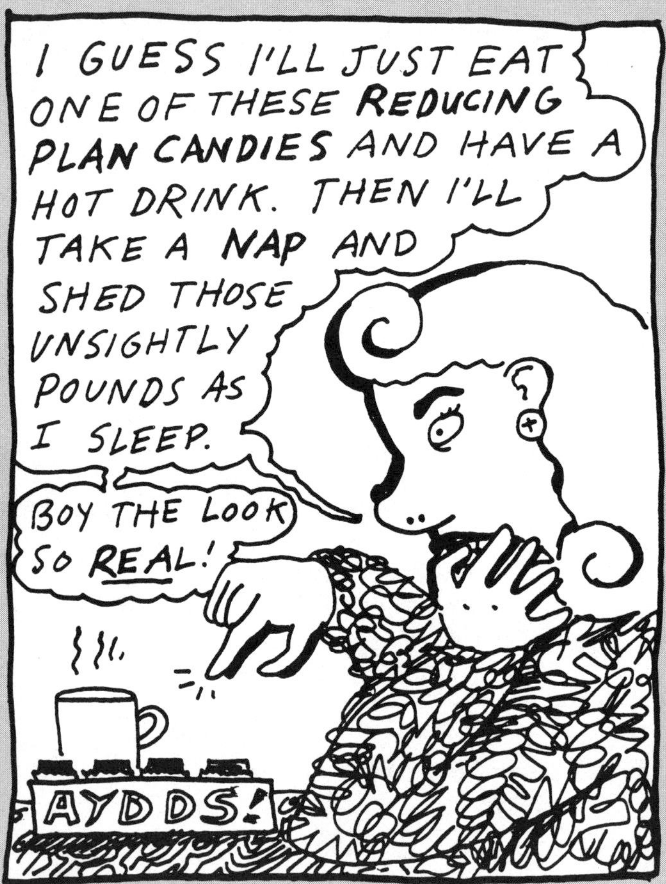
I GUESS I'LL JUST EAT ONE OF THESE REDUCING PLAN CANDIES AND HAVE A HOT DRINK. THEN I'LL TAKE A NAP AND SHED THOSE UNSIGHTLY POUNDS AS I SLEEP.
BOY THE LOOK SO REAL!
AYDDS!

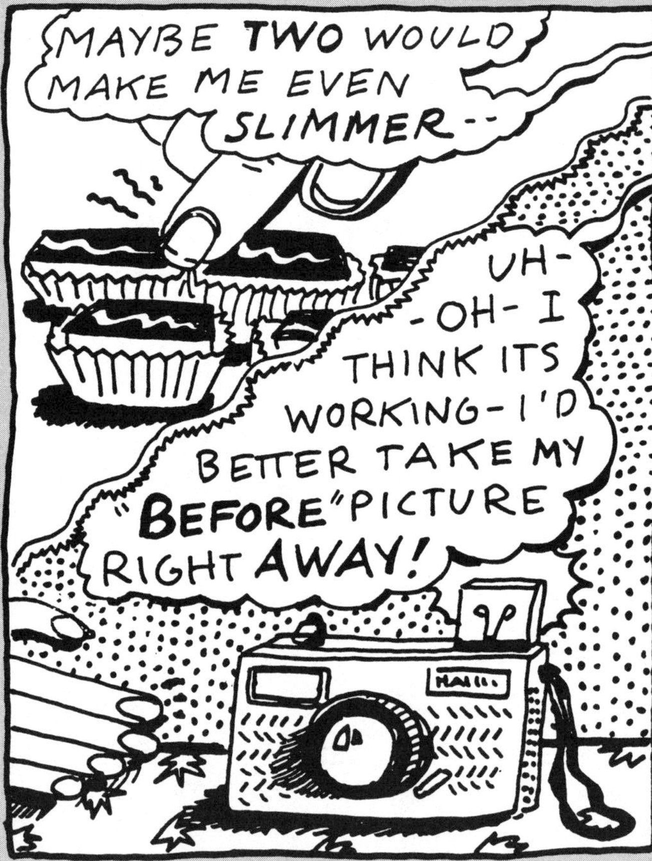
MAYBE TWO WOULD MAKE ME EVEN SLIMMER--
UH--OH- I THINK ITS WORKING-I'D BETTER TAKE MY "BEFORE" PICTURE RIGHT AWAY!

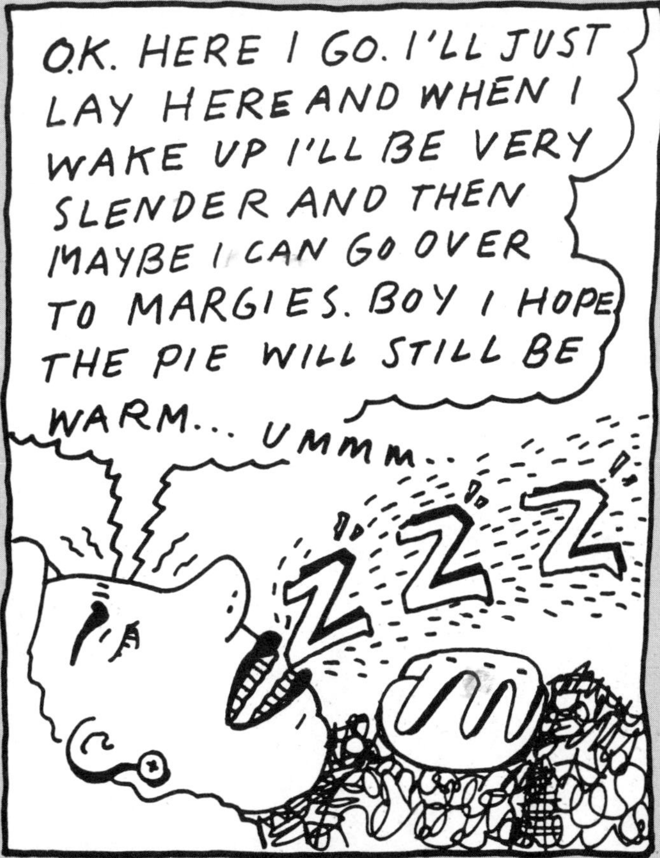
O.K. HERE I GO. I'LL JUST LAY HERE AND WHEN I WAKE UP I'LL BE VERY SLENDER AND THEN MAYBE I CAN GO OVER TO MARGIES. BOY I HOPE THE PIE WILL STILL BE WARM... UMMM
ZZZ

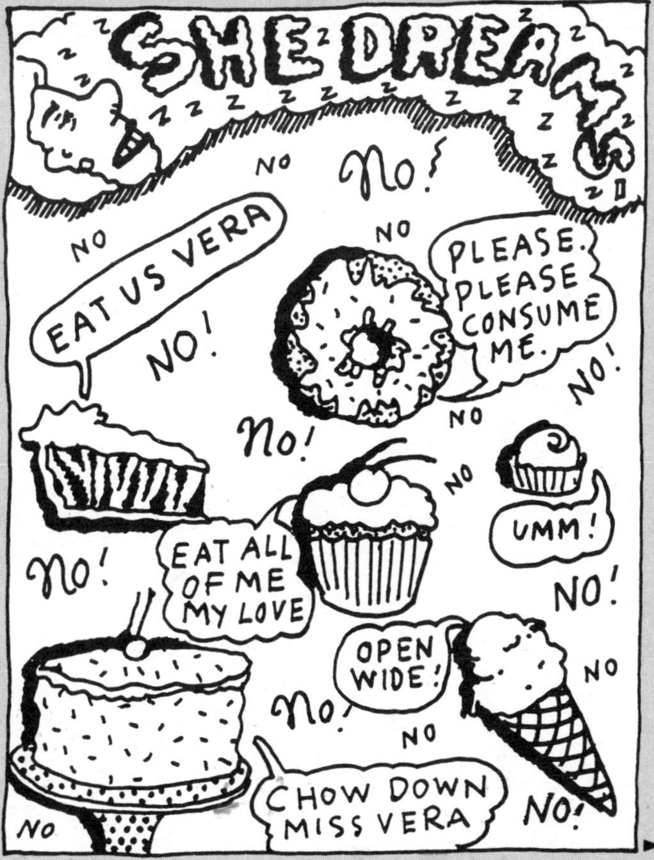
SHE DREAMS
NO
NO!
EAT US VERA
NO
NO
PLEASE. PLEASE CONSUME ME.
NO!
NO!
NO
NO!
NO
UMM!
NO!
EAT ALL OF ME MY LOVE
NO!
OPEN WIDE!
NO
NO!
NO
CHOW DOWN MISS VERA
NO
NO!

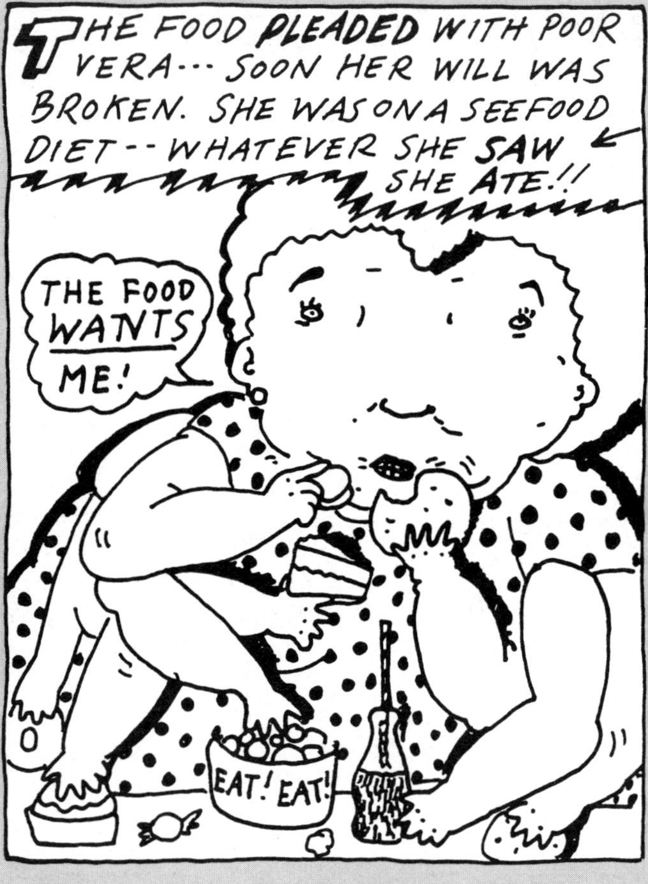
THE FOOD PLEADED WITH POOR VERA··· SOON HER WILL WAS BROKEN. SHE WAS ON A SEEFOOD DIET -- WHATEVER SHE SAW SHE ATE.!!
THE FOOD WANTS ME!
EAT! EAT!

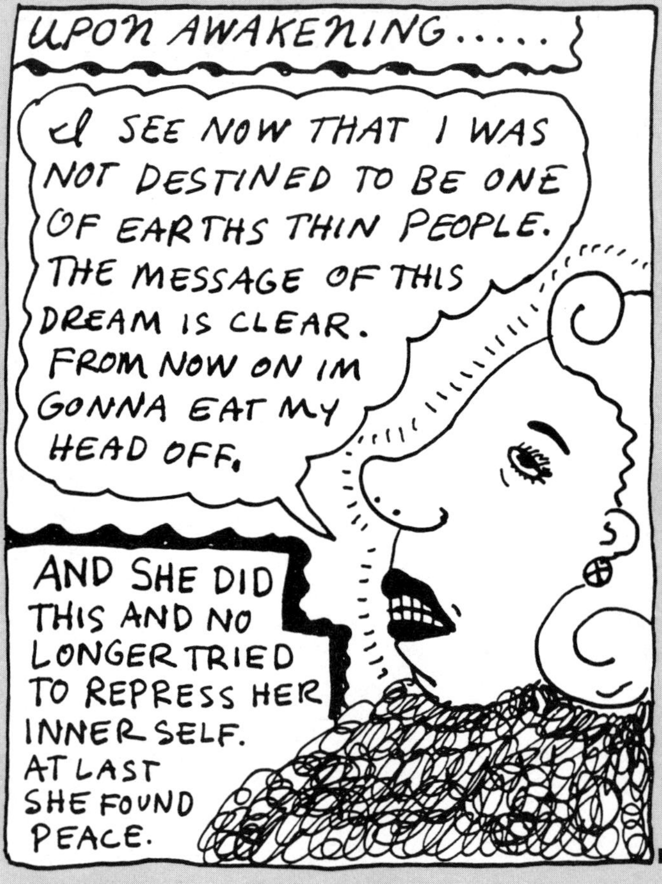
UPON AWAKENING.....
I SEE NOW THAT I WAS NOT DESTINED TO BE ONE OF EARTHS THIN PEOPLE. THE MESSAGE OF THIS DREAM IS CLEAR. FROM NOW ON IM GONNA EAT MY HEAD OFF.
AND SHE DID THIS AND NO LONGER TRIED TO REPRESS HER INNER SELF. AT LAST SHE FOUND PEACE.

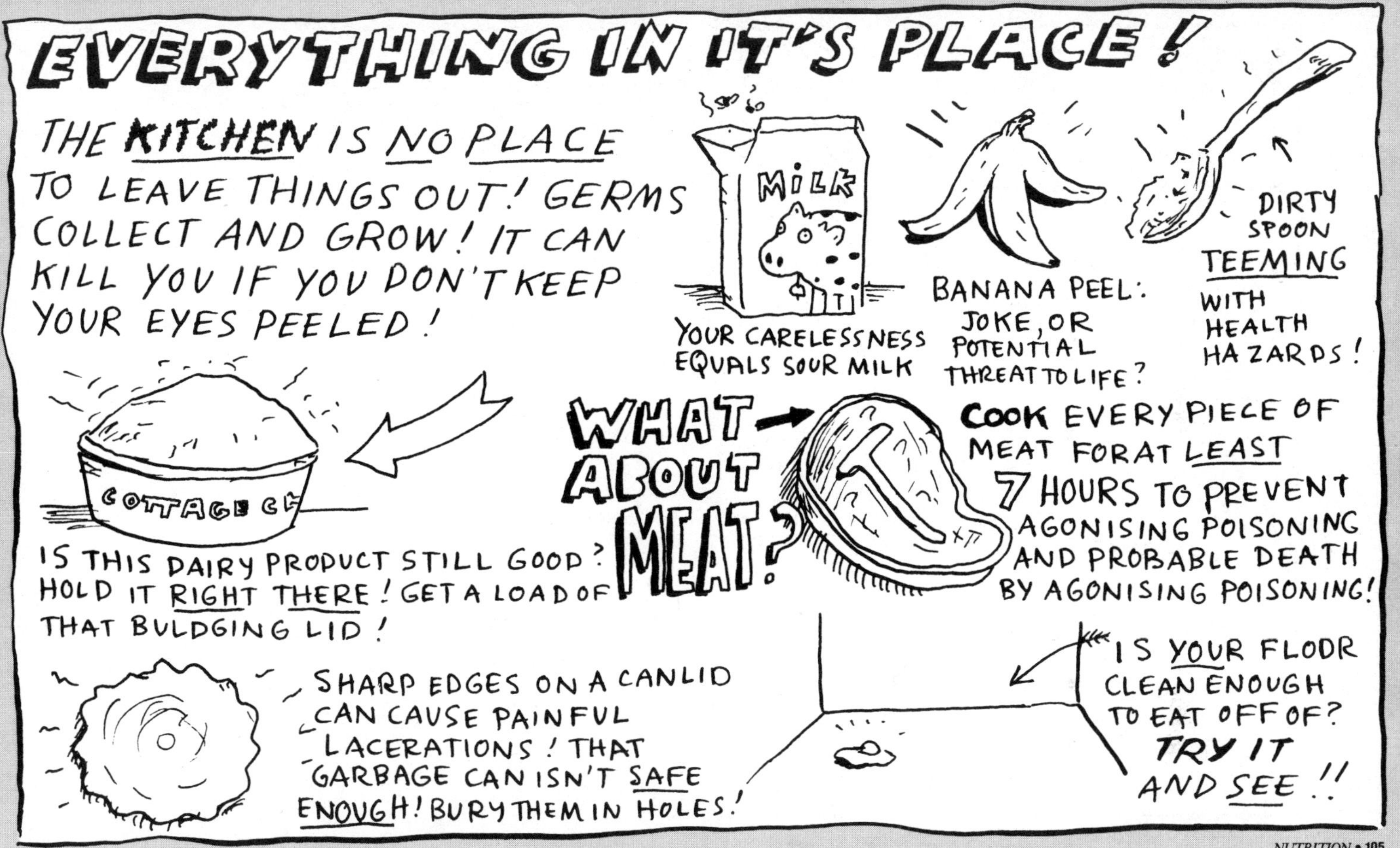

EVERYTHING IN IT'S PLACE!
THE KITCHEN IS NO PLACE TO LEAVE THINGS OUT! GERMS COLLECT AND GROW! IT CAN KILL YOU IF YOU DON'T KEEP YOUR EYES PEELED!
MILK
YOUR CARELESSNESS EQUALS SOUR MILK
BANANA PEEL: JOKE, OR POTENTIAL THREAT TO LIFE?
DIRTY SPOON TEEMING WITH HEALTH HAZARDS!
COTTAGE CH
IS THIS DAIRY PRODUCT STILL GOOD? HOLD IT RIGHT THERE! GET A LOAD OF THAT BULDGING LID!
WHAT ABOUT MEAT?
COOK EVERY PIECE OF MEAT FOR AT LEAST 7 HOURS TO PREVENT AGONISING POISONING AND PROBABLE DEATH BY AGONISING POISONING!
SHARP EDGES ON A CAN LID CAN CAUSE PAINFUL LACERATIONS! THAT GARBAGE CAN ISN'T SAFE ENOUGH! BURY THEM IN HOLES!
IS YOUR FLOOR CLEAN ENOUGH TO EAT OFF OF? TRY IT AND SEE!!

Advice

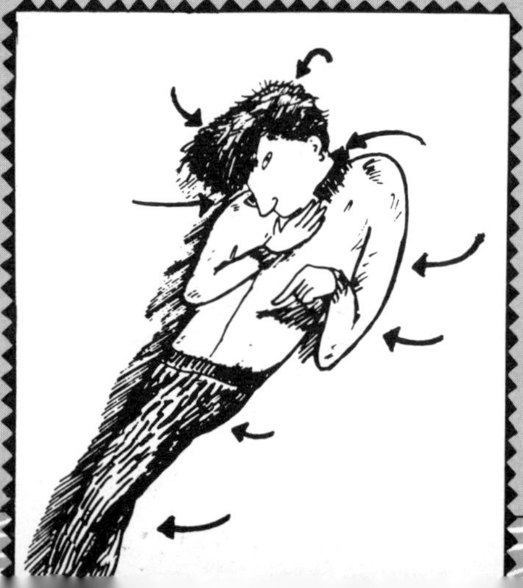

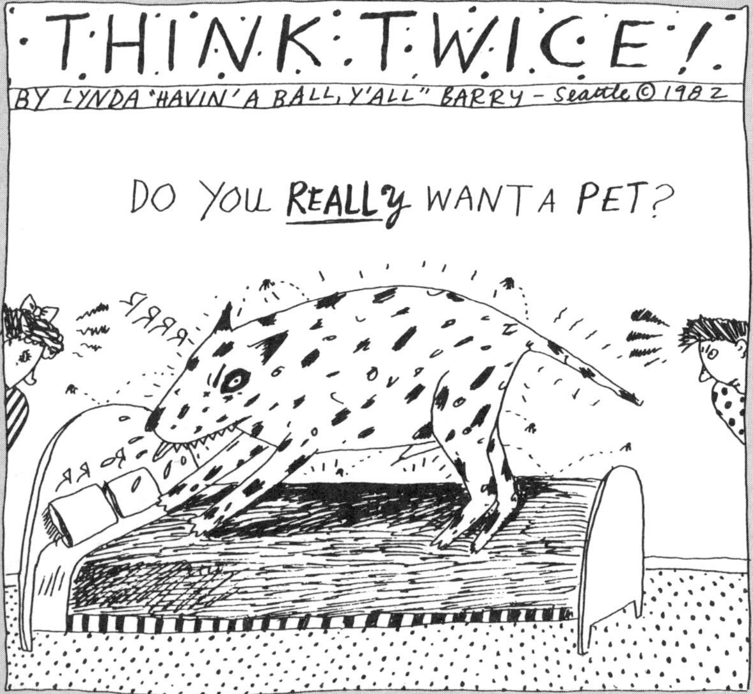
THINK TWICE!
BY LYNDA "HAVIN' A BALL, Y'ALL" BARRY - Seattle © 1982
DO YOU REALLY WANT A PET?
RRR
RRR

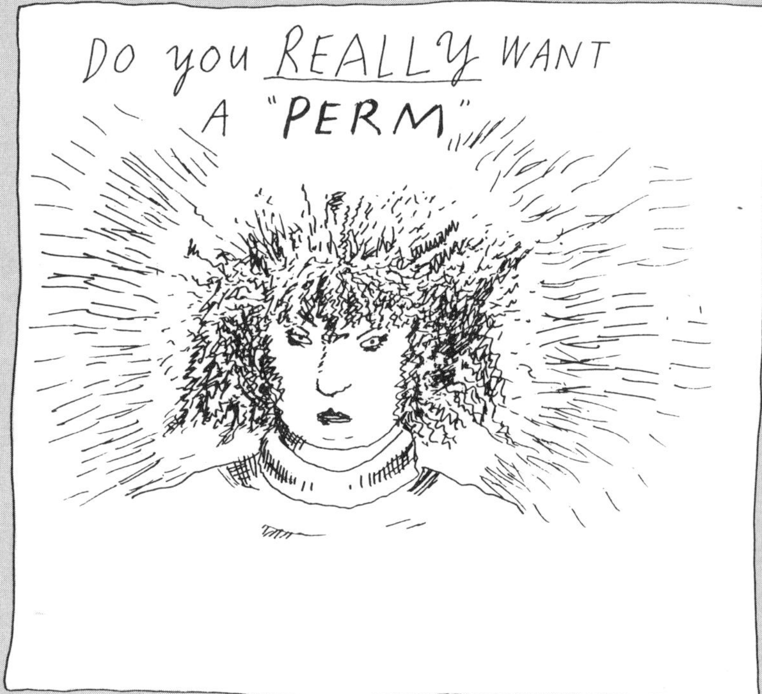
DO YOU REALLY WANT A "PERM"

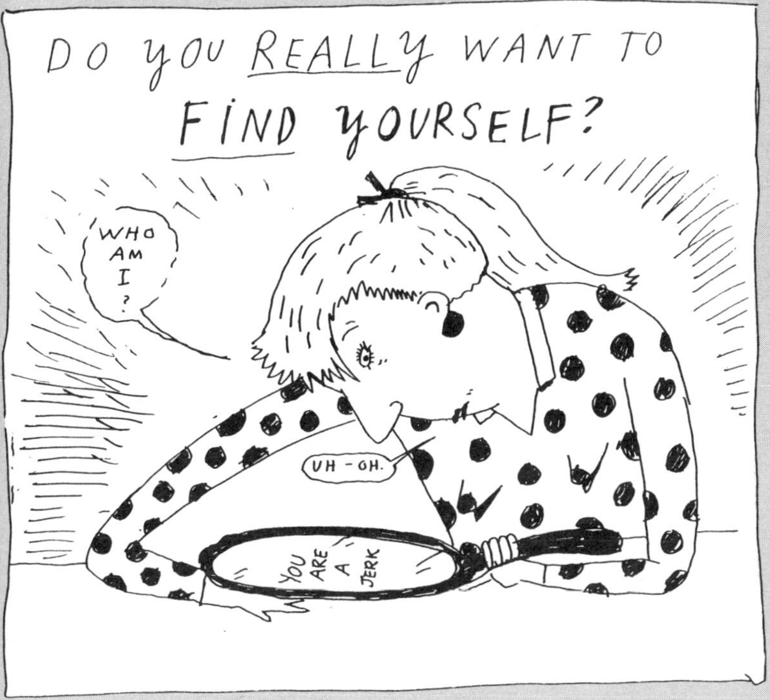
DO YOU REALLY WANT TO
FIND YOURSELF?
WHO AM I ?
UH-OH.
YOU ARE A JERK

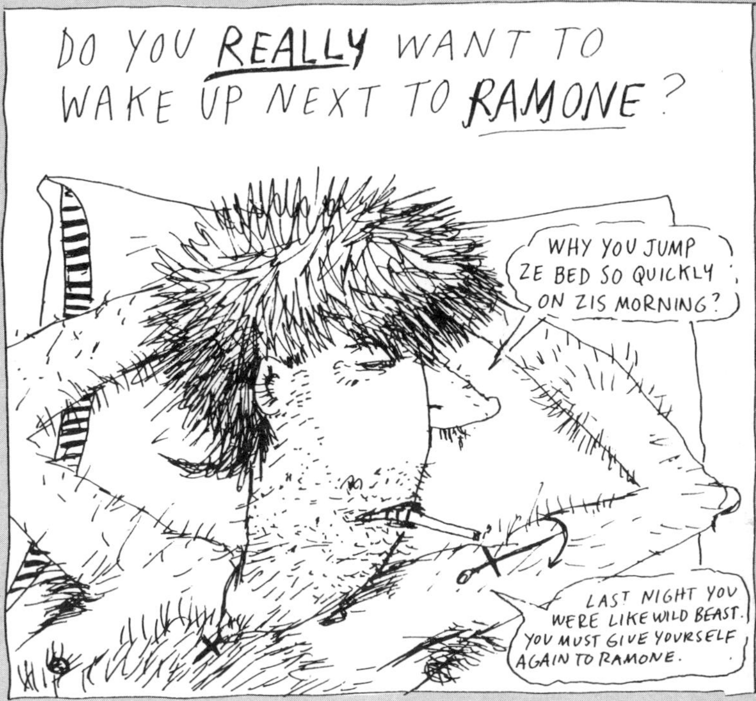
DO YOU REALLY WANT TO
WAKE UP NEXT TO RAMONE?
WHY YOU JUMP ZE BED SO QUICKLY ON ZIS MORNING?
LAST NIGHT YOU WERE LIKE WILD BEAST. YOU MUST GIVE YOURSELF AGAIN TO RAMONE.

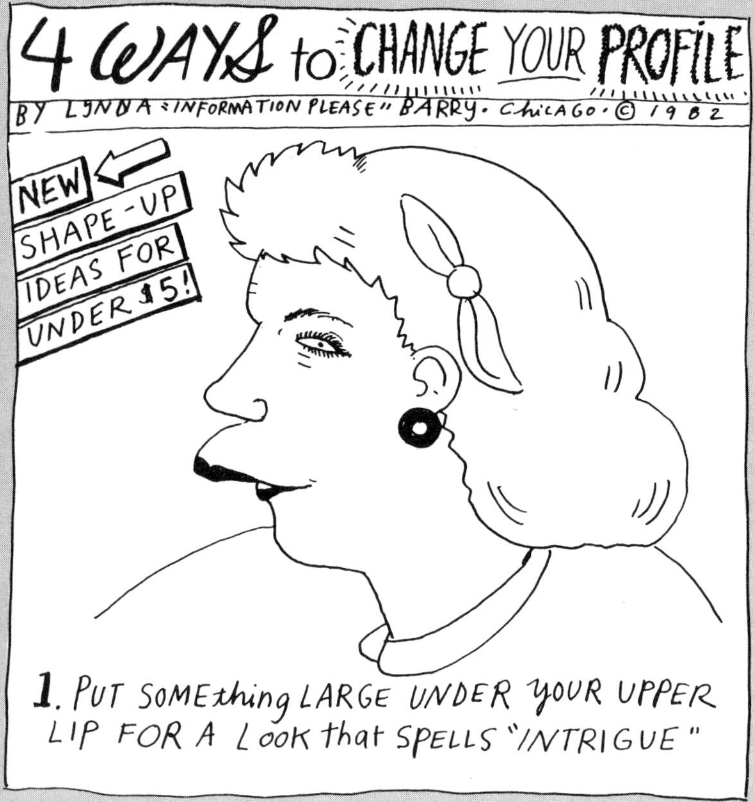
4 WAYS to CHANGE YOUR PROFILE
BY LYNDA "INFORMATION PLEASE" BARRY · CHICAGO · © 1982
NEW
SHAPE-UP
IDEAS FOR
UNDER $5!
1. PUT SOMEthing LARGE UNDER YOUR UPPER LIP FOR A Look that SPELLS "INTRIGUE"

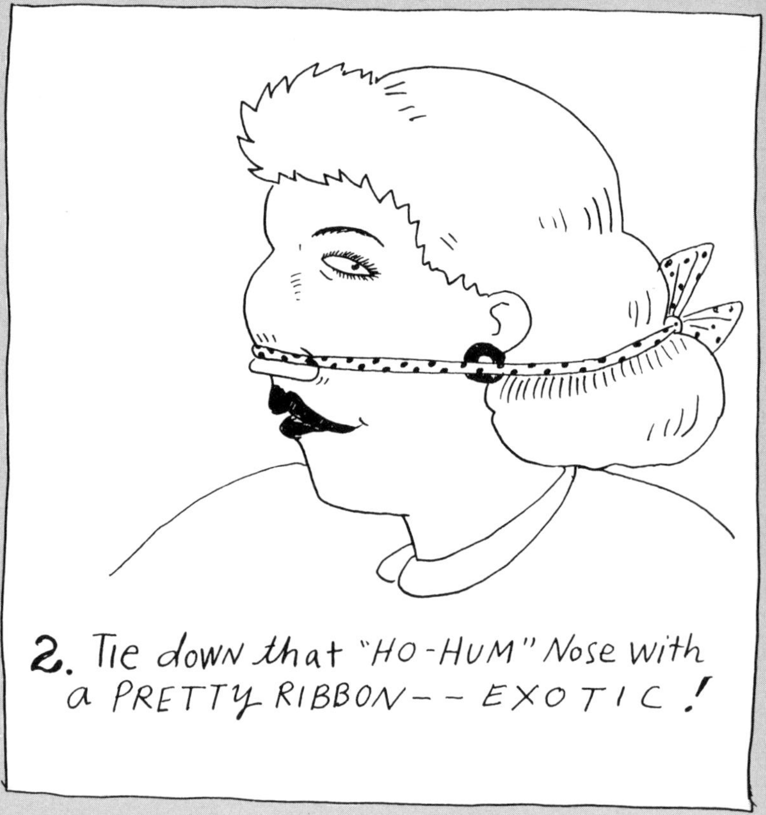
2. Tie down that "HO-HUM" Nose with a PRETTY RIBBON -- EXOTIC!

3. FAKE teeth CAN help **ANYONE** Look JUST A LittLE MORE FRIendLy!

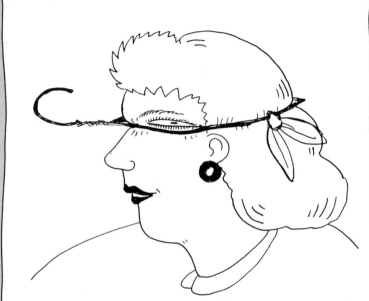

4. A ReGuLAR CoAT HanGeR CAN Lend bLAND EYes AN AIR Of ORIENTAL FLAiR AND The HooK IS A LOOK IN ITSELF.

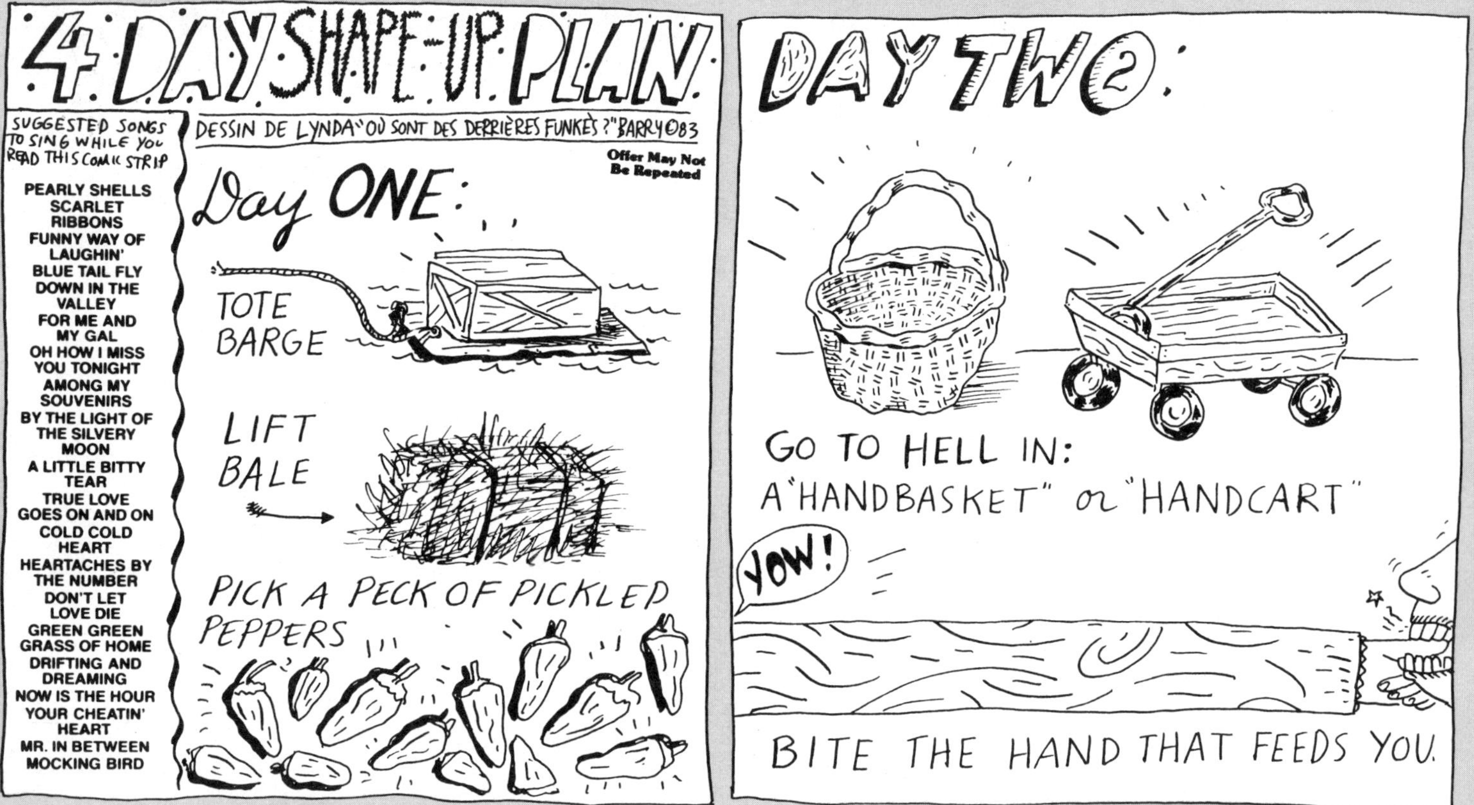
4 DAY SHAPE-UP PLAN
SUGGESTED SONGS TO SING WHILE YOU READ THIS COMIC STRIP
PEARLY SHELLS
SCARLET RIBBONS
FUNNY WAY OF LAUGHIN'
BLUE TAIL FLY
DOWN IN THE VALLEY
FOR ME AND MY GAL
OH HOW I MISS YOU TONIGHT
AMONG MY SOUVENIRS
BY THE LIGHT OF THE SILVERY MOON
A LITTLE BITTY TEAR
TRUE LOVE GOES ON AND ON
COLD COLD HEART
HEARTACHES BY THE NUMBER
DON'T LET LOVE DIE
GREEN GREEN GRASS OF HOME
DRIFTING AND DREAMING
NOW IS THE HOUR
YOUR CHEATIN' HEART
MR. IN BETWEEN
MOCKING BIRD
DESSIN DE LYNDA "OU SONT DES DERRIÈRES FUNKÈS?" BARRY©83
Offer May Not Be Repeated
Day ONE:
TOTE BARGE
LIFT BALE
PICK A PECK OF PICKLED PEPPERS
DAY TWO:
GO TO HELL IN:
A "HANDBASKET" or "HANDCART"
YOW!
BITE THE HAND THAT FEEDS YOU.

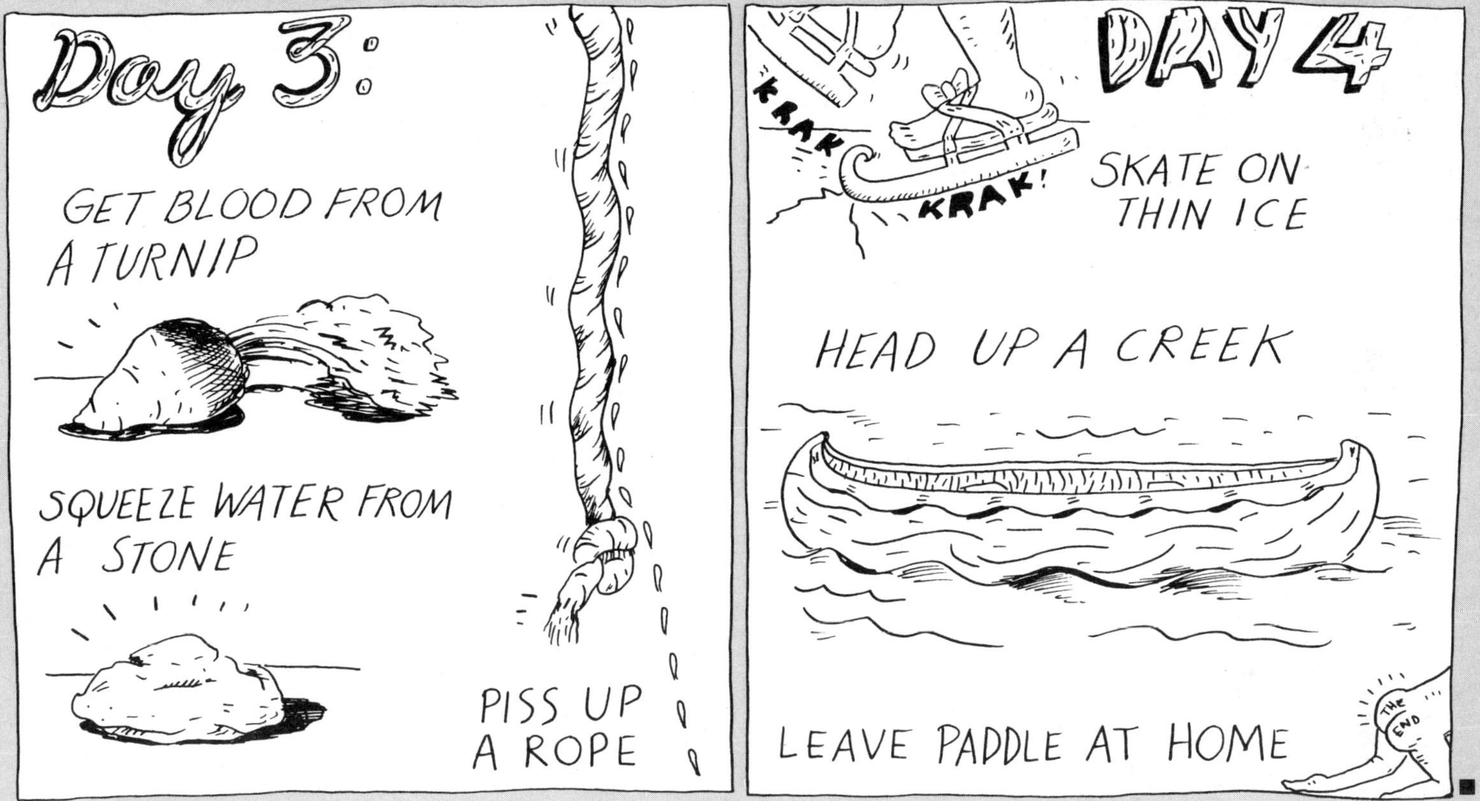
Day 3:
GET BLOOD FROM A TURNIP
SQUEEZE WATER FROM A STONE
PISS UP A ROPE
DAY 4
KRAK KRAK
KRAK!
SKATE ON THIN ICE
HEAD UP A CREEK
LEAVE PADDLE AT HOME
THE END

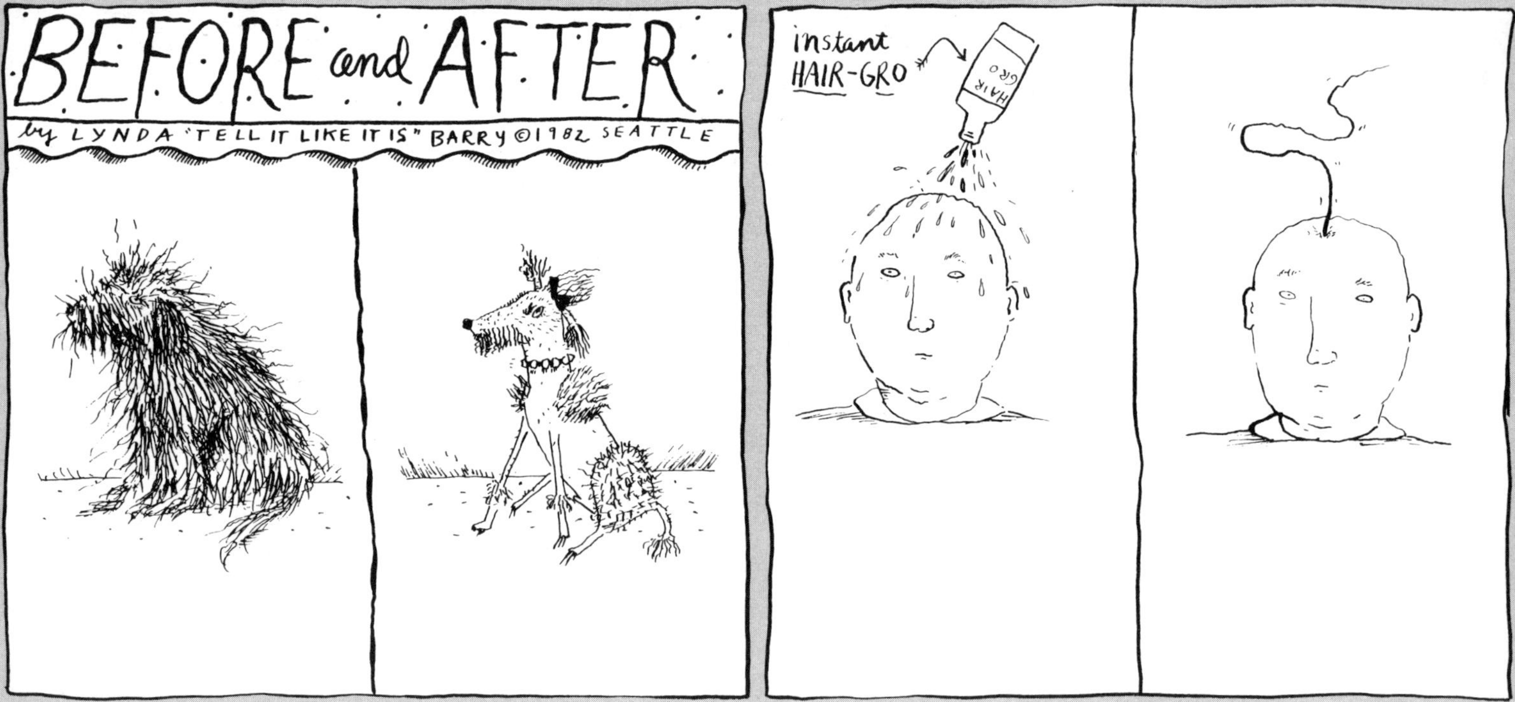
BEFORE and AFTER
by LYNDA "TELL IT LIKE IT IS" BARRY ©1982 SEATTLE
instant HAIR-GRO
HAIR GRO

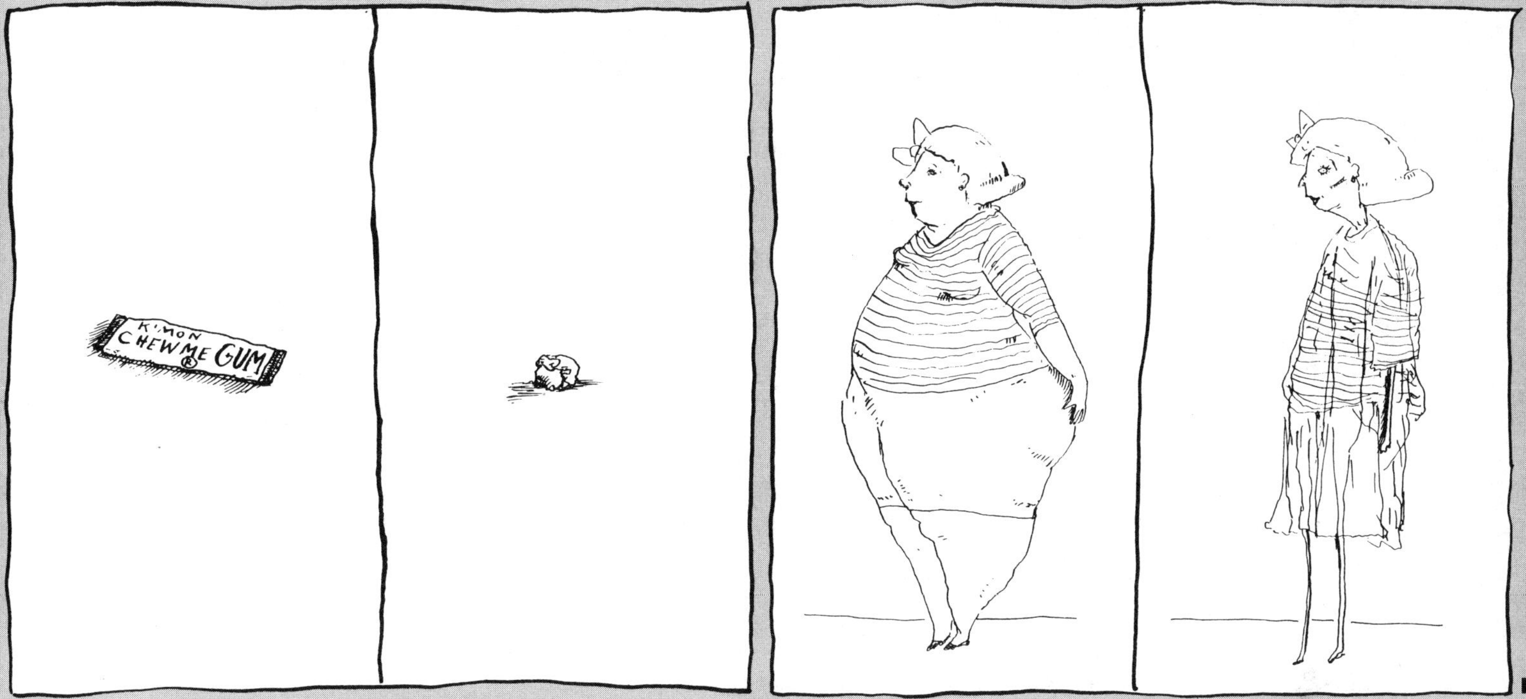
K'MON
CHEWME GUM

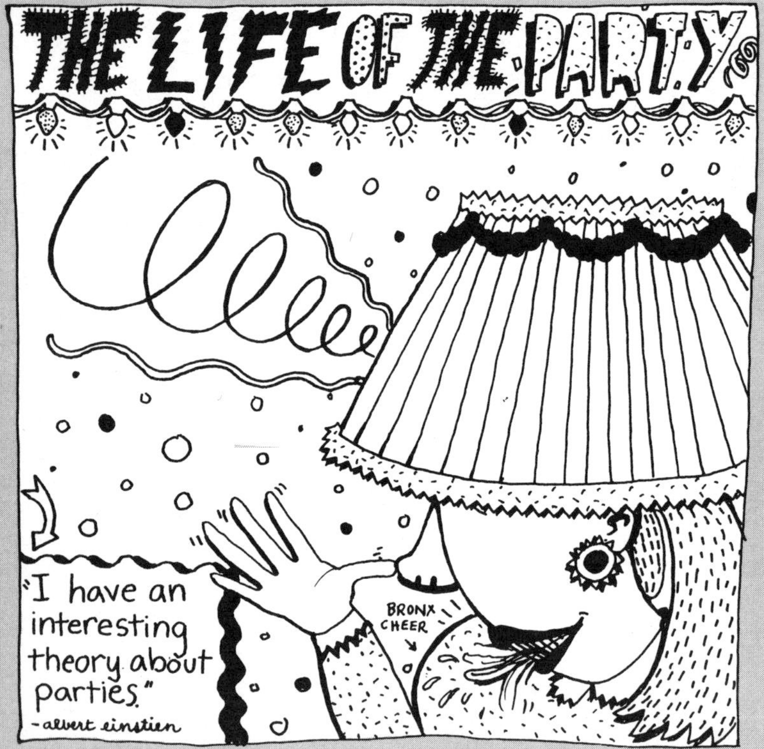
THE LIFE OF THE PARTY
"I have an interesting theory about parties."
-albert einstien
BRONX CHEER

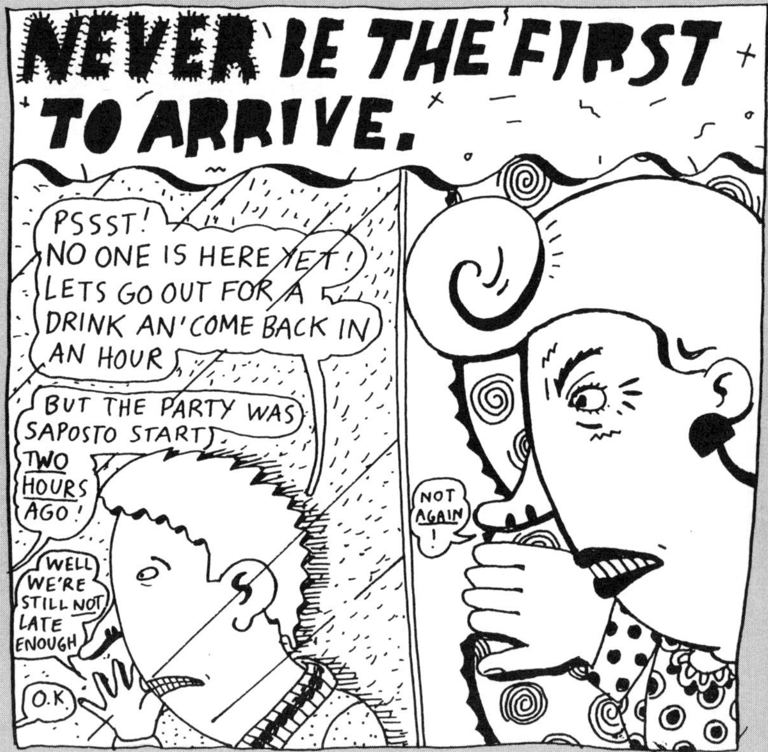
NEVER BE THE FIRST TO ARRIVE.
PSSST! NO ONE IS HERE YET! LETS GO OUT FOR A DRINK AN' COME BACK IN AN HOUR
BUT THE PARTY WAS SAPOSTO START TWO HOURS AGO!
WELL WE'RE STILL NOT LATE ENOUGH
O.K.
NOT AGAIN!

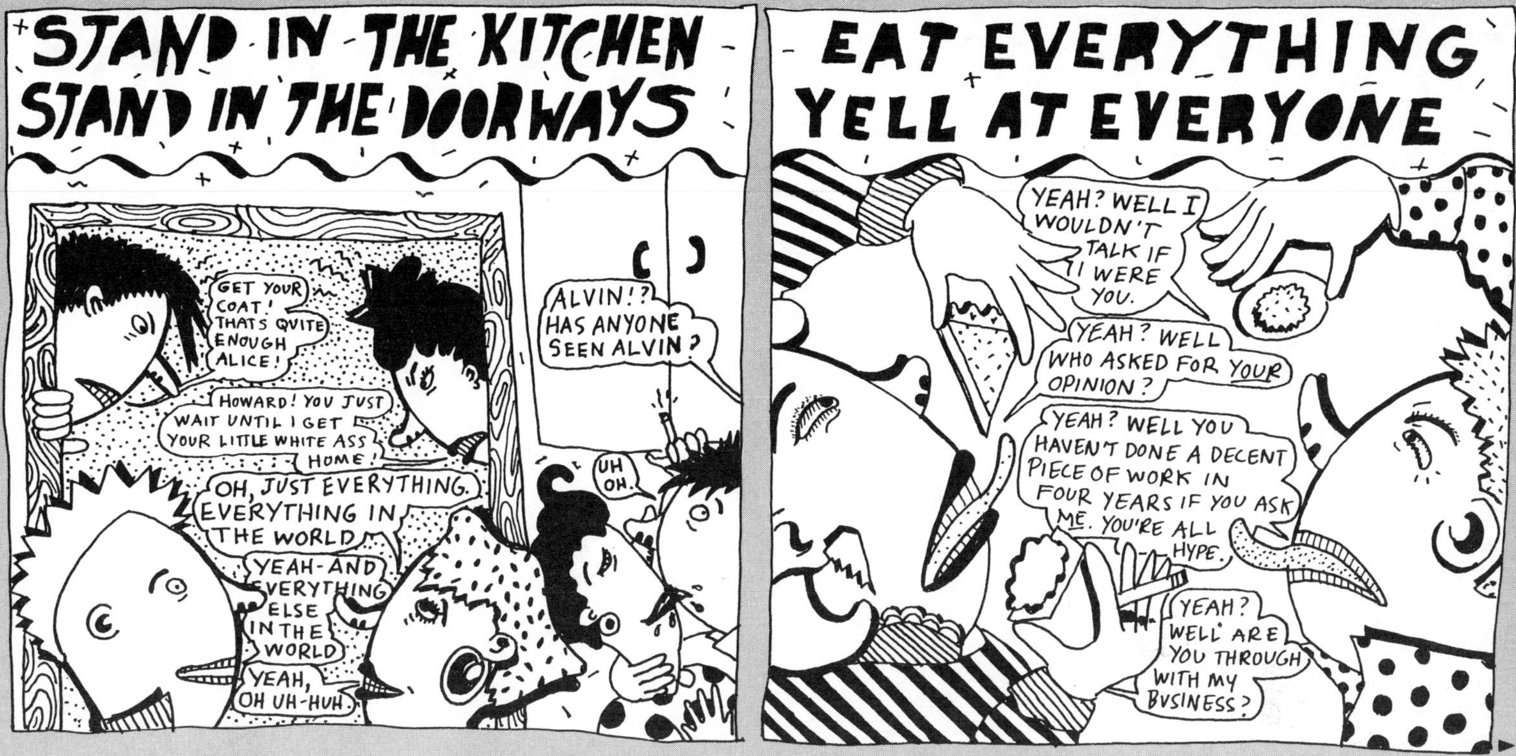
STAND IN THE KITCHEN
STAND IN THE DOORWAYS
GET YOUR COAT! THATS QUITE ENOUGH ALICE!
HOWARD! YOU JUST WAIT UNTIL I GET YOUR LITTLE WHITE ASS HOME!
ALVIN!? HAS ANYONE SEEN ALVIN?
UH OH.
OH, JUST EVERYTHING. EVERYTHING IN THE WORLD
YEAH-AND EVERYTHING ELSE IN THE WORLD
YEAH, OH UH-HUH
EAT EVERYTHING
YELL AT EVERYONE
YEAH? WELL I WOULDN'T TALK IF I WERE YOU.
YEAH? WELL WHO ASKED FOR YOUR OPINION?
YEAH? WELL YOU HAVEN'T DONE A DECENT PIECE OF WORK IN FOUR YEARS IF YOU ASK ME. YOU'RE ALL HYPE.
YEAH? WELL ARE YOU THROUGH WITH MY BUSINESS?

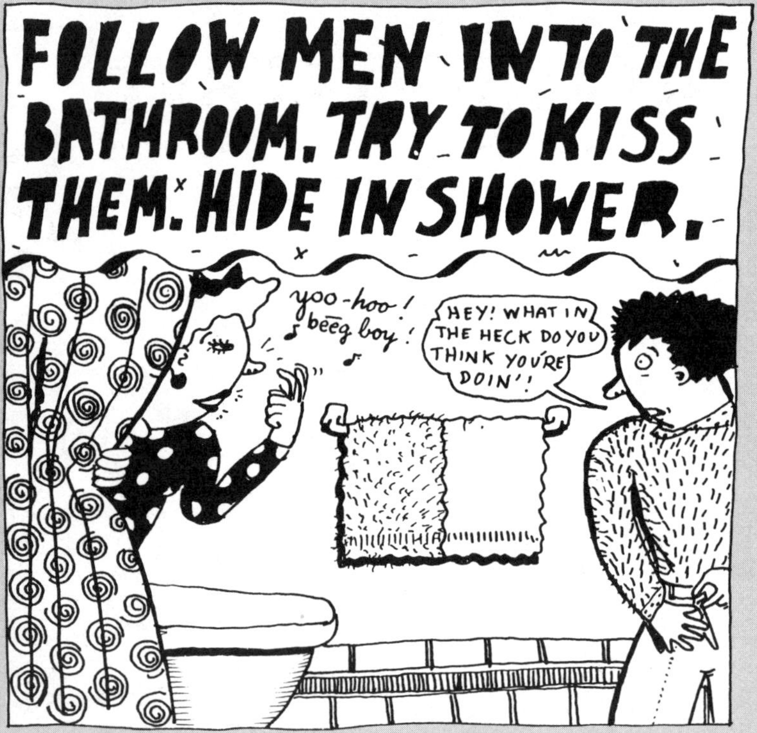
FOLLOW MEN INTO THE BATHROOM. TRY TO KISS THEM. HIDE IN SHOWER.
yoo-hoo! beeg boy!
HEY! WHAT IN THE HECK DO YOU THINK YOU'RE DOIN'!

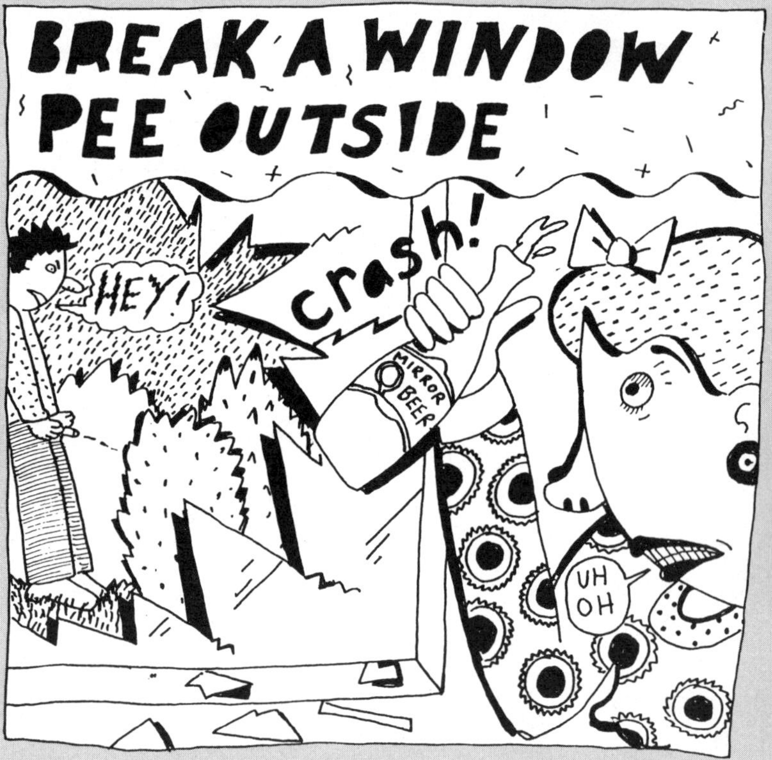
BREAK A WINDOW PEE OUTSIDE
HEY!
crash!
MIRROR BEER
UH OH

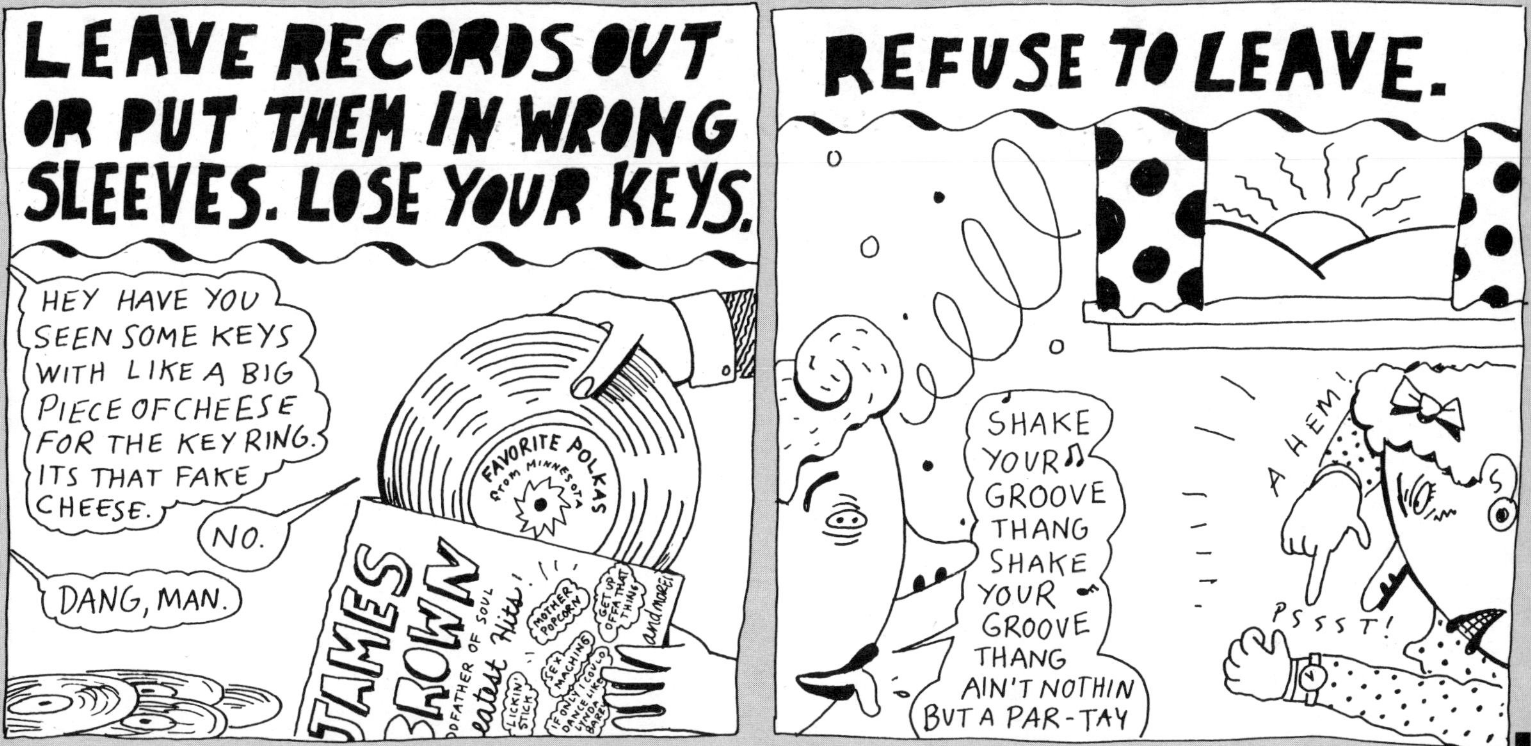
LEAVE RECORDS OUT OR PUT THEM IN WRONG SLEEVES. LOSE YOUR KEYS.
HEY HAVE YOU SEEN SOME KEYS WITH LIKE A BIG PIECE OF CHEESE FOR THE KEY RING. ITS THAT FAKE CHEESE.
NO.
DANG, MAN.
FAVORITE POLKAS from MINNESOTA
JAMES BROWN
ODFATHER OF SOUL
eatest Hits!
MOTHER POPCORN
GET UP OFFA THAT THING
and more!!
SEX MACHINE
LICKIN' STICK
IF ONLY I COULD DANCE LIKE LYNDA BARRY
REFUSE TO LEAVE.
SHAKE YOUR GROOVE THANG SHAKE YOUR GROOVE THANG AIN'T NOTHIN BUT A PAR-TAY
AHEM!
PSSST!

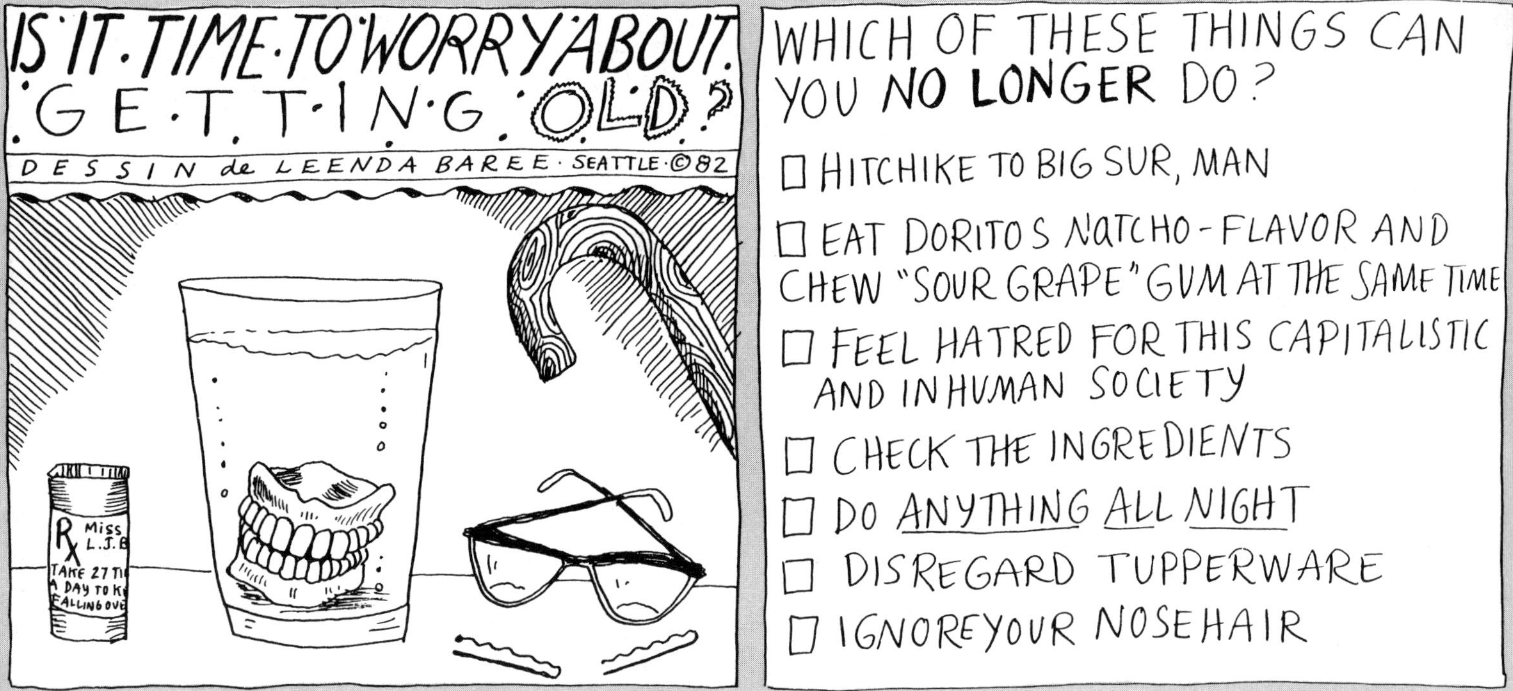
IS·IT·TIME·TO·WORRY·ABOUT·
GE·T·T·I·N·G OLD?
DESSIN de LEENDA BAREE · SEATTLE · ©82
WHICH OF THESE THINGS CAN YOU NO LONGER DO?
☐ HITCHIKE TO BIG SUR, MAN
☐ EAT DORITOS NATCHO-FLAVOR AND CHEW "SOUR GRAPE" GUM AT THE SAME TIME
☐ FEEL HATRED FOR THIS CAPITALISTIC AND INHUMAN SOCIETY
☐ CHECK THE INGREDIENTS
☐ DO ANYTHING ALL NIGHT
☐ DISREGARD TUPPERWARE
☐ IGNORE YOUR NOSEHAIR

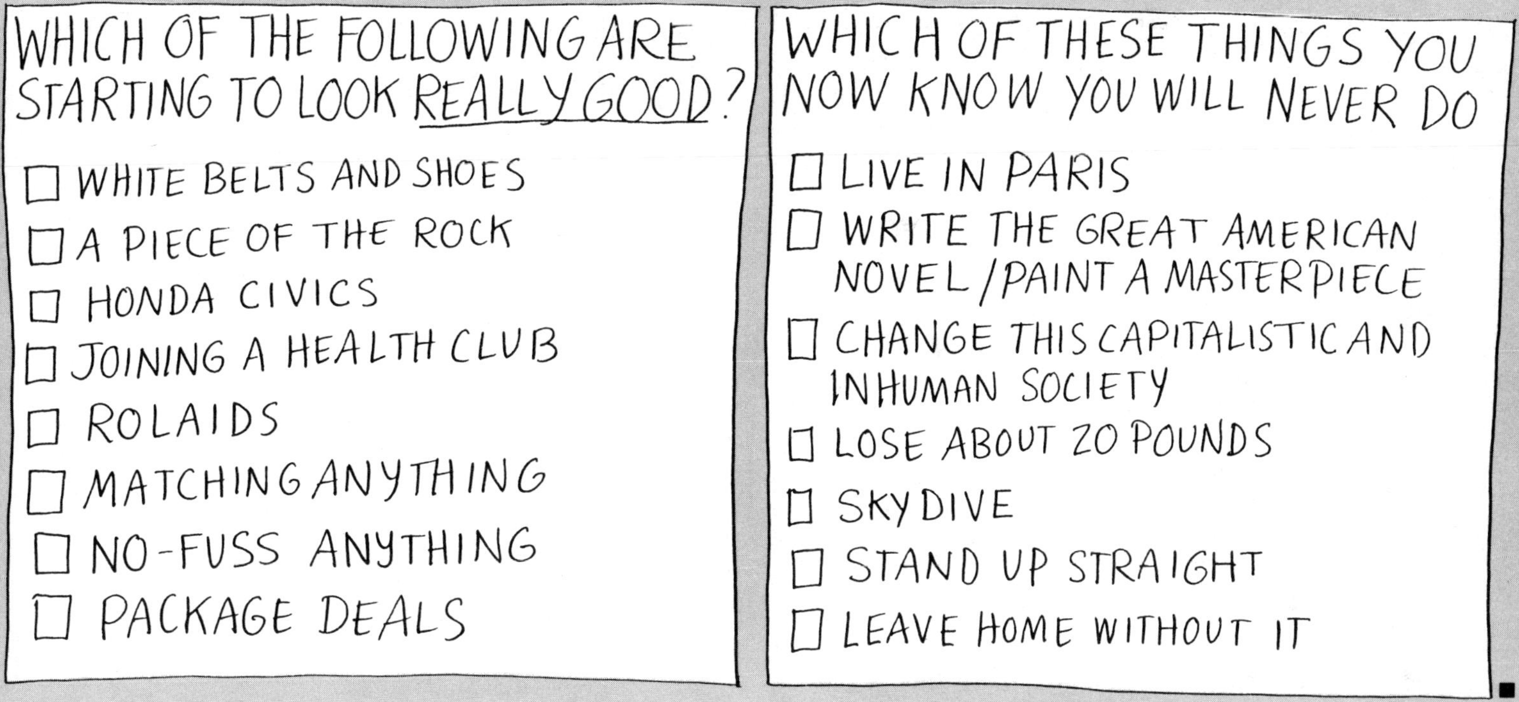
WHICH OF THE FOLLOWING ARE STARTING TO LOOK REALLY GOOD?
☐ WHITE BELTS AND SHOES
☐ A PIECE OF THE ROCK
☐ HONDA CIVICS
☐ JOINING A HEALTH CLUB
☐ ROLAIDS
☐ MATCHING ANYTHING
☐ NO-FUSS ANYTHING
☐ PACKAGE DEALS
WHICH OF THESE THINGS YOU NOW KNOW YOU WILL NEVER DO
☐ LIVE IN PARIS
☐ WRITE THE GREAT AMERICAN NOVEL/PAINT A MASTERPIECE
☐ CHANGE THIS CAPITALISTIC AND INHUMAN SOCIETY
☐ LOSE ABOUT 20 POUNDS
☐ SKYDIVE
☐ STAND UP STRAIGHT
☐ LEAVE HOME WITHOUT IT

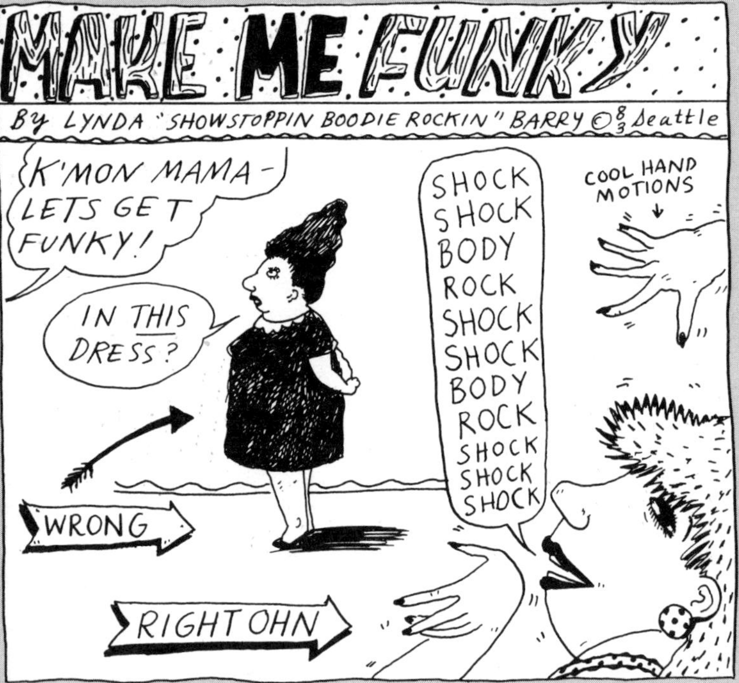
MAKE ME FUNKY
BY LYNDA "SHOWSTOPPIN BOODIE ROCKIN" BARRY © 83 Seattle
K'MON MAMA - LETS GET FUNKY!
IN THIS DRESS?
SHOCK SHOCK BODY ROCK SHOCK SHOCK SHOCK BODY ROCK SHOCK SHOCK SHOCK
COOL HAND MOTIONS
WRONG
RIGHT OHN

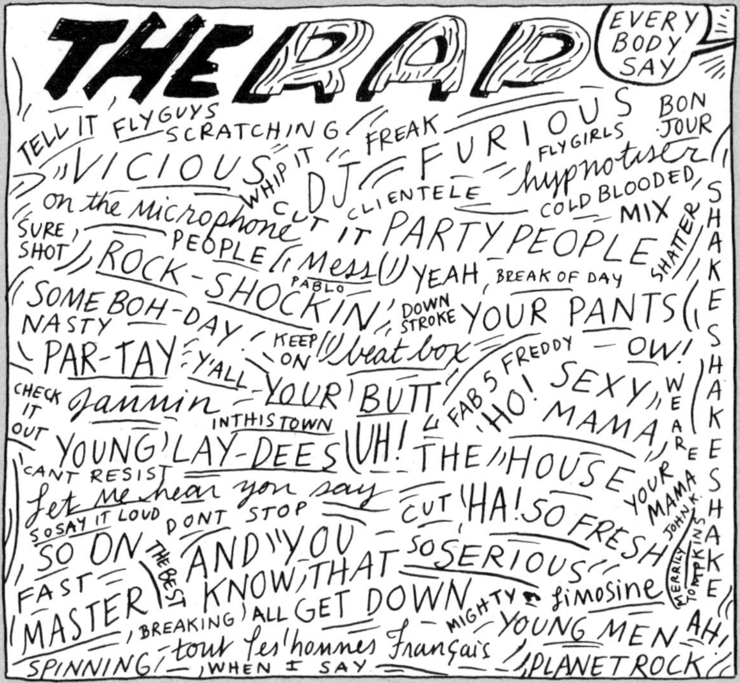
THE RAP
EVERY BODY SAY
TELL IT
FLYGUYS
SCRATCHING
FREAK
FURIOUS
BON JOUR
FLYGIRLS
VICIOUS
WHIP IT
DJ
hypnotiser
on the microphone
CUT IT
CLIENTELE
COLD BLOODED
SURE SHOT
PEOPLE
PARTY PEOPLE
MIX
SHATTER
ROCK-SHOCKIN'
Mess
PABLO
YEAH
BREAK OF DAY
SOME BOH-DAY
NASTY
DOWN STROKE
YOUR PANTS
PAR-TAY
Y'ALL
KEEP ON
beat box
FAB 5 FREDDY
OW!
CHECK IT OUT
Jammin
YOUR BUTT
HO! SEXY MAMA
IN THIS TOWN
YOUNG LAY-DEES
UH!
THE HOUSE
WE ARE
CANT RESIST
Let me hear you say
YOUR MAMA
SO SAY IT LOUD
DONT STOP
CUT
HA! SO FRESH
JOHN K.
SO ON
THE BEST
AND YOU KNOW THAT
SO SERIOUS
FAST
MASTER
ALL GET DOWN
MIGHTY
Limosine
MERRILL
TOMPKINS
BREAKING
YOUNG MEN
AH!
SPINNING
tout les hommes Français
WHEN I SAY
PLANET ROCK
SHAKE SHAKE SHAKE SHAKE SHAKE

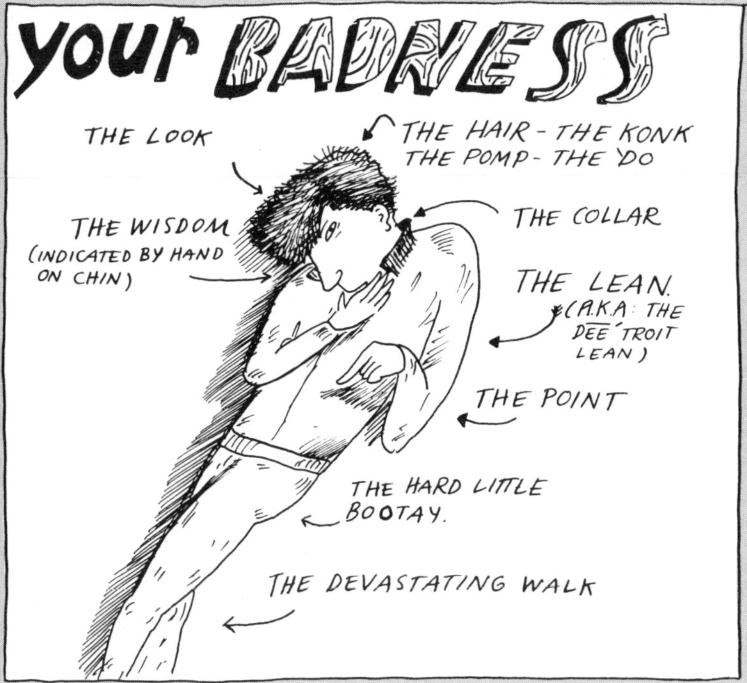

your BADNESS
THE LOOK
THE HAIR - THE KONK
THE POMP - THE 'DO
THE WISDOM
(INDICATED BY HAND ON CHIN)
THE COLLAR
THE LEAN.
(A.K.A: THE DEE'TROIT LEAN)
THE POINT
THE HARD LITTLE BOOTAY.
THE DEVASTATING WALK

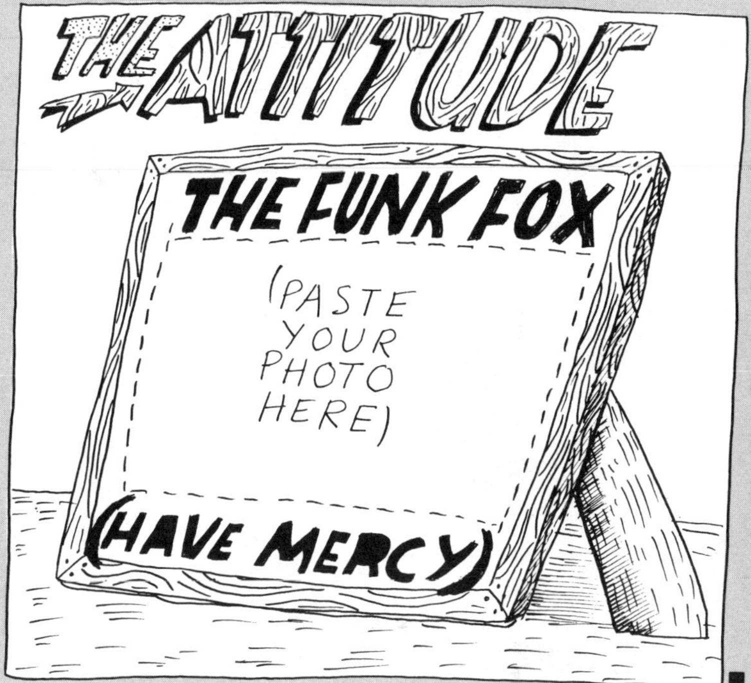

THE ATTITUDE
THE FUNK FOX
(PASTE YOUR PHOTO HERE)
(HAVE MERCY)

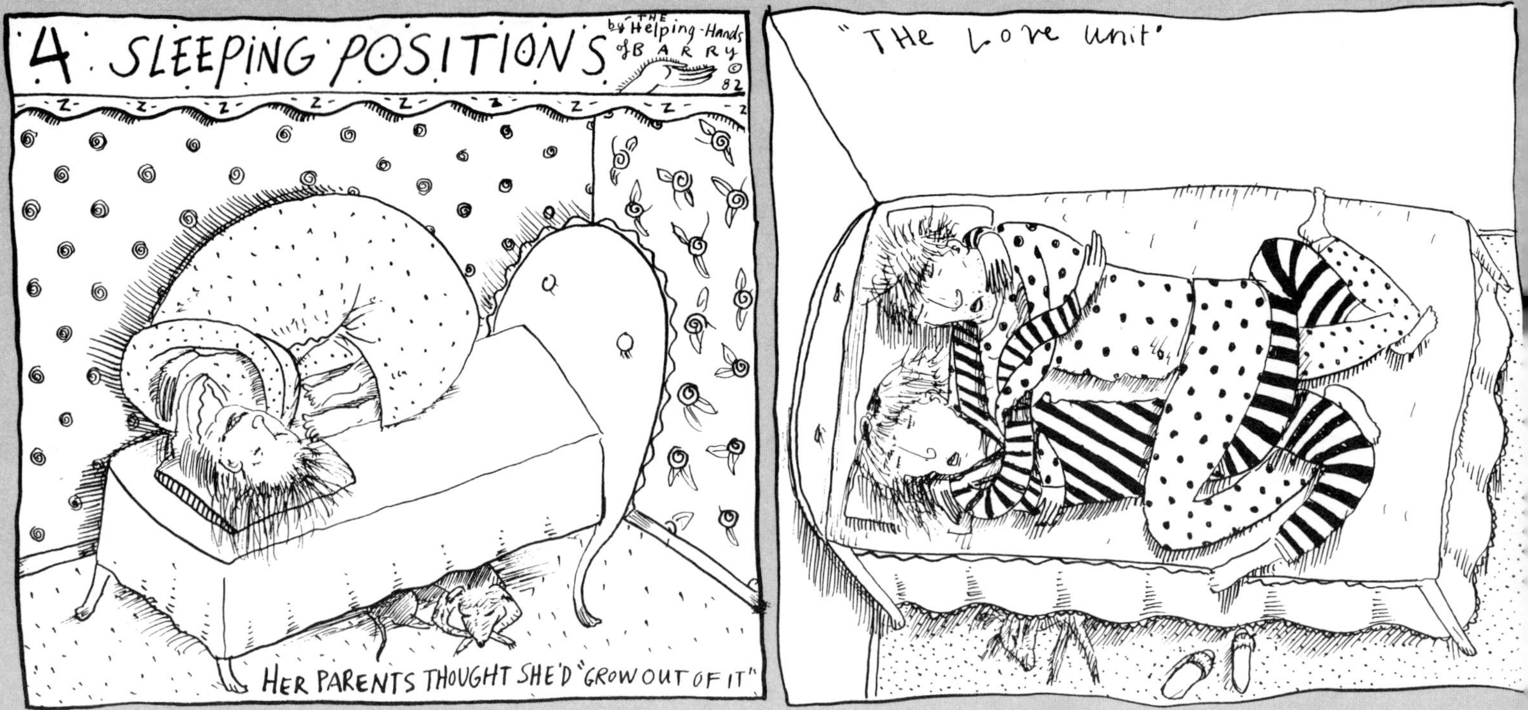
4 SLEEPING POSITIONS
by THE Helping-Hands of BARRY © 82
HER PARENTS THOUGHT SHE'D "GROW OUT OF IT"
"THe Love unit"

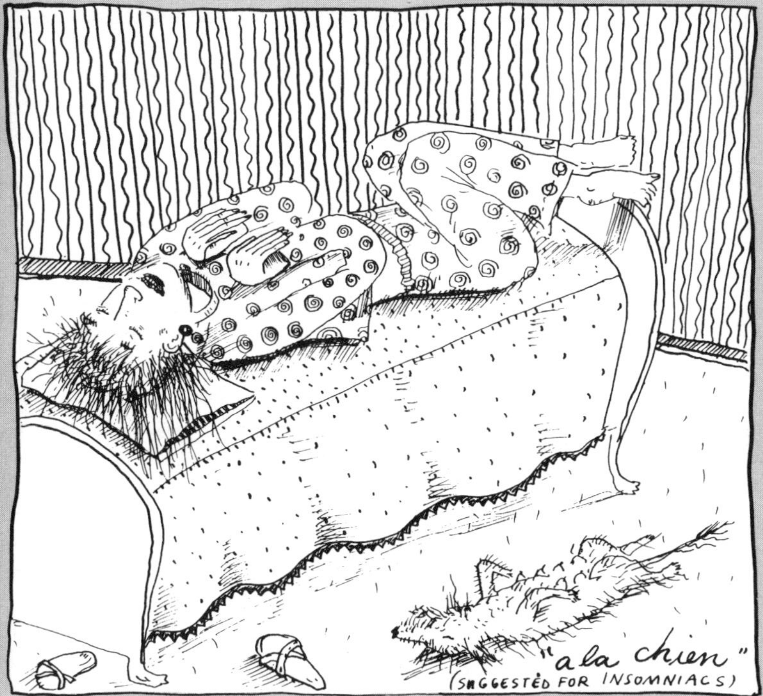
"a la chien"
(SUGGESTED FOR INSOMNIACS)

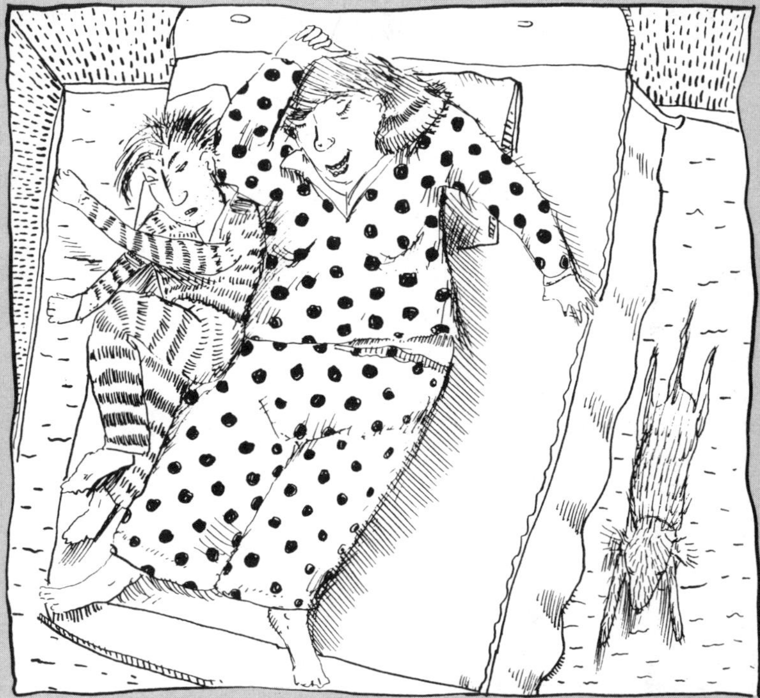

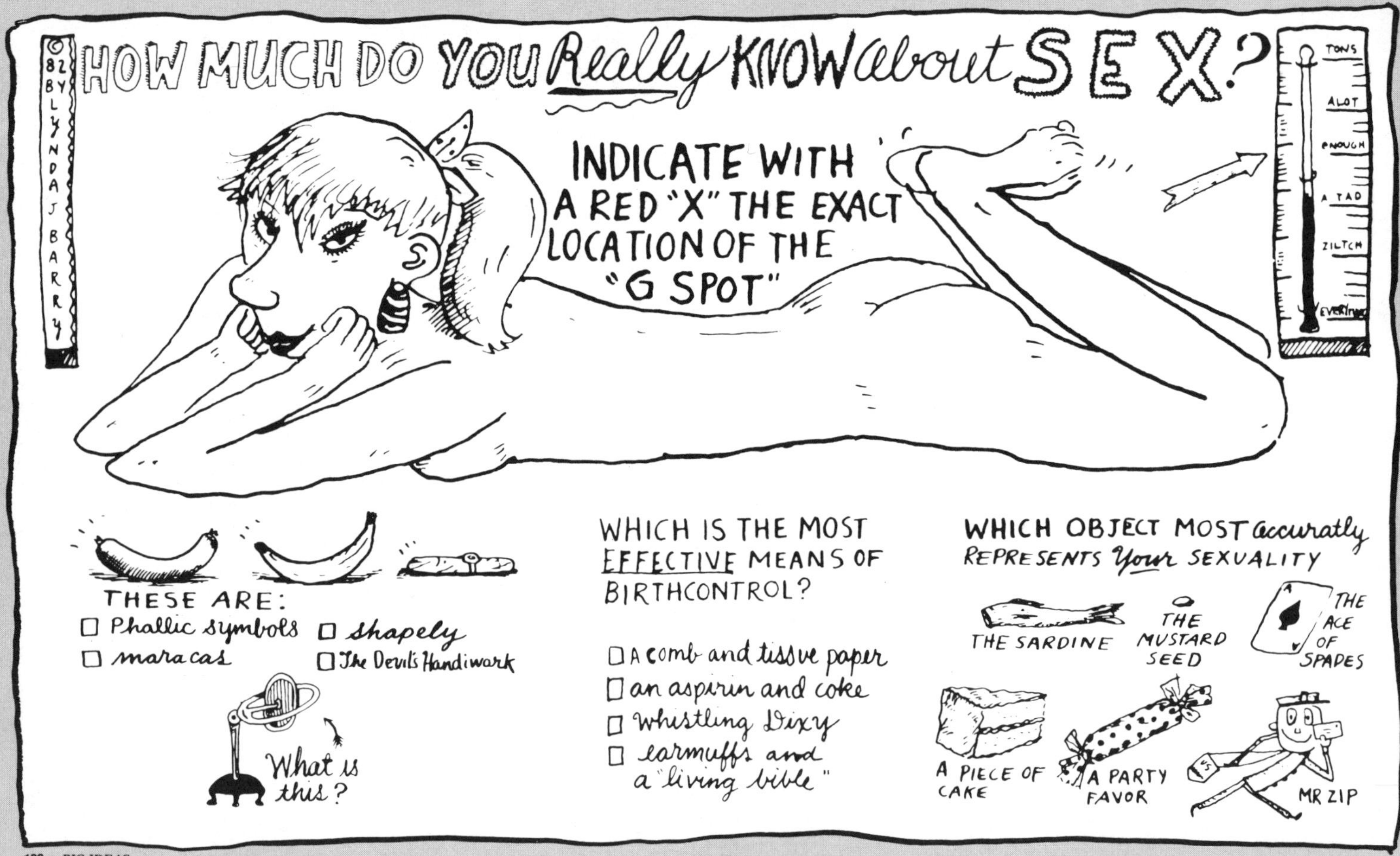

HOW MUCH DO YOU Really KNOW about SEX?
© 82 BY LYNDA J BARRY
TONS
ALOT
ENOUGH
A TAD
ZILTCH
INDICATE WITH A RED "X" THE EXACT LOCATION OF THE "G SPOT"
THESE ARE:
☐ Phallic symbols ☐ shapely
☐ maracas ☐ The Devil's Handiwork
What is this?
WHICH IS THE MOST EFFECTIVE MEANS OF BIRTHCONTROL?
☐ A comb and tissue paper
☐ an aspirin and coke
☐ Whistling Dixy
☐ earmuffs and a "living bible"
WHICH OBJECT MOST accuratly REPRESENTS Your SEXUALITY
THE SARDINE
THE MUSTARD SEED
THE ACE OF SPADES
A PIECE OF CAKE
A PARTY FAVOR
MR ZIP

This book is
dedicated to
Merrily Tompkins
and
John Keister.

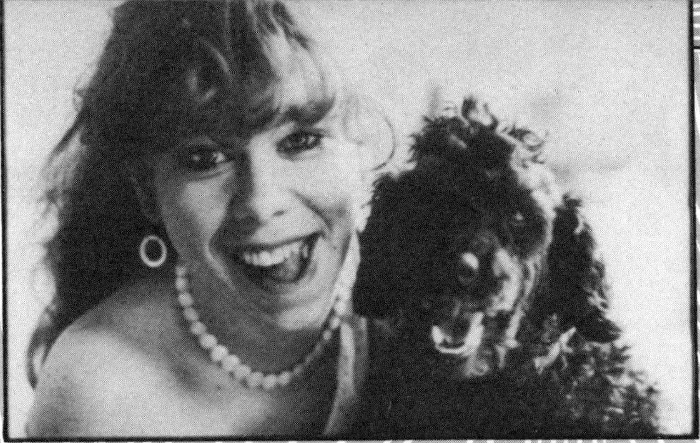

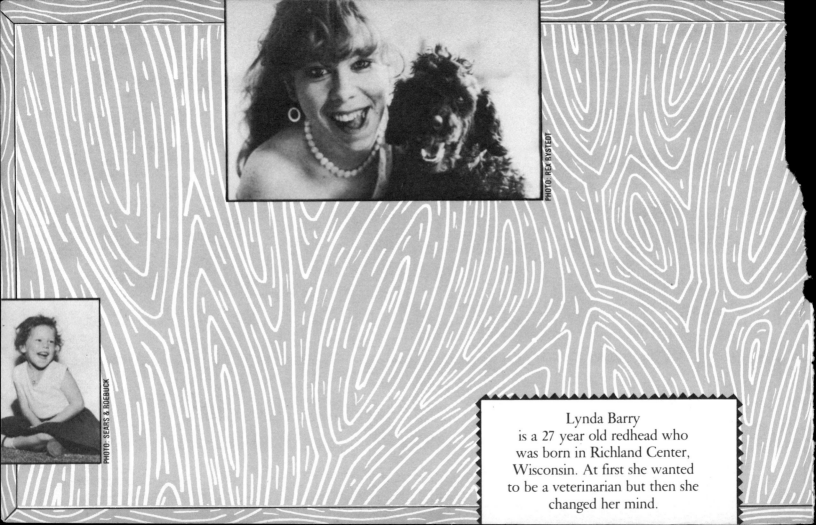

PHOTO: REX RYSTEDT

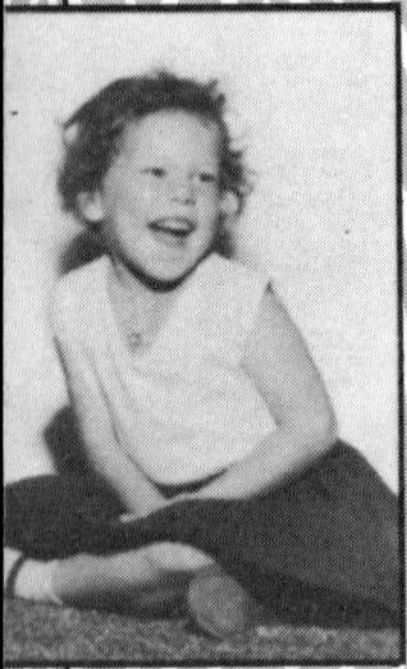

PHOTO: SEARS & ROEBUCK

Lynda Barry
is a 27 year old redhead who
was born in Richland Center,
Wisconsin. At first she wanted
to be a veterinarian but then she
changed her mind.